Canaries Among Us

A Mother's Quest to Honor Her
Child's Individuality in a
Culture Determined to Negate It

Kayla Taylor

SHE WRITES PRESS

Published 2022
Printed in the United States of America
Print ISBN: 978-1-64742-293-6
E-ISBN: 978-1-64742-294-3
Library of Congress Control Number: 2022910424

For information, address:
She Writes Press
1569 Solano Ave #546
Berkeley, CA 94707

Interior design by Tabitha Lahr

She Writes Press is a division of SparkPoint Studio, LLC.

For my children.
I love you to infinity plus one.

And to my husband,
who encouraged me to tell my story
even as others refused to listen.

Author's Note

Advocates keep reminding me that the First Amendment protects my right to tell my story. But my trials are intertwined with the lives of others. While I want my experience to be heard and believed, I think children should be able to define and share their own narratives. As a result, key features of all youth characters have been altered to protect their privacy.

Surprising even myself, I concluded that adults, including those who behaved egregiously, must be protected as well. My intention never has been to "get even." Moreover, I've learned that public disclosures of poor conduct induce shame. And shame is a destructive beast, often causing people who mistreat others to transgress even further. As behavioral researcher Brené Brown notes, "Shame corrodes the very part of us that believes we are capable of change." I hope we all have the capacity to support one another, to value our collective humanity, to do better. As a result, all adult characters you are about to meet, except nationally known figures and published authors, have also been altered.

I've taken great lengths to change names, identities, and locations. I've altered facts, and I've created composites, all in an effort to protect both the innocent and the guilty. I also took the liberty of adjusting the timeline to connect dots and convey meaning more coherently.

So, with all of these revisions, what's left?

I believe what remains is the most relevant part: one parent's unvarnished look at the ways we treat children who don't conform to society's expectations of "normal" or "average" and the daunting challenges parents face when raising them. While the characters and events on the following pages might be altered, the underpinnings of my personal experience—my confusion, my hopes, my joy, and my sorrow—are very real.

In an ideal world, no reader would identify with the narrative that follows, but I've listened enough to know that many will. In fact, I wouldn't be surprised if a saga similar to this one is unraveling in your own town at this very moment. My greatest hope is that if you relate to any portion, this account might help you feel less isolated or abandoned. You are not alone.

I hear you.

I believe you.

I see you.

We are in this together.

Goldfish

I join the other adults at the curb and wait. Students from various grades shuffle away, but second-grade parents remain, rechecking watches and raising eyebrows at one another.

We are annoyed.

Then curious.

And now we are worried.

I'm grateful my two boys are on playdates so I don't have to contend with their impatience in addition to my own.

After about ten minutes, the missing class finally bounds toward its assigned bench to await pickup. My daughter is released from her seat, and we walk to the car hand-in-hand. She's still young enough to reach for me out of habit.

"Sorry I'm late, Mom." She explains, "Some kids created an 'I Hate Hannah Club' today, and the teacher needed to talk about kindness." She reminds me of a reporter, objectively conveying the news of her community.

But "Hannah" is my child.

My emotions lock down as I halt the instinct to console her. First, I want facts. "What do you mean, an 'I Hate Hannah Club'?" Softening my voice, I ask, "Can you tell me more about that?"

"Umm, Daniella created a club and got the other kids to join. Everyone wrote their names down on a paper."

I question, "There's a club charter?" while I think, *Second graders have actually formalized this cruelty?*

She asks, "What's a charter?" but doesn't wait for my answer. Instead, she rushes to another concern. "And, uh, Mom, at lunch the other day, Daniella yelled to all the kids, 'If you like Hannah, raise your hand!' And nobody did."

"How many kids were there, Sweetie?" I modulate my voice to appear calm and controlled.

"About twenty."

Her whole class.

Since the second month of school, we've heard reports of disruptive classroom behavior, and the frequency has only increased. We're now six months in, and some people estimate our teacher spends eighty percent of her time trying to manage one child. Parents of a few of the more docile kids have requested that their child not be partnered with Daniella. And I recently learned that admissions tours are no longer allowed to visit the classroom, suggesting the administration knows this is not the shining example of joyful learning they wish to project.

So far, my husband and I have stayed in the background, opting to trust school leaders to manage the situation. We chose the Global Citizens Academy because of its commitment to developing kind children and instilling good values. The school's mission is particularly attractive given the power and money seeping into our neighborhood from the looming city nearby. Manhattan might be a dozen train stops away, but its influence is inescapable.

Not only do we believe in GCA's principles, but we resolved to be patient when we first heard about Daniella's classroom disruptions. Her parents are divorcing, and we believed she needed support rather than judgment. We wanted to give the teacher the leeway to address specific needs. After all, who knows? It might be our kid who requires extra support next time.

But now it feels like it's time to engage more intentionally. In the past few weeks, Daniella's behavior has escalated rather than improved. While she was once a general, albeit almost constant, disruption to the class, her actions are now meaner. Hannah comes home from school complaining regularly that Daniella spit, pushed, and teased. Just last week, Hannah reported, "Daniella grabbed one of my arms and got Lauren to take the other one, and they spun me around till I fell to the ground."

I assumed these behaviors were indiscriminate, but now I'm wondering, *Have we crossed a new boundary? Is Daniella focusing on our child specifically? And encouraging other children to do the same?*

When we arrive home, I help Hannah find a snack before stealing away to email her teacher:

Leslie, Hannah just told me about her day, and my heart sank. Before I rush to any conclusions, can you please share your understanding of what happened?

I've heard the eight-year-old version, and I'm hoping there's a more benign explanation.

Leslie responds within the hour:

My heart is aching as well. Can you come and talk before class tomorrow?

That evening, I ask my husband to corral our preschool and first-grade boys, Jake and Theo, so I can focus on Hannah. She follows her bedtime routine but with none of her usual ebullient chatter. Instead, she's silent and seems vacant. Her shell is going through the motions but there's nothing visibly alive inside.

I try to play the part of a casual bystander so she doesn't sense my concern. After all she's been through, I don't want to add to her stress or make her feel pitied. But I do want her to know she's loved.

chaos to lead his budding technology company, leaving him little energy to debate what's obvious to him at home. So we email the head of school and request a meeting. But before receiving a response from Richard, I get another email—from Daniella's mother:

Hi, Kayla, I don't know what to say. I was so sorry to hear about Daniella's behavior today. It was so out of character. I have taken away all her stuffed animals tho. I'm very adamant that bullying is not ok. She is sad she lost her toys, but she's looking forward to playing with Hannah again tomorrow!
Fondly, Kara

My fingers fly across the keyboard:

Kara, thank you for your kind note. We appreciate your concern. It would be nice if the girls could play together tomorrow. However, it sounds like you might not be aware that Daniella has been teasing Hannah for a few months now? Did the school not inform you of the various incidents?

Her next email does not quell my concern:

No. Really? I had no idea. Let me talk to Daniella. I'm sure she didn't mean anything bad by it. She's a very sensitive child and probably doesn't understand how she comes across. But I'll talk to her. Thanks for letting me know!

I'm perplexed. How could she not know about *months* of misbehavior? Didn't the school contact her? Not sharing crucial information seems akin to denying Kara the right to parent her own child. It also seems counter to the school's values and mission. It is, after all, the Global Citizens Academy. Or, maybe the school *did* contact her, but Kara refuses to hear what she's been told?

I'm anxious to speak with the head of school, but Richard doesn't respond for over twenty-four hours. When he does, he suggests a meeting on Friday at 4:00 p.m.

I sigh in Jim's direction, "Wow, busy guy. He can't fit us in for three more days?" I feel bullying should be a priority, but it seems Richard has other concerns.

Later that night, I hear from Daniella's mom again:

I spoke to Daniella, but she says she has never teased Hannah. All I can do is go off what she says. Maybe there was some confusion? Anyway, I reminded her that she needs to be kind, so hopefully everything's good. Daniella is looking forward to seeing Hannah tomorrow!

Good Lord, I think. *"All I can do . . ."*? It hasn't occurred to her that Daniella might lie to avoid getting in trouble? It looks like I won't be able to co-parent with this mother.

■ ▨ ■ ▨

Over the next three days, Hannah becomes needier. I first notice her insecurity when she begs me to walk her into school rather than use the car drop-off line. Delivering Hannah directly to her classroom is a time-suck during already busy mornings. But as I stand in her doorway, I hope my presence reminds the staff of Hannah's situation and compels them to address any mean behavior swiftly.

I turn to depart, and a fusion of emotions pervades me. Yes, I'm stressed by my towering to-do list, but I'm also grateful I was able to take leave from my management consulting job. Had I been working today, I likely would have been on a plane or in another state right now, unable to attend to Hannah's needs. And then I marvel—and recognize several undue benefits I have—when I consider all the working parents who somehow contend with similar situations. *How do they do it?* It's impossible to earn a paycheck and protect kids at the same time. As a result, schools hold such powerful roles for the parents who entrust their children to them.

I cross my fingers that Hannah will slide back into a regular routine and regain the bounce in her step. Unfortunately, she can't seem to get a break. Hannah tells me after pickup the next day, "Mommy, my stomach hurts," and her appetite wanes. I consider canceling the barbeque I'm hosting for friends at the end of the week. This school drama is wearing my family down! But a thermometer insists Hannah's temperature is normal, so I commit to keeping our plans and resist Hannah's pleas to stay home.

When Friday finally rolls around, our babysitter retrieves the kids from school so Jim and I can convene at Richard's office. "Jim! Kayla!" Richard greets us wholeheartedly. "It's so great to see you! Please, take a seat!" His handshake almost doubles my knuckles around, but I suppress a wince. I refuse to show any signs of weakness today.

As I scan the room, I note a picture of Richard's beautiful wife but none of children. He has no kids of his own, but I've always thought it odd that he doesn't at least display some of the cute drawings and lopsided pottery that students must have given him over the years. Instead, his walls exhibit awards of all types, including a high school diploma from upstate New York, a college degree, and certificates documenting his participation in various training programs. In fact, the only potentially playful things I see are two goldfish gliding lazily around a tank.

Richard pulls my attention from the fish when he says, "I just want you to know I spoke with Leslie about everything. I love Hannah and Jake, and we can't believe Theo's almost old enough to join us! They're important parts of our GCA family." His use of the word "love" feels incongruous with this clinical office, but

I listen as he continues. "Now, as you know, scuffles are a regular part of elementary school, and it's our job to help children learn from them." He's charming and convincing, although he does direct his comments primarily toward Jim. Other moms have told me Richard focuses his attention on their husbands as well.

Jim thanks Richard for his concern but reminds him that this class has had issues for a while now.

"It's been a rough year," I chime in. "We only have three months left, and we're hopeful we can get things back on track." I've heard parents often come here to complain, so I want to signal my intention to be constructive. Since I've heard several other families have already voiced concerns about the continuous classroom disruptions, I pivot to our personal concern. "It seems Hannah's the target of some pretty mean behavior. And when I spoke with Daniella's mother, she was unaware that Daniella's been teasing her most of the year."

I know that if *my* child was taunting another, I'd want someone to tell me, and I'm tempted to tell Richard so. But I restrain myself. Other mothers have warned me that he doesn't appreciate suggestions from "the cheap seats." Just recently, the parent who chaired the last school fundraiser revealed, "The only way I could get Richard to agree to anything was to make him feel like it was his idea in the first place."

Apparently, Richard doesn't appreciate my restraint. His response is curt. "I assure you, we're actively involved." Before I can probe for details, he admonishes, "I would ask that you not talk to Daniella's parents directly. We'll handle that."

It takes me a second to rebound from his evasion and condescension. I ask, "Um, really? Don't you think we should all be engaged together? I mean, an I Hate Hannah Club is just cruel. We're supposed to just sit on the sidelines? Especially when Daniella appears to be screaming for help. When we don't address her behavior, we're neglecting her needs as well. Shouldn't all the adults be working together on this?"

Richard insists, "We're handling it."

Jim nods. "I'm glad to hear that because this behavior is completely inconsistent with the school's mission and values." I smile as I realize he's parroting some of the phrases I spewed last night. "We came to this school for its commitment to raising good, kind kids. And we've been trusting your process for months now, but things are getting out of hand."

"You might not see all we're doing, but we're engaged," Richard tells us. "In fact, I've been handling this situation personally." He stalls for a second and then stammers, "What's the best way to say this? Umm . . . Daniella's therapist isn't great, so I've been meeting with Daniella personally. She comes to my office once a week."

I'm confused. Part of me is glad he's involved, but I also wonder, *Is his approach ethical? Is he trained to do this kind of counseling? Is he now biased toward one child in particular?* I later learn that Richard even visited each of Daniella's parents' homes to "set consistent schedules."

Maybe Richard senses my concern over his focus on one child because he reveals, "I invited *both* girls to my office last week, and we had a wonderful chat. See the two goldfish over there? We decided to name them Hannah and Daniella!" He then declares with satisfaction, "Look! They're swimming together!"

I'm speechless. Is he really equating Hannah's experience with her classmate to a relationship between two goldfish? Is bullying this trivial to him? Am I supposed to be as enamored with the fish as he is?

I peer at the tank and then turn to study Richard's proud face, but his smile and raised eyebrows beckon me to look again at the fish. I wonder if he appreciates that he's comparing young children to creatures trapped for others to admire. There's no escape route if one decides to attack the other. What would he do if one of the two goldfish behaved more like a beta fighter? Would he sit here so blissfully?

Richard's stance seems so distant, so unsympathetic, that I sense he's no longer available to us . . . to Hannah.

I want to grasp the tank and heave it against the wall. I can envision the glass and pebbles as they ricochet around the room while I sweep up the fish and escape. Might a display like that wipe the smug look off his face and get him to care about a little girl who's hurting? The image is tempting, but I force myself to remain calm. I've learned over the years how swiftly women are dismissed when they appear "dramatic."

Clenching my jaw, I allow my husband to wrap up the conversation. We've always been a good tag team this way. Sometimes Jim takes the lead, sometimes I do. Today, I have no desire to participate in the banal conversation expected prior to a civilized departure. So I watch the aimless fish while Jim manages the goodbyes.

We stand, and I force myself to offer a nod and a handshake. My lips are pursed, but I turn them up at the sides. It's a submission I resent, but I know I must appear respectful if I want anyone to help Hannah.

As we depart, I hope Richard feels at least a little pressure to ensure the school is as uneventful as his ridiculous fishbowl seems to be.

She's for Real

I'm relieved to escape Richard's office, but I immediately wish I weren't hosting this barbeque tonight. I'm going to need to work quickly to prepare dinner for three other families!

The boys are excited to have guests, but when I recruit them to help, they scurry away. Fortunately, Hannah volunteers to set the table. She begs to use the tablecloth and settings I reserve for special occasions, but I insist we keep things casual. "Let's make it easy on ourselves!" She gets to work while the babysitter scoots the boys toward the living room to collect their toys.

When I pass the dinner table an hour later, it's organized flawlessly except for a book strewn on the floor nearby. I lean down and see it's open to a page diagramming a proper place setting. Noting the similarity between the drawing and our table, I'm both pleased and annoyed. I told Hannah I wanted to keep things casual, but the scene before me is almost ostentatious with unnecessary utensils and plates.

I decide to contain my frustration. She's been working hard to demonstrate her competence lately, and the table does look gorgeous. My only adjustment is to swipe up the butter knives and bread plates, leaving fewer things to clean later.

Hannah enters the room with an armful of flowers. I pray she didn't strip the yard of all its color as I say, "Are those for the table? It's amazing, by the way. Thanks for your hard work!"

But she looks violated. "Mom, why did you ruin it?" And she huffs away.

Ugh. Why must she be so sensitive?! Her constant need for validation can be exhausting, and it's only gotten worse lately. Parenting her is different than nagging my boys to clean up their messes. She requires nuanced and emotionally draining responses, and now she's diverting my attention from preparing for our guests, who will be here shortly!

I find Hannah curled up on the couch. The babysitter's trying to console her, but I know she won't be pacified by someone she doesn't know well. Realizing it's time for the sitter to leave anyway, I hand her some cash and turn my attention back toward my daughter.

"I see you're angry, and I'm sorry. But do you remember me saying I wanted to keep things simple? Extra plates just create more mess and complication." I think she might be swayed, but she's clearly still dismayed. "Why don't you come with me to the kitchen? You can be in charge of the salad!"

She contemplates, then nods. As I suspected, the allure of being "in charge" appeals to her. She gallops down the hall and almost trips on her way, but she catches herself and beats me to the kitchen.

Hannah gathers vegetables from the refrigerator, and I hand her an avocado.

"Eww!" she squeals. "No way!" Amid the drama, I forgot her aversion to mushy foods. She grabs a cucumber and some carrots and then reaches for a knife with an eight-inch blade.

I sigh. If I take the knife away, she'll feel insulted and demoralized, assuming I don't think she's capable. But if I don't grab the blade, she could slice her finger off.

I make an offer, but in a tone that suggests my parameters are firm. "I'll make the first cuts, and then you can do *all* the rest." I want to slice the vegetables in half and place the flat sides down so they'll stay in place as she works. Her face first registers frustration but soon fades to pride as she realizes she'll have responsibility for most of the work.

Of the families I invited to join us tonight, two I know well. The third is new to the school—a mom and her son who joined Jake's class after winter break. I stood near them during pickup a few weeks ago and immediately appreciated her friendly, laid-back demeanor and the way the two shared giggles over inside jokes.

This new family arrives first, and I'm flustered. I was hoping to be further along with the dinner prep by now. Fortunately, Jim bounds into the entryway to greet our guests. He's usually running late from work, so my heart leaps at his presence. *He's on time!*

We crowd awkwardly inside our front door, offering introductions until Jim suggests, "Why don't we all head out to the yard? We just hung a swing!"

Jake dashes out first with Theo and our young guest in tow.

I encourage Hannah to join the boys, but she insists, "No! They're too chaotic! I want to be a chef with you!"

I clench my jaw and inhale deeply.

Maya must notice my stress because she offers, "I'll join you! How can I help?" I knew I liked this woman. She rolls with whatever's thrown her way.

Hannah leaps ahead while Maya raises an eyebrow questioning me with one word: "Chaotic?"

I respond, "Yeah, Hannah prefers things calmer than her brothers." But then I realize Maya was likely referring more to Hannah's advanced vocabulary than to her inclinations.

Maya settles in with Hannah while I prepare the marinating chicken for the grill.

When Hannah asks her, "How has your day been?" Maya appears taken aback.

"Wow! Thank you for asking, Hannah! It's been great."

"You're welcome!"

They chat for a while, and I worry Hannah's dominating our guest's time. I encourage again, "Hannah, why don't you head outside?" But the two ignore me and continue chatting about school and work.

My daughter's eyes pop when Maya explains that she's a math professor at the local university. Hannah exclaims, "Cool! Do you know Euler's formula?"

Maya scrunches her eyebrows and looks at me as if to say, *Is this kid for real?*

I sigh, wondering if I should explain Hannah's interest in math and physics and how she stays up late with her dad to discuss complicated concepts, like the dimensions of black holes. But I'm still worried about getting dinner ready, so I let a nod suffice. *Yes, she's for real.*

Maya and Hannah remain engrossed in conversation while I focus on the meal. I spy Maya resting her head in both hands with her elbows propped on the counter. She looks intently at my child as Hannah asks, "Did you know a lot of calculus is just about finding the area under a curve? Look, you can see how to do it if you draw a bunch of tall skinny boxes . . ."

Now she's just showing off.

I worry Maya might judge this peculiar conversation, and the little girl, too, but one look tells me she's enchanted. Some people take delight in my kid's quirks, and others judge and dismiss her for the very same reasons.

When the doorbell rings, I prod, "Hannah Banana, let Maya come with me so I can introduce her to some friends!" Maybe the third time is the charm?

Hannah remains still, except for a slow movement of her head to the left and then the right. She has found somebody who "gets" her, and she doesn't want to budge.

Maya smiles, "It's okay! Go attend to the others. We're having fun!"

"Are you sure?"

Maya gives me a thumbs up, and I give Hannah the warning that often helps her prepare to switch gears. "How about five more minutes with your new friend, and then we're going to let her hang out with the adults, okay?"

Hannah smiles as I head off to greet the other guests at the door. But since the remaining families have been to our home many times before, the gang has already found Jim and the boys in the yard. I steal back to the kitchen to save Maya, but she remains thoroughly amused. Still, I insist, "Hannah. It's time to head outside. Let's help everyone get to know one another."

"Okay, Mom, just let me finish up the salad, okay?"

"Hah!" Maya laughs. "Can you teach my son to be that responsible?"

I lead Maya out before Hannah can dominate her any longer, but Maya lags nervously as she asks, "Are you okay leaving her with that knife?"

"Trust me. Leaving her with that knife is lower risk than telling her she can't use it." When the world is right with Hannah, the whole house runs more smoothly. And I'm comforted knowing she already completed the chopping. All that remains is dressing and tossing.

Maya checks on her son and then introduces herself to the dads nearby. She looks comfortable, so I sidle up to my friends, Ellen and Heather, and hug them as I ask, "How was your week?"

They respond simultaneously. "Fine. Busy!"

When they ask me about mine, I consider how honestly I should answer. Since they're two of my closest friends, I decide to bare the truth. "It was a rough one."

I explain about the targeting of Hannah without mentioning any names. Ellen is on the board of the school, so I want her to know what's happening. Dynamics like these not only affect my child but can impact the entire school culture.

She responds, "Really?"

I nod. "We met with Richard today, but he wasn't very responsive. He equated Hannah and the girl who's taunting her to goldfish."

"Huh." They seem to find the notion more entertaining than ridiculous, but before I can elaborate on the analogy, Heather changes the subject.

"Have you guys decided what you're doing for spring break?"

I stifle the half-formed sentence in my mouth.

Apparently, there are more interesting things to discuss.

The Canary

I feel somewhat victorious as I get Hannah and Jake to school on Monday morning a minute before the bell rings. It's a small win, but I'll take any I can get.

Once Theo is settled at his preschool nearby, I check my watch and note I have an hour to kill before my next commitment: a board meeting for one of my favorite nonprofits. I hit the coffee shop to grab my morning caffeine and then wander into the adjoining bookstore. I'm always on the hunt for a good read, especially something that invites me to widen or shift my point of view. Today, I'm drawn to a memoir a friend recommended. Sprawled on the cover is a large red heart and the words, *Love Warrior*. I swipe it up, pleased to have a distraction from the parenting guides stacked on my nightstand.

That evening after reading a story to the kids and tucking them in, I pick up my own book and indulge. It begins like an easy beach read, but on page twenty-nine, it shoves me sideways, clear off my footing. Here, author Glennon Doyle flashes back to a period in high school when she was admitted to a mental health facility. She recalls befriending her roommate and sharing with her a description of her great-grandfather, a coal miner who worked alongside a canary each day. Doyle writes,

"When the toxin levels rose too high, the canary stopped singing, and the silence was the miners' signal to flee the mine."
She then wondered aloud to her roommate if perhaps neither of them was "crazy" as society seemed to suggest. Maybe they were sensitive instead. Doyle's teenage-self asked, "Could it be
. . . that we aren't making any of this up—we're just sensing the very real danger in the air?" She continued, "I think the world is more than a little poisonous, and that [we] were built to notice that." She told her new friend that "in lots of places, canaries are appreciated. They're the shamans and the poets and the sages, but not here."

I'm blown away by the metaphor. The shock of recognition lands like a meteor, morphing the landscape I thought I knew well. *Oh my God, Hannah is a canary!*

I flash back four years to Hannah's early weeks in preschool. She was the first child to say, "That teacher isn't nice," and all the adults, myself included, ignored her. The teacher started reporting to us that Hannah was not compliant, and I sided with the teacher. I didn't want Hannah to "play the adults off one another." When the teacher suggested Hannah was a bad child, poorly mannered and obstinate, I worried that I had a kid with behavior problems. Eventually, I was invited to visit the classroom to observe Hannah's problems firsthand, but when I went, I witnessed something very different. The teacher didn't appear to like children, nor adults for that matter. And she provoked dissidence. For example, she insisted that one of Hannah's classmates sign his name to the attendance list before allowing him to join the other children. When he resisted, I wondered if the boy was embarrassed because he was unable to accomplish the task. He was in preschool, after all. But the teacher was adamant and directed him to sit on a bench until his name was signed. When I left the classroom at the end of my visit, the boy was still confined to the seat. The teacher had effectively given a three-year-old a two-hour timeout.

For the rest of that afternoon, I reconsidered my original reactions to what Hannah had been trying to tell me, and I wondered why I had chosen to dismiss her. I resolved never to ignore my children so readily again.

Later that day, I sat on the floor in Hannah's room and searched deep in her eyes as I explained, "Hannah, I believe you. I saw what is happening at school. You have good instincts. Let's listen to them. I love you *so* much."

She peered at me with such overwhelming gratitude, I almost broke. I could tell she was trying hard not to cry as she threw her arms around me in an embrace that was unusually long and intense for a preschooler. It was then that I started to recognize her "old soul."

Four years later, I can still feel the magnitude of the message delivered in that hug: *Thank you for believing me. Thank you for not letting me be alone.*

Jim and I switched schools the very next day, and the teacher was asked to resign a few months later. It took a little time, but adults eventually caught up to Hannah's assessment.

Still overwhelmed by the canary metaphor, I consider another event that took place about eight months after Hannah transferred preschools. We had hired a new babysitter, and as I was tucking Hannah into bed, she shared, "Jenna makes my heart turn brown."

I wasn't sure that such a young child knew much about anatomy, especially the colors of her insides, so I asked, "What color is your heart normally?"

"Red or pink or something like that." And then she added, "But when I think of Jenna, my heart turns brown, or gray. Or what color is it when things burn and they die?" Her round eyes questioned me innocently.

I was speechless. Hannah had complained about Jenna several times, but I assumed she just wanted to be with a parent rather than a babysitter. Yet, the day after Hannah's heart turned brown, another adult visiting our home approached me and said, "Kayla, I feel awkward saying this, but I think you should know that Jenna acts very differently when you're not around." We fired Jenna, and I later learned that she was released by her next employer after only a few days.

Now, as I continue to reflect, I start to appreciate my daughter's sensitivity and understand that perhaps it's more complex than I previously imagined. She's living her life like a canary sensing toxins. And when she voices concerns, people regularly dismiss her. "In lots of places, canaries are appreciated," Doyle wrote, "but not here."

I'm not sure how to proceed, so I decide to seek advice from someone who can give me a gut check. I want to understand how to support a young child like Hannah, and I'm worried about the recent developments at the Global Citizens Academy. I want a safe place to work through my thoughts—a place where I won't be considered "high maintenance" as I determine what's reasonable to expect from a school like GCA.

I find a local therapist with a strong reputation. Gail impresses me immediately when I see that her perspectives are rooted in science and reason. I need an approach like hers because I often don't trust my own instincts and judgment, especially when others are dismissing me, as they have been lately.

When I tell Gail about the goldfish, she validates my assessment. "It's disappointing your head of school isn't taking bullying seriously." She notes his stance both reflects poorly on his leadership and puts the school in jeopardy, increasing its liability.

I appreciate her insights, but I'm still insecure. She's just one person, after all, and most others seem complacent. Yes, Hannah's teacher expressed concern about the bullying, but few others have. And yes, parents are upset about the unruly classroom behavior, but nothing's being done about it. Daniella's mom seemed unaware there was even a problem. All of this adds to my lack of confidence. And I worry that the more I advocate for Hannah, the more I'll be considered the problem: a mom who's too quick to indulge her kid. Worse, Hannah could be considered a spoiled, hypersensitive brat who perhaps deserves what she gets.

I complain to Gail, "With all the talk about bullying, you'd think the school would be more proactive. And parents would be more concerned."

She agrees. "Yes, it's discouraging. There's a lot of talk about how we can do better, but actions don't always follow. People often don't get concerned until it affects their own kid."

I then divulge, "I feel guilty. I imagined I would be a rock for my children. Reliable. But I saw the warning signs, and I did nothing."

She encourages me to see that we *have* done something. We met with teachers and administrators. We spoke with friends. And I am here, after all.

She then tells me about a growing body of science on "high sensitivity." I want to support my canary-like daughter, so following the session, I dive into multiple books and articles. The research findings challenge many common assumptions, including my own.

I feel vindicated, and like my family is a little less peculiar, when I learn that roughly twenty percent of the human population is genetically wired with a more sensitive nervous system. So Hannah isn't alone! Not even close. Apparently, this predisposition is too common to be written off as an aberration. In fact, the tendency toward sensitivity exists because it's evolutionarily *desirable*. For example, during the times of hunting and gathering, clans benefited from an association with individuals who assessed environments before rushing in to gather berries or attack prey. Who knows what kind of predator might have been lurking?

And many advantages remain today. Multiple books, like Elaine Aron's *The Highly Sensitive Child*, identify several characteristics that are overrepresented among highly sensitive people. For example, they regularly demonstrate elaborate cerebral processing; sensitive individuals often think at a deeper level, a finding documented by brain MRIs. They are also known to be exceptionally kind and conscientious and more likely to react to heartlessness, injustice, and cruelty. This, too, is documented by brain studies; imaging shows highly sensitive people tend to have more activation in the neural structures involved with empathy.

Scientists agree that while high sensitivity allows individuals to be especially aware of nuances in their surroundings—like subtle sounds, unique smells, and different textures—it also causes people to feel overwhelmed. Stadiums and concerts and busy markets can be exasperating rather than enjoyable. So too can loud classrooms and testy tones of voice. To survive, sensitive people might try to control their surroundings, they can become less emotionally flexible, and they might even flee. Essentially, life is richer yet harder for individuals with high sensitivity.

Unfortunately, rather than appreciate the valuable attributes of sensitive people, modern society often regards them disdainfully. The exceptional skills related to sensitivity are disregarded as "soft," and the people themselves are devalued for being delicate, inhibited, reactive, rigid, and anxious. Aware of the excessive scrutiny they face, sensitive kids might feign composure at school and then break down at home. They also might become perfectionists and react intensely to even the slightest error. Many seek constant affirmation to calm their nerves and perform poorly when watched or tested. Given these distinct responses, experts encourage adults to allow for calmer environments, gentler forms of guidance, and more compassion.

I find the research consistent with my personal experience, and it stills some of my nagging concerns. I've been parenting Hannah differently than my other children because I've noticed for years now that an authoritarian posture and a stern voice don't work with her. Jake might respond swiftly to a command like "Hurry up!" but Hannah is likely to quiver and insist, "I'm trying!" I use a softer approach with her, to the extent that I've wondered if my differentiated parenting tactics are fair. But now, they seem necessary.

While many assume sensitive children underperform compared to "more resilient" children throughout life, researchers like Jay Belsky and Michael Pluess disagree. In several studies (a favorite of mine is titled "Vantage Sensitivity"), they demonstrated that while highly sensitive children do, on average, lag behind their peers in difficult environments, like unsupportive homes or rigid classrooms, they also *outperform* less sensitive children in healthier, more constructive arenas. I take this to mean that the outcomes of sensitive children can be more binary, with the possibility of failure or success highly dependent on their situations and the way they're treated.

Summarizing his research findings, W. Thomas Boyce compares highly sensitive children to orchids and their counterparts to dandelions. He acknowledges that the latter often outperform the former in many settings, especially ones that are arid and rough. But he explains that when orchids are placed in hospitable environments, they often outshine their dandelion counterparts in dazzling ways.

I consider the implications of the research for schools. We all revere the educators who change a child's trajectory for the better, and I imagine many enter the teaching field with just such aspirations. It seems, given the science, that if educators want to induce positive inflection points for children, they might have the greatest chances if they create classrooms that support the orchids and canaries of the world. In so doing, they also might also teach the rest of us how to respect people who learn differently or are unique in any number of ways.

I exhale, relieved Leslie is one of these teachers. She sees Hannah's vulnerabilities but also appreciates her strengths. She was genuinely upset when classmates targeted Hannah and is trying to teach her peers to be "upstanders." I realize Leslie must answer to Richard, but I'm grateful to have her on Hannah's team.

■　▩　■　▨

A few weeks after my canary revelation, a friend invites me to join her in Manhattan's West Twenties, an area studded with art galleries. We step into a building with bleached hardwood floors and monumental white walls, each paired with a single painting. I note how every single piece, even the smallest, dominates its wall. No matter how minimal, each work has presence.

As I turn the corner to the final room, I'm shocked to find myself face-to-face with a colossal yellow canary on a bright turquoise background. The painting is about five feet square, but it would have been striking at any size. I think, *There you are. I know you.*

I'm transfixed by the bird's presence, by the simplicity of her beauty. Then I notice the demoralizing reality of her existence. She stands proud, so I was initially deceived into believing her position here is intentional—as if she had chosen this very spot to greet me all by herself. But the artificial perch and silver band on her leg suggest otherwise. I can't help but wonder, *Is this what we do to our children? We display them proudly, but we clip their wings and assign them restrictive, self-serving roles. And then we stifle anything that's especially unique about them because honoring that beauty, that distinctiveness, would be so much more difficult to manage.*

The painting is at once glorious and heartbreaking. I decide I must have it, even though I'm not sure I have a wall to house her. Still, somebody who understands this creature must give her space. I tell the gallery associate about my own canary, and she nods. I wonder if she's paid to agree with whatever potential customers say, but I sense she gets it. Perhaps she has her own canary at home.

The associate then reveals the price, and my excitement plummets. My husband would choke if I told him the cost. In my conscience, where what is right is aligned with what is, this bird belongs with my family. But if I want to avoid conflict, I probably need to keep strolling. As I exit, I sign my name to the gallery's contact list in hopes that I might at least be emailed images of such beautiful things.

A week later, the associate from the gallery calls me. She says she conveyed the story of my canary to the artist, and he would like for the bird to live with me. Apparently, he was reluctant to let his baby go in the first place and priced her accordingly. Maybe this explanation is part of a sell job, but I decide I don't really care. I haven't stopped thinking about the bird. When I'm offered a healthy but doable price, I'm overjoyed.

Sometimes, what should be, is.

Upside Down

We settle into spring slowly. Shoots pop from the turf as soft winds and green tracery remind me nature doesn't stop, not for concerned mothers nor their sensitive daughters. While I can manage the home environment, I have no control over the school setting. So after each drop-off, I hold my breath and hope to greet a smiling child at the end of the day.

Today my kids are clearly appreciating the warmer weather because they all ask to play in the yard after school. I lift Theo on my hip, hand him a snack, and let the other two run off. I keep my eye on Hannah, though, surveying as Daniella initiates a game of tag. I'm relieved to see Hannah's included. She squeals while running after the girls who are not "It." But after a few rounds, I realize the tagged girls never actually become "It." They continue running away, despite Hannah's successful efforts.

My daughter's exuberance turns to indignation as she stops, crosses her arms, and stomps the ground. I call her over and suggest, "Babe, if a game isn't working for you, maybe you can find someone who plays the way you like? I see Aisha over there on the swings." Aisha is a joyful girl who doesn't seem to engage in playground power-plays.

While Hannah often has difficulty being redirected, she rushes to join her friend.

Good choice, I think.

■　▧　■　▧

The next morning, I pull her teacher aside and say, "Leslie, I noticed more mean-spirited behavior on the playground yesterday. It wasn't flagrant, but it was there. Have you seen anything?"

She responds, "I get my break at recess so, unfortunately, I'm not there. But Hannah *has* been telling me about some teasing on the playground. I've already alerted the monitors."

I'm frustrated to learn that Hannah's main ally is not around when she might need her most. I remember the perils of the playground from my own childhood.

Leslie must see my disappointment because she responds, "I'm frustrated too; I'll do everything I can to fix this. On a positive note, I've been impressed with Hannah's ability to articulate her feelings and advocate for her needs. She should be proud of herself."

■　▧　■　▧

A few weeks follow without incidents, lulling our apprehension and raising our hope that the worst is behind us. Then one evening, as I turn off her bedroom lights, Hannah drops a bomb in the safety of the dark. "I'm fat," she asserts.

I'm confused as I try to decipher what she's *really* telling me. At Hannah's recent checkup, the pediatrician confirmed her weight and height percentiles are solidly average.

I want to scream. *Already? We can't get past second grade without body image issues? Are you kidding me?* All women of my generation are aware of the potentially devastating effects of idealized, unattainable expectations for body shapes and any related weight-shaming. So with all my children, I've emphasized the values of strength, nutrition, and a healthy lifestyle. And I've strived to validate the natural beauty in all sorts of body shapes. I rack my brain to determine the source of Hannah's new concern, and I mentally start berating the advertising industry—so ready to make a quick buck on the back of people's self-confidence.

"Hannah, Sweetie. What makes you say you're fat?"

"Daniella told me I look like a whale. And then Lauren said I'm so fat and ugly that my mom puts a bag over my head to kiss me goodnight."

It seems even second-graders know the tools to induce insecurity and shame.

I insist, "Hannah. You are beautiful and healthy. Daniella and Lauren are just trying to be mean, but nothing they say is true."

"They told me there's so much fat on my arm, it's going to fall off."

"Now that's just ridiculous. Do you think that could actually happen?"

Hannah starts to laugh, but the absurdity of the notion only distracts her for a moment. Her voice turns earnest as she asks, "Mom, why are they being mean to me?"

What can I say? I try, "Sometimes when people aren't happy, they are mean to others. They think that by bringing others down, they'll feel better. But it never works because being mean doesn't make you feel better. It makes you feel worse. Happy people don't do mean things."

My words have no effect, and Hannah clarifies why. "But Mom, why are they being mean to *me*? They could be mean to anyone. Why *me*?" Tears pool in her eyes.

I console her with a hug, which also serves to block her view of my own sad face. They shot an arrow with so much force that it blew through her and punctured me. It's not just the mean words; it's the way they were targeted so precisely at *her*.

How do I respond? Do I explain how her uniqueness makes her vulnerable? She loves math and science, while her peers prefer dolls and tag. She has a vocabulary significantly outsized for her age. She moves inefficiently as if she's forever almost falling. Kids notice these things.

It's true. She *is* unique. And interesting. And fabulous. And endearing. And fun. I *love* her differences. But they make Hannah the perfect target for children looking to assert their own warped need for dominance. And today, their aim was swift and devastating.

"Oh, Hon. You have so many qualities that make you special. Often, the kids who feel bad about themselves pick on the kids who have their own wonderful way."

I know this isn't enough, but what is? I'm powerless to protect her from the pain. No bandage in my medicine cabinet can heal a sinewy, deep-seated wound like this.

Sticks and stones, my ass. Words cut like a serrated knife, penetrating to the core.

I decide that, despite Richard's directive to avoid other parents, I believe communication among adults can be a constructive means for addressing challenges. But since Daniella's mother was a dead-end last time, I call Lauren's mom this evening.

After we exchange greetings, I try to sound casual as I say, "So, there's been a little problem at school, but I'm hoping that if we put our heads together, we can solve it. Apparently, Lauren teased Hannah about her weight."

"That's awful. But are you sure it was Lauren?"

"Yes." I'm surprised she's suggesting otherwise—as if my assertion is somehow inconsistent with her daughter's past behavior—so I remind her, "I think it was especially hurtful given all the other teasing this year."

"What do you mean?"

"The school hasn't mentioned anything to you?" I'm noticing a pattern here.

"No, honestly, this is the first I've heard of any problems between the girls, besides the Club thing."

I'm thrown. *Is this woman for real?* Is she really being dismissive of "the Club thing"?

I take a long breath and ask, "Would you mind talking to Lauren? Maybe help her understand the impact of what she's saying?"

"Oh, sure! No problem!"

I'm relieved, and I consider saying more, being more direct, but I worry she might judge *me* rather than help the girls if I push too much.

When we hang up, I can only hope she follows through. I sigh as I realize I might have said both too much and not enough.

■ ▨ ■ ▨

The next morning, a Wednesday, Hannah scurries to our bed before dusk and burrows under the covers. When the alarm sounds, she stays buried. I reach to massage her back to help her wake and realize her chest is heaving.

"Honey, are you okay? What's bothering you?" I envelop her in a hug.

Amid gasps, she's barely able to say, "I . . . don't . . . know . . ."

This girl is unrecognizable. Jim is awake now, and while we can guess the source of her distress, we try to encourage her to articulate it. The incidents she mentioned are enough to humiliate anyone, but maybe there's more she has yet to describe?

Despite my prodding, Hannah refuses to speak. She's usually the most loquacious child we know. Yet everything about her body language signals that she's closed herself off to us. This is the first time I haven't had access to my own child, and I'm anxious and frustrated by my incompetence.

Jim and I agree to let her stay in bed. If she can't get up to go to school today, we won't make her. New rules apply under these unique circumstances.

We email the nurse and Leslie and copy Richard:

Hannah has not stopped crying since she awoke this morning. And for the first time in years, she is unable to put her feelings into words. Apparently, she was taunted again, this time about weight. We will bring her to school when she is ready. In the meantime, can the adults please convene to figure out how to resolve this ongoing problem?

We hear from Richard at the very end of the school day. Why it took him this long to get back to us is beyond me. He says:

Thanks for letting us know. I think this is better discussed in person. My assistant will get back to you with times.

My husband muses, "Do you suppose he's trying to avoid a paper trail? He never has much to say on email."

My mind flashes with clarity as I realize almost all our interactions with the teachers and staff to date have been in person. I have always believed difficult issues are best handled face-to-face, but now I see my naivete. We have no documentation. I also grasp that while I assumed Richard was working on the problem since our last meeting, I have no proof he's done a thing.

I rush to my computer and start drafting.

Dear Richard,
We are writing to express our concern for the children in second grade. Leslie is a skilled, veteran teacher who is doing her best to manage this particular cohort of students. It's apparent, however, that she could use more support.

Several families have spoken to you about troubling classroom dynamics and the behavior of two children in particular. For months you have promised concerned parents that your team is working with the children and their families, but the situation has become more concerning with time. To date, we have not heard of any

consequences to troubling behaviors, and we are regularly
dismissed when we try to discuss important issues.

The email goes on for a few more paragraphs, detailing my
concerns, explaining the impact on Hannah's well-being, and
asking for transparent communication and policies. I also suggest
the school's response to date is inconsistent with its purported
values. I finish the email explaining that we are considering
withdrawing our children from GCA. I want to get Richard's
attention. I want him to recognize the significance of what is
going on here. I want him to pull his head out of the sand and
support *all* the children at this school.

I'm shaking when I hit the send button, and this time I don't
have to wait long for a response:

Kayla and Jim, Let's discuss this in person. Are you
available tomorrow at 4 pm?

We agree, and then we email Leslie and her assistant teacher
to determine if Hannah will be safe at school the next day. They
promise to remind the playground *and* lunchroom aides to
monitor closely, so we encourage Hannah to return. We can't
let her remain home all year. (Or can we? Might that be a more
humane option?) We then try to arm Hannah, encouraging her
to play near the aides, at least for the next couple of days. And
we share advice that our pediatrician insisted was effective. She
believes that girls like Daniella and Lauren are trying to get a rise
out of people, so Hannah's best response would be a dismissive,
"Whatever." We explain to Hannah that if she reacts to their
taunts, Daniella and Lauren will likely keep coming at her.

I wonder if I should also teach Hannah an uppercut. Or
at least a few good swear words. Our world has clearly turned
upside down.

I Love Your Children

When we awake, Jim and I force cheer and confidence into our voices as we vie to reclaim harmony in our home. Who would have thought we'd need to put so much effort into creating normalcy? Our efforts feel both artificial and vital, as though any misstep could set us back again. Allowing zero margin for error is beyond draining.

When we meet Richard later that day, he greets us warmly, but his whole demeanor seems duplicitous to me. While I once considered him professional and engaging, he now feels like a fraud who uses charm to obfuscate. I'm disgusted by him. But I need him to help my child, so I try to sound nonthreatening when I say, "Richard, this keeps happening. We're exhausted."

He sees we're past the point of small talk, so he cuts to the chase. "We've decided we'll implement a behavior plan next year in case we need it."

I'm astounded. "Next year? After all these months of disruptive behavior and bullying, you're pushing this off to *next year*? We still have six weeks of school left. Let's finally address what's happening!"

Richard looks taken aback. He actually seems surprised that we expect him to deal with this now.

I explain, "We trusted you were doing something. Privately, with the family. But now you tell us nothing has happened? We have to wait until *third grade* to see any consequences?"

Jim piles on. "If what happened this year didn't qualify for an action plan with teeth, what would? In the past few months alone, Daniella has created an I Hate Hannah Club and recruited others to exclude her from games and class activities. She spits and pushes and teases Hannah regularly. And Lauren's right there with her."

I fall a little more in love with my husband as I watch him defend our daughter. And I feel less alone. We are a team. But I don't revel too long. As the sole female in the room, I feel it's important to add, "Don't forget the weight-shaming. That kind of taunting can have disastrous effects on a child's health. Any of these kids could end up with eating disorders, and we'd have ourselves to blame. We need to teach them to respect all kinds of body shapes."

Richard responds, "I completely understand your concerns, but I think there's been some confusion. I met with Hannah and Daniella myself and asked them each about the fat comments. Hannah says she doesn't remember being called 'fat.'"

Huh? This is at direct odds with Hannah's reports to me and entirely inconsistent with what we're witnessing at home. And Richard's glib reference to "the fat comments" feels dismissive of some pretty big issues. Yet, the ease with which he is glossing over my concerns makes me wonder, *Have I analyzed things incorrectly? Am I totally off base?*

Something's not right. I start to wonder if Richard questioned the girls together in the same room. If he did, or if he was similarly dismissive of Hannah's concerns, she easily could have retracted her account. I wonder if Richard is cunning or just plain clueless. In any case, I'm disheartened, and doubts continue to creep in. I concede, "Look, we realize Hannah's sensitive and has unique needs. Maybe this just isn't the right school for her."

"We absolutely want her here," he interjects. "I've spoken with her teachers, and we all very much believe your children belong at GCA. This is a good fit. And we love your children. *I* love your children."

Does he? Or is he just worried about losing our tuition? Instead of asking, I tell him, "Richard, I don't need you to love my children. I need you to see them."

He nods and continues, "I do, Kayla. I see *all* our students."

I doubt he understood the depth of my statement as I push on to the question I need answered most. "Do you believe *any* shaming or bullying occurred? At all?"

Richard looks me straight in the eye (a gesture he usually reserves for Jim) and responds, "No, I don't. In fact, I'm hesitant to use labels like that on children. It's against good pedagogy."

His condescension is infuriating, as is this weaponizing of industry jargon. He's using fancy language to suggest he's more knowledgeable and to put me in my place. I try to remain calm as I say, "Richard, I understand not wanting to pigeonhole young children with restrictive labels, but if we don't acknowledge their *behaviors*, we can't help them learn and grow. We're failing both Daniella and Lauren when we ignore their actions. In fact, we're failing all the kids. The school stands for certain values. Now's our chance to actually embody them!"

Richard finally concedes, "What if I agreed to separate Hannah from Daniella and Lauren next year? They could be placed in different classrooms."

This seems possible. There *are* two classes in each grade. But what about all-grade activities? And recess?

Jim has had enough. He stands and responds, "Thanks, Richard. We'll go home and think about it."

In the parking lot, Jim and I debrief. Right now, he's the only person I feel comfortable talking to without varnishing my words. And I know he'll give it to me straight. He has a brilliant way of sifting through complicated situations and distilling them down to the most crucial elements. Some people find his crisp directness off-putting, but I find it stabilizing. I can trust what he says. So I ask the questions that are taunting me, "Are we crazy? Hannah *is* sensitive. Maybe she's blowing things out of proportion?"

Jim retorts, "No, we're not crazy. But we need to be rational here. Are you serious about pulling the kids out? Our public school is huge, and I thought we agreed Hannah needs a smaller setting. But if you've changed your mind, just say it. Because our negotiating position is only as strong as our next best alternative."

"If only GCA *did* what they *say* they do! Their mission and values are plastered all over their walls! We have a sensitive child, and we *need* them to be as kind as they say they are!"

"Well, we only have so much power. We don't run the school. So right now, our only decision is whether we keep the kids at GCA or pull them."

I want to shake the pragmatism straight out of him. I want the school to be what it promises. But I know he's right. Which leaves us with two imperfect options. I try to remind myself that we're fortunate to have an alternative. Too many kids don't.

Damn it. I feel no better than I did before our meeting with Richard started.

As Jim departs for his office, an acquaintance approaches. The last time we spoke, Melanie complained about bullying in her son's class, the one below Hannah's. I share what's going on with us, including details about our meeting with Richard.

"He's doing to you what he did to us," she says. "He's gaslighting you, Kayla. Trust yourself. You *know* what happened. And you're not the only family experiencing this. There is a *systemic* issue here. When I tried to talk to Richard about Luke—and I mean he was *punched* and *slapped* in the face—Richard literally yelled and said, 'How dare you say this about our youngest learners!' And he told me not to talk to anybody else about it!"

When I slide into my car, I open my phone's web browser and type "gaslighting." The screen reminds me of its meaning and ripple effect: gaslighting is a psychological tool used to manipulate others, negate their experiences, and create a new storyline. The effort often causes people to doubt their own sanity.

It seems Melanie pretty much nailed it.

An hour later, I return to school for pickup and run into Lauren's mother. I'm still upset, so when she diverts her gaze, I dive in and ask her whether she's spoken with her child, as we agreed on the phone.

"Well, actually, no. I have a better idea. What if our nanny takes the girls on a playdate so they can patch things up? They could get ice cream!"

I'm incredulous. "So you think the nanny can manage this?"

Lauren's mom nods cheerfully.

"Including the comments about Hannah's body?"

"Oh, let's just leave that in the past. I think if the girls just get a chance to play together, they'll figure it out."

She actually thinks Hannah might want a playdate with a girl who's been tormenting her for months. And she wants to let her nanny handle everything. *What the hell?* Maybe Richard was right about avoiding Daniella's *and* Lauren's parents after all.

With all the talk about "villages" these days, I assumed more parents would lean in and help kids in need. But each time I ask for support, I feel my community get smaller and smaller.

■ ▨ ■ ▨

That evening, as I tuck Hannah into bed, I ask her what she'd think about trying a different school.

"But Mom, I like GCA."

I know she's terrified of change. As she gets more insecure, her anxiety increases, and her fear of new things rises with it. So the more unsafe her environment becomes, the more scared she is to leave it. It's an ironic, vicious cycle.

"Maybe it would be nice to go to a place where there's more kindness?"

"But Mom," she protests again, "why should I have to go? Why can't the mean kids leave the school?"

Once again, I'm at a loss. This young child gets it. Why can't the adults? How do I explain that her injustices have only just begun? She's heard us say "life is not fair" many times, but we've arrived at a whole new level. We're not talking about learning how to distribute unevenly sized cookies anymore.

I share Hannah's sense of injustice but am still taunted by Richard's assertions that bullying has not occurred. I wonder yet again, *Am I being irrational? Am I misperceiving what's happening?* So, I decide to send one last email before bed:

> *Leslie, I want to ensure that I am not misunderstanding what has transpired. I realize that much of my information comes from an eight-year-old, so I would appreciate your adult perspective. Do you think Hannah has been bullied, or is she being too sensitive?*

The pit of my body believes it knows her answer. It remembers how Leslie told me the school "failed" Hannah and recalls her looks of concern as we discussed the repeated, targeted assaults. But the gaslighting is working, so I hope she'll confirm in writing what I already know to be true.

I head to bed admitting I'll be lucky to sleep.

I don't hear from Leslie the following day, which is concerning given how responsive she usually is. I consider reaching out again, but I don't want to seem pushy. So I wait.

The following day, we *do* receive a response, but it's not from Leslie. Richard writes:

> *Kayla,*
> *Leslie forwarded your email. She said she felt more comfortable having me respond. We have discussed the matter, and we both agree that no bullying has taken*

place. As I said during our last meeting, I am handling
this matter and will be in touch with any updates.
Regards, Richard (in conversation with Leslie)

This escalates things to a new level. It was one thing to learn Hannah was being shunned by her class, but now it seems that Leslie has been restricted from communicating directly with me. Both Hannah and I are being isolated. This level of manipulation and obfuscation is unnerving. *What is this? Second grade or the Pentagon?*

One thing's becoming apparent: If I want to advocate for my child, I need to know *precisely* what I'm talking about. Even one misrepresentation or false fact could undermine my credibility— and Hannah's well-being.

As I'm contemplating what to do, on the periphery of my consciousness I hear, "Mommy, can you please open this?"

I look down and am embarrassed to register that Jake has just asked the same question three times, yet I'm only hearing him just now. The fact that he's showing no frustration over my inattentiveness makes me feel even worse. *This can't go on. Jake and Theo need attention too!*

After dinner, we all sit on the floor, and I help Jake build the biggest, baddest Lego police station he's ever seen—a three-story behemoth, replete with a helipad, chopper, jail, motorcycle, two vehicles, and a canine officer. The boys are thrilled, and Hannah joins to voiceover the dog's role. Jim and I later tuck in the kids, grateful to close out the day with a small sense of normalcy.

With the children in bed, I head to my computer. I want to understand this phenomenon of bullying. I want to gather as much information as possible so Richard can no longer manipulate my ignorance. I want truth.

Rite of Passage—or Wrong?

I feel like I'm presenting multiple fronts to the world. Around my kids, I feign composure. I want to create a haven distinct from the disorienting school environment. With my peers, I play the part of an amiable, approachable adult. And then on my own, I'm a dogged researcher. I need to make sense of the strange, unspoken conventions that condone bullying and drive children to feel worthless. I'm realizing that without evidence, without a better understanding of the relevant social and developmental science, I won't be able to stand up to further gaslighting. With any luck, my research will enable another dimension of my persona: capable advocate.

I cast a wide net and visit the websites of several bullying prevention organizations like Stop Bullying, PACER, Stomp Out Bullying, Bystander Revolution, and even the Center for Disease Control. I then click deeper into their links and references. I pay the fees to gain access to peer-reviewed research, and I purchase the books cited in the notes. I want to know everything the experts know. Our school administrators are intimidating in their confidence, despite the fact that I've seen no signs of bullying training nor scholarly backup. So, I want facts to support me.

After many nights investigating, I feel better prepared for future conversations with Richard. Crucially, I now know the definition of bullying. Most authorities agree: bullying is the act of *repeatedly* and *intentionally* causing physical and/or emotional *harm* to another person with *less power*. Hannah's experience qualifies on every level.

The literature is clear that a one-off or random incident is not bullying, but Hannah has been suffering targeted attacks for months now. Intentionality can be difficult to discern, but experts explain that if children are not cognitively impaired and are told they hurt someone yet continue with their behavior, their actions qualify as intentional. At GCA, Hannah's teachers have repeatedly admonished Daniella and Lauren, all to no avail. Hannah reports that the girls laugh when they tease her, which I consider a further sign of cognizance and intentionality. They are aware of, and are even taking pleasure in, my daughter's pain.

For years now, scientists have known that children identify power differentials at astoundingly young ages. Bullies often seize on the cushy safety provided by others' perceived inferiority. Hannah's wiggly body, high sensitivity, and adult vocabulary set her apart. It doesn't help that Hannah is one person up against a duo. I hoped the school would celebrate individuality and diversity, but it now seems Hannah's uniquenesses aren't appreciated there. Instead, her differences make her a prime candidate for ridicule.

I reflect on the other students whose parents reported bullying over the past few years. I'm not intimate with all their stories, but I can see most of the children have characteristics that place them outside the realm of what society considers normative (or what kids call "normal"). The targeted children are shy, sensitive, poor, nonathletic, anxious, hyperactive, socially awkward, or otherwise distinct. Some face significant changes (like a new school) or personal loss (like divorce or abandonment), which amplify these frowned-upon traits. The literature holds that the most common targets of bullying are racial minorities, kids trying to define their gender or sexual identity, and students with disabilities or learning differences. Aggressors home in on these distinctions, like sharks circling prey, often exacerbating preexisting insecurities and traumas.

Some scientists suggest that the children who bully suffer from low self-esteem. They might mistreat others in hopes of feeling better by comparison. They also might participate in cruelty to be accepted by the "in crowd," especially in cultures that condone bullying or glamorize "toughness." Children can also misbehave when confused about constructive ways to get attention. And, sadly, kids who are mistreated at home might mirror the behavior at school.

Other scientists believe bullies *don't* exhibit low self-esteem. Rather, the aggressors consider themselves superior and even flaunt their social power, demonstrating little tolerance or compassion for others. Instead of feeling guilty when they hurt people, they cite their targets' vulnerabilities as justifications. Ringleaders are also known to recruit "henchmen" to do their dirty work, obscuring who instigated the mean behavior.

I'm bolstered when I discover that the United States' own StopBullying.gov identifies bullying as "a form of victimization." I've been hesitant to use such substantial language because I want to appear reasoned and calm, but Hannah's experience feels significant, and the weight of the word "victimization" is commensurate with the child who couldn't climb from my bed the other day.

The wide body of literature repeatedly suggests that a school with safeguards that limit bullying is a "human right"; that children deserve to learn in environments free of "abuse"; and that children are no longer safe or able to reach their academic and social development potentials when bullying threatens their cognitive and emotional functioning. Brains become inhibited— they can literally feel frozen—when people feel threatened, making learning nearly impossible. The scholars also hold that bullying prevention is an issue of "social justice," especially since, by definition, bullying entails an imbalance of power and often targets minorities or people considered "misfits." In general, bullying dehumanizes people and perpetuates warped views of superiority. As a result, schools that tolerate it send terrible messages contrary to civil rights principles and human decency.

Richard promotes GCA as a model community. He insists bullying is nonexistent. But several researchers equate assertions like his to "red flags." They say they would be more concerned about a school that reports no bullying than one that documents many cases. Bullying occurs everywhere. The challenge with bullying does not lie in its appearance. It lies in authority figures' negligence in addressing poor behavior effectively when it arises. Adults who refuse to name bullying for what it is miss opportunities to stand as role models and instead become complicit bystanders. In the most toxic environments, leaders not only ignore aggression but actively side with the perpetrators.

Sadly, students generally believe adults in a position to help— including parents, teachers, and other community members—are failing to address the issue of bullying adequately. I learn that bullying is more prevalent than people realize, perhaps because the vast majority of children don't report abuse to adults. After seeing how the school responded to my child's needs, I can understand why many are hesitant to come forward.

But GCA administrators aren't the only obstacle. I consider my own peers, parents themselves, who trivialize our predicament. One of my closest friends asked recently, "Isn't bullying just part of elementary school? Just something we all had to deal with?" Unfortunately, this kind of social acceptance perpetuates the problem. By contrast, experts reject the notion that bullying is a harmless rite of passage. In fact, it is very, very wrong. Especially since bullying can have significant, lifelong consequences.

Research shows that bullied students are at increased risk for adverse outcomes, like social isolation, low self-esteem, academic impairment, stress-related ailments (headaches, stomachaches, and problems sleeping), mental health issues (anxiety, depression, and suicidal ideation), substance abuse, and crime. An article in the *Harvard Review of Psychiatry* entitled "How Well Do We Understand the Long-Term Health Implications of Childhood Bullying?" reveals some scary statistics like male bullying victims are eighteen times more likely to experience suicidality, and female targets are almost twenty-seven times more likely to contend with panic disorders. The article also suggests the chronic stress of bullying can potentially elevate body inflammation and lead to significant long-term health risks like obesity, diabetes, and heart disease. As a result, loving adults and communities must intervene early to decrease the likelihood of these consequences, and I resolve to do my part.

I also learn that targeted children are not the only ones at risk. Bullying affects witnesses as well. When children see wrongdoing but do not intervene, they often struggle with feelings of inadequacy, powerlessness, and moral failure. They can also feel unsafe and neglected themselves when they observe adults' apathy or reluctance to hold those who bully to account. When justice appears convoluted, children can even start to doubt their own consciences, judgment, and ideas about right and wrong. As a result, bystanders, too, exhibit higher than average rates of substance abuse, mental health problems, and school truancy.

Ironically, the children who instigate bullying behavior demonstrate many of the same outcomes as children who are bullied. In fact, research suggests they are prone to *even more* alarming behaviors later in life, like dating aggression, spousal or child abuse, difficulty holding jobs, and criminal activity. We fail these children when we don't address their behaviors and needs when they arise. If we don't guide them toward constructive social codes when they are young, we should not be surprised that they continue to violate them as adults.

Often, juveniles who bully are bullied themselves or they regularly witness loved ones being mistreated. Children who both dole out and suffer from aggression have the worst outcomes of all. Adults who ignore their behaviors are doing them no favors.

The further into the research I get, the more I recognize the parallels between bullying resolution and restorative justice principles, which aim to reestablish the injured parties' sense of safety and rightful place in their communities. They also encourage transgressors to acknowledge and address the damage they inflicted with the hope that they can reintegrate into society as constructive members. While severe consequences, like expulsion or suspension, might be the last resort for individuals who create unsafe environments for others, restorative justice first offers students the skills and opportunities to repair harm and behave pro-socially.

Unfortunately, I find studies that suggest restorative justice practices are ineffective in schools. I wonder, though, if the fault lies less with the underlying principles and more with program implementation. This could happen easily if people gloss over or don't address the deep wounds inflicted by abusive behaviors, or if they commit what StopBullying.gov refers to as "Misdirections in Bullying Prevention and Intervention," such as treating bullying as a mere "conflict" rather than a form of victimization.

Several bullying prevention efforts have been successful, but outcomes across the field are varied. I learn that endeavors are especially ineffective when administrators neglect to implement transparent policies and when they refuse to identify power imbalances, especially in diverse environments. Short-term, half-hearted, and limited approaches (that don't integrate all community members and all portions of the campus, including specialist/elective rooms and the playground) are unlikely to have long-term effects.

So what does work?

One of the most important elements seems to be the most obvious: strong, compassionate leaders who take bullying seriously and set the tone for the entire community. They establish clear policies and enforce reasonable consequences for misconduct. StopBullying says a victimized child must hear, "No one deserves to be bullied, and we will do everything we can to stop it." And an aggressor must be told, "Your behavior is inappropriate, and you must stop it." Personal experience and anecdotal evidence tell me statements like these are important but insufficient on their own. Instead, the entire community benefits from witnessing words being reinforced by corroborating actions.

Experts also recommend reporting systems and surveys, especially ones that provide anonymity to preserve the safety of the people who speak up. Apparently, these tools don't just identify current problems; they enable schools to detect landmines before they explode. Upon reading this advice, I sigh. At GCA, if injured parties like Hannah want to come forward, they must do so unprotected—they must expose themselves and increase their vulnerability. By contrast, obscurity is afforded to the offenders, whose transgressions are managed in seclusion, if at all. The provision of privacy and protections seems backward if the goal is to be compassionate and just and help those in need.

A common theme I notice throughout the reading relates to the power of culture, which can be influential enough to prevent bullying in the first place. Without a truly caring environment, few programs are effective. Values must be role-modeled from on high and rest on a foundation of authenticity, not rhetoric.

Culture is particularly important because it facilitates one of the most effective deterrents to bullying: peer intervention. Studies show that when bystanders speak up, bullying rates drop precipitously. Unfortunately, this doesn't seem to happen at GCA, perhaps because children there believe that an intervention could lead to their own ostracism or attack. The I Hate Hannah Club and lunchtime call-out "If you like Hannah, raise your hand" are cases in point. Not one child stood up to the malice. So Hannah surmises her peers endorse her mistreatment—that they believe she deserves it.

I'm heartened to read that, in fact, most young people don't support mean behavior. They crave safe, kind communities. But a few bullies can command significant attention, causing students to assume that bullying is more pervasive than it is. When adults promote and validate acts of kindness, they create new norms and fuel a cycle of goodwill.

As I wrap up my investigation, I perform one last search and make a list of well-known people who experienced bullying in their youth. The names include the likes of Lady Gaga, Lin Manuel Miranda, Rihanna, Justin Timberlake, Simone Biles, Eminem, Michael Phelps, Selena Gomez, Drew Brees, Demi Lovato, Elon Musk, and Wayne Gretzky, many of whom are also known to have learning differences. I'll tell Hannah some of their stories so she can know she's not alone. She's more than what people have done to her. She has agency and a worthwhile future—potentially, a very bright one.

Empathy Warrior

The ballroom I'm entering is bright and lively, but I'm braced for the upcoming discussion, which will likely be neither. The event is being hosted by the local clinic that supports children dealing with mental health challenges, learning differences, and attention issues.

When I received the invitation, I was tempted to decline. I've been overwhelmed and harried, with little time to spare. And we've never used this organization's services, so I don't have a personal connection. But over the previous years, too many local teens have ended their lives in what psychologists call a "contagion" (whereby each child's death somehow led to another). While I'm unable to fathom the depth of suffering endured by these families, I feel it's important to show up. This is my community, and I want to lean in and see how I can help.

Maybe I'm also seeking a distraction from my own life. They say one of the best ways to feel better is to support others. So here I am, seeing what I can do.

The keynote speaker takes the stage and unfolds her story. A few guests remain chatting among themselves as she reveals, "I was at my previous job when a young employee came to me and said, 'I just got an anonymous note, and I'm not sure what to do with it.' And then she read, 'He keeps raping me, and he

49

won't stop. Is anyone listening?'" The speaker now has everyone's attention. She continues, "My colleague just stared at me, dumbfounded. And then she asked, 'What should I do?'" The woman on stage pauses before she explains to the audience, "This isn't our business. We're not in the line of supporting rape survivors. But I decided, yes, somebody *is* listening! And so I started a crisis response organization to help people in their darkest hours."

When she took the stage, the speaker appeared to be just another professional in chic, smoke-hued attire. Now, her words reveal something much more dynamic: her empathy. Her cool quotient just rose immeasurably in my book, and I'm transfixed. I realize I'm probably especially receptive to her story after months of watching adults dismiss Hannah's pain. I've pleaded with people to hear me. To believe me. To see my daughter. To help her. All with little progress. Yet when this woman heard a message from somebody she didn't even know, she didn't just listen. She started a whole new enterprise to support her and people like her. Her response is the antithesis of our experience at GCA.

The speaker then mentions her organization's many volunteer counselors, and I'm shaken by the depth of the effort. Individuals undergo at least forty hours of training and donate at least one hundred hours a year, all to help protect the lives of people they will never ever meet.

I feel buoyant and optimistic for the first time in weeks. This is the definition of philanthropy. I read recently that the word's roots come from the Late Latin and Greek *philanthrōpía*, which translates to "the love for mankind." We can all give money or donate time to our own schools and communities, but to help people you will never know (by the system's design) represents an entirely new level of caring.

And *love*.

Someone in the audience asks the speaker why she pursued something so heart-wrenching. She responds, "Others are interested in less emotionally draining ventures. I get it. I do. But these souls . . . they have such compelling stories. I just couldn't turn away."

Thank God.

I realize I'm eager to join her ranks. I want to be impactful beyond my immediate sphere. And I've always been interested in human psychology. When the speaker describes the online training class, I recognize her organization presents an opportunity to pursue my interests in both the cognitive sciences *and* supporting young neighbors in crisis. So I do a full-court press, buckling down to study while my kids are at school or sleeping. After each lesson, I'm given an evaluation, during which I must role-play what I've learned with a computer-simulated texter. Even though I know the texter isn't real, I still get nervous before each test. Will I get flustered? Will I say something insensitive? Will I end up hurting people more than helping them? Am I really up to the challenge? Who do I think I am getting in so deep?

With practice, however, I get into a groove, especially as I realize I'm not expected to know all the answers. Instead, I'm mandated to be an "empathy warrior" who listens compassionately and works alongside texters as they define their own paths forward. This is not my journey. I'm here to bear witness to theirs.

As I work through the material, I begin to appreciate that the lessons don't apply just to counseling. I need them in everyday life! And the formal training is especially useful because much of it is contrary to my natural instincts and social norms.

One of the key things I learn is: ***When somebody shares a painful experience with you, sit in it.*** Until this point, if people I cared about told me their fears or troubles, my impulse was to diminish their problems—to take them away or fix them. When my child said, "I'm scared to go to a sleepover," I responded, "You'll be fine! It will be so much fun! There's nothing to worry about." This is true but doesn't recognize—nor help my child confront—some very real feelings. So I'm now learning to restrain myself and concede calmly, "Doing something new can be scary. What worries you most?"

In the same vein, I'm taught to *resist all temptation to prescribe.* People don't need advice as much as they yearn for a comrade to sit in the trenches with them. Individuals are usually quite capable of solving their own problems. They just don't want to feel alone doing it. Rather than suggest solutions, I'm told to ask things like, "What can I do to be most helpful to you right now?" instead of assuming I know the antidote. Even children can benefit from brainstorming their own solutions before adults dictate possible answers.

I also learn to *resist relating my own story to someone else's.* While my gut tells me that recounting my similar experiences will demonstrate that I sympathize, the training teaches me the opposite is true. The second I mention myself, I pull the spotlight toward me. And while my situation might be analogous, it's never the same. If I want to help people, I need to understand their experiences, not insert my own.

I'm surprised when I'm told to *use strong words to validate feelings.* Too often, to diminish a loved one's pain, I have minimized the language I used to describe it. I worried that a comment like "How devastating!" would inflame the issue and exacerbate trauma—that it might even immobilize my friend. But now I know the opposite is true. Sure, I don't want to introduce hysteria. But when loved ones hear me validate their feelings with expressive language, they are more likely to feel heard, supported, and emboldened to move forward.

I'm also told to *avoid inquiring "Why?"* Of all the question words, "why" is the one that implies judgment. When my husband asks me, "Why are the kids still up?" I feel defensive. Jim might just be wondering if someone is sick, but I assume he's upset that I failed to get them to bed on time. So now I avoid "why" like the plague.

All of this makes me reconsider—at the most basic level—how I interact with people. I used to assume I could see people the moment I laid eyes on them. After hearing them speak, I could decide if I believed or agreed with them. The process was fraught with judgment, but the order was simple: See. Hear. Believe. (Or not.)

I now wince at my arrogance. Who am I to pass judgment on someone else's truth? I have not walked in their shoes. I have not faced their demons. I now know that if I'm lucky, people might share their concerns with me. I then have the opportunity to try to understand them. And only if I'm successful in acknowledging their beliefs and experiences—in understanding their truths—can I truly see them.

The order for me now is: *Hear. Believe. See.*

People's truths don't necessarily have to become mine. But when I listen well, they most often do.

■ ▩ ■ ▩

After I finish the training, I sit at my computer, anxious to log on to my first night of counseling. I passed my evaluations, so I should feel confident. But I don't. Not even close. The weight of responsibility looms large. While I had committed to work for two hours, I end up staying for five, unable to walk away from the long queue of texters seeking support. I'm inspired by their bravery and remind myself, *If they can do this, so can I.*

Among the individuals I connect with is a fourteen-year-old girl who needs somebody to believe her when she confides that her father is molesting her. Apparently, nobody in her family does. So I do my best to convey the same message in every way I can imagine: *Yes, you are believed.* From the outset, she tells me she's scared someone will catch her reaching out for help. She promises that if we're interrupted, she'll text back at a safer time. I initiate the legal process required to help her get her abuse reported, and then I get the one message I don't want: "dads here. gotta go." Our connection evaporates as my brain races to devise a way to grab her through our screens and yank her to safety. My incapacity to help such an obvious need leaves me incredulous and fuming. I'm then deflated when I realize she's not unlike any person approaching a clinic who gets spooked at the last minute and turns away. I don't like becoming resigned to her tragic circumstances, so I pray she finds a safe time to text again.

I sit staring at the screen for a while, and then, somehow, I gather the composure to continue. I end up speaking with four people contemplating suicide, two with imminent intent. This is *way* above the advertised ratio, so I buckle down. Each time, I find myself humbled by the texter's courage and authenticity. Their abilities to reach out to others and articulate their stories, even when they are at their lowest points, are awe-inspiring. I try to rise to the challenge. It's a frenetic, taxing night, one I couldn't have prepared myself for emotionally even if I'd tried. Fortunately, the key principles I gathered during training end up enabling each individual to choose life, at least for tonight. I've been taught this is a huge win, but I still wish I could guarantee so much more.

When I finally allow myself to sign out, I climb in bed and stare at the dark ceiling for hours, praying for the well-being of each person at the other end of the line, especially that girl, who I sense will live with me forever.

Each person I spoke with tonight has unique challenges, but as I rehash the conversations, I recognize two common themes: all of the texters either had their feelings and experiences diminished when they talked to the people who matter to them *or* they are not accepted for who they truly are deep down. As a result, too many feel utterly alone, even when they live in a house full of people who care about them.

This realization makes me consider the kind of person I want to be: I want to be someone friends can talk to, with whom they can share their ugliest truths. I want to help battle the unspoken loneliness I see festering in our society. And I never want my children to feel alone in our own home—or outside of it, for that matter. I must help my children build relationships with other reliable adults so they'll have people to confide in besides their own parents. Kids should know there are decent and trustworthy people out there in the world.

This belief makes me even more agitated by GCA's reluctance to support Hannah. How can so many adults be so apathetic and insensitive?

But then I recall several times when I, myself, said or did the absolute wrong thing when someone else was in need. I had the best intentions, and I wanted to help—but I didn't know how. I once even tried to diminish the trauma of my friend's cancer treatments. I told her that other people had survived chemo and radiation, so she could too. *She was a warrior!* My goal was to inspire her and lessen her pain, but I only left her feeling negated and misunderstood. And probably angry and annoyed too. When I challenged her to be a cancer warrior, I missed the opportunity to be an empathy warrior.

I now wish I had taken counseling training so much earlier. The insights could have helped me throughout every single stage of life. They could have enabled me to be a much better friend, partner, neighbor, and now mother.

I wonder, *Why aren't we all taught to be empathy warriors from the outset?* After all, couldn't we all benefit from supporting one another and being truly seen? Even when we're not in crisis?

Winding Down

Jim and I decide we need help bringing joy to our home, so we enlist an unsuspecting twelve-week-old puppy. I was hesitant at first. We only *just* got our son Theo out of diapers. Am I really up for more potty training? But I know the gift a puppy can be to a child: the ultimate source of unconditional love. Given the difficulties of the past year—the hits to Hannah's self-esteem, the countless sleepless nights, the degree to which the boys felt the fallout as we triaged the most immediate threat to our family—a pet seems like the perfect antidote. Our very own support animal.

When Jim walks through the door cuddling our adoptee, the kids' eyes widen. They look at me quizzically, and when I smile, they leap toward their father.

"Daddy, what is that?"

"What do you think it is?" He laughs.

"Can I touch him?"

"Can I hold him?"

"Please?!"

Each child presses closer.

"Yes, everyone can get a turn. But it's a 'her.' And everyone first needs to calm down. She's shaking. This is a whole new place to her, so we need to be very quiet. And she's small and fragile, so be very gentle with her. Okay?"

"Okay!" all three sing in chorus.

Jim places the puppy on the kitchen floor, and the kids surround her. She moves timidly at first, vacuuming scents through her snout. The children are enthralled.

After a few minutes of introduction, Hannah disengages and skulks toward me.

I worry, *Is this too much? Is this not what she needed?*

Hannah sits on my lap and pets my hair as she whispers into my mouth. I remind her, "Honey, my ear is up here."

She whispers again, "Mommy, what do you think the puppy is thinking?"

I try to assure her. "I think she's happy. She's probably also a little scared after a long day of traveling. But she wants to get to know us. See her sniffing? That's one of the ways she's checking us out."

Hannah is tentative. "I hope she feels at home."

"It might take a little time, but she will. Look how she's already starting to be comfortable around all of you. And check this out." I lead Hannah toward a corner of the living room where I'd piled up some dog supplies without the kids noticing.

"If I were a dog, I'd love these toys and this little private space when you need some alone time," Hannah says, pointing toward the crate that will serve as the puppy's bed. She picks up a chew-toy, and we walk back into the melee together. "I hope she's happy." And then she wonders aloud, "Are we giants to her? How can we make her feel safe?"

Jake is trying to lift the puppy, while Jim reminds him to be gentle. And Theo can't seem to decide if he wants to smother our new pet with hugs or hide behind Jim's legs. It's a glorious cacophony.

I look back at Hannah observing intently, and once again, I'm struck by how different each of my children is.

Hannah continues, "I want to be in charge of combing her and walking her. And who's going to train her?"

"It'll be a team effort. We all need to help."

"Okay," says Hannah. "But I want to be in charge."

The puppy is gnawing the fringe of our rug, so I bat her head away softly. "Maybe we should call her Chewbacca or Chewy," I suggest. "She seems to want to gnaw on everything. Even my fingers!"

The boys laugh, but Hannah is quick to disagree. "No, that's not official. Or kind. We need to come up with a respectful name. One that shows how sweet and wonderful she is."

By the end of the day, everyone agrees on our new family member's name: Grace Gummybear Garrett. Hannah only capitulates when I promise she'll never have to say the word "Gummybear." To her, our puppy is simply "Gracey."

■　▦　■　▦

A few days later, Jim takes Jake and Theo to gymnastics class while I escort Hannah to her end-of-school-year party in a classmate's backyard. The air is warm, but the Northeast humidity has yet to set in. It's a gorgeous June day, perfect for a celebration.

When we arrive, Hannah's eyes pop. The host installed a colorful tent to shield beverages and treats from the sun. But what really draws her attention is the inflated structure arranged in three sections to form an obstacle course. Hannah loves bouncing, but confined spaces with masses of jostling children, like traditional jump houses, can be hard for her. This version, which does not congregate children in one small area, could be perfect.

Hannah is sheepish at first, clinging to my legs. But when she spies Aisha and Amanda, she scurries to join them.

The mother next to me exclaims, "This is amazing! Leave it to Lena to create an amusement park in her backyard! I'm going to need some Advil when I get home!" She has a way of giving compliments with a little bite at the end.

Our host smiles, unwilling to take the bait.

I'm tempted to join a group of parents chatting under a large beech tree, some of whom are clinking glasses of rosé, but Hannah yanks on my arm before I can make my move.

"Mom, they're pushing!"

The activity at the jump house looks raucous, but nothing out of the ordinary for seven- and eight-year-olds. Still, I let Hannah lead me toward the mass of children.

The host hired a teenager to manage the line, but it's a lot for her to oversee. She's admitting one child at a time, presumably to diminish collisions along the course, but the bottleneck makes the queue more tumultuous. I know if I can just get Hannah settled, I'll be able to join the parents lounging under the tree canopy. So I shield Hannah from unintentional bumps, and I wonder, *How can she feel so comfortable standing directly on my feet but be annoyed by nudges from peers?* Her sense of personal space is confounding.

When Hannah enters the course, I beeline for the tree. Of course, I want to relax, but I have an ulterior motive. This cohort of parents has never gelled, ever since I first met them when Hannah joined GCA in kindergarten. I want to get to know them better. I want to help create some comradery. Maybe we can support one another when future problems arise.

I'm offered a glass of wine—a few moms are now on to their second pour—but I stick to sparkling water and wonder if I'll get the chance to let my guard down.

Five minutes later, I feel another tug on my sleeve. "Mom, they're pushing again!"

I guess I have my answer.

A mixture of resentment and embarrassment washes over me. Can't I enjoy the afternoon the way these other parents do? And why must the adults stare at me as I lean over to address my child? I stifle the urge to tell Hannah to *suck it up* and instead offer, "Sweetie, look over there. At the beanbags and bullseye. And the bucket of balloons! Do you want to play with those?" The lure works, and she's off to investigate the options.

Fifteen blissful minutes pass before I hear, "Mom, that babysitter isn't nice!"

"What do you mean?"

"She won't let me stay in the jumpy. I like it in there! It's calm."

Calm? The jumpy? I think, *That can't be.*

But sure enough, I look up and see the jump house is deserted. The swarm of kids is now buzzing around the bucket of balloons, which are loaded with water. The children also found long Styrofoam noodles and are employing them as swords. Between the bombs of water and the whipping blades of foam, the lawn is now a laughter-filled war zone. But Hannah isn't having any of it.

She leads me to the vacated jumpy and recounts, "I was playing with the bean bags, but they came and threw water balloons at me. So I came in here. It's nice here. But that mean lady won't let me stay."

I'm willing to bet the balloons weren't thrown with malice. It's one big free-for-all, but the scene was probably overwhelming for Hannah.

Turning to the young babysitter, I ask, "Is it okay for Hannah to play in here?" I nod to the middle section of the obstacle course, through which children are expected to shimmy to get to the next stage.

She responds, "I was told to keep traffic moving and not let any child stay in one place for too long."

I acknowledge her predicament. "I get it. That makes a ton of sense to keep the kids safe when it's busy. But right now, no one else is here. Would it be okay to let Hannah play inside and then ask her to move along if other kids decide they want to turn this into an obstacle course again?" If I had a count of the number of times I asked people to use their own common sense rather than hard and fast rules around Hannah, the tally might reach the thousands.

"Yeah, okay," she agrees.

But after only a few minutes, Hannah finds me under the

tree again. It's all I can do to contain my exasperation as I turn toward her.

"Mom, other kids came in, and I don't know what to do. They want to run, but they're knocking me over." Her refuge transformed, and with it, my independence.

I notice several mothers watching me as their fingertips dangle from their wine glasses. I see nonchalance in their fingers but not in their eyes.

I'd love to unwind under this tree like they do, but rest is clearly not in the cards for me today. Inhaling deeply, I suppress the urge to scream: *Hannah! Why can't you be like the other kids? Chill out and grab a balloon! Play with the bean bags. Ask some friends to hunt for dandelions with you. I don't care. Anything! Just stop being so needy! You're freaking eight!*

I flash my eyes toward hers and, with one glance, my stance transforms. How did I not notice before? She's on the verge of tears. And her rigid muscles are bracing her entire body, vying to hold it together. She probably senses the moms' judgment as much as I do.

I have a choice to make. I can push my child to rejoin her peers so I can socialize with my own, or I can spend the afternoon as her companion. Essentially, I can encourage her to adapt to the environment, or I can offer her a sanctuary. I know I'm expected to help her stretch herself. Parents are supposed to push their children, not coddle them.

I open my mouth to urge her to go, but as I point toward the lawn, I recall the metaphor that knocked me sideways several months ago: the canary—the stunningly perceptive canary.

I peruse the scene and acknowledge the very real toxins in the air, especially under this tree. I had dampened my senses to tolerate the judgment, but is denying her truth a beneficial survival technique for either of us?

Hannah only just finished second grade, yet it seems she already knows she's different. She doesn't thrive in pandemonium the way many of her peers do. She worked hard to adapt today, but a few eyes under the tree tell us that her effort was not enough. Hannah must act like the other kids if she wants to be accepted here. Nobody will create a quiet space with a calm activity, a place safe from water bombs. So she will need to contort herself to fit in.

I reevaluate the disorderly mass on the lawn, and I motion for Hannah to come closer. I whisper, "To be honest, I wouldn't want to be out there either. It looks a little hectic. Would you like to head home? We can wind down together there."

Hannah nods, her eyes moist and her mouth twitching. But she's resolved to remain intact here. She's learned enough to know that she's better off not letting them see her vulnerability. So instead of bearing witness to her truth today, the others will see only her idiosyncrasies. In another environment, they might be considered desirable. But not here.

I find Hannah's understanding remarkable. She's already learned to hide her tears and her needs. She knows they won't be accommodated.

As I collect my bag, I see the mom who mentioned the need for Advil whispering to a friend, both sets of eyes tracking our trail. Wasn't she the one who suggested this event was a headache waiting to happen? And now she wants to judge Hannah for agreeing?

I remind my daughter to thank our host, who graciously hands over a popsicle.

As we depart through the side gate, relief floods me. We were both trying too hard to adapt. To be something we're not. I might be more adept at conforming to social expectations, and I can hold my own with one or two judgmental moms, but I realize I'd rather spend the afternoon relaxing with Hannah at home. And Hannah clearly couldn't stand the chaos. Why were we even trying? The escape route now allows us to reclaim ourselves.

When we arrive home, Hannah flies toward Grace's crate. The two cuddle, playing quietly until I hear Hannah giggle.

"Mom, she's licking me! What do I do?"

"That's her way of kissing you. She loves you."

It appears the feeling is mutual. Thank God for unconditional love.

Out of the Box

With jaws clenched, Jim and I reenroll Hannah and Jake for another year at the Global Citizens Academy. As Jim said, our negotiating position is only as strong as our next best option, and we're nervous about moving Hannah to a school of nearly five hundred elementary school students. We can send Jake anywhere, but Hannah will do best in a small, structured environment. Who knows about Theo, so we'll watch how he progresses in pre-K.

Despite being apprehensive about giving GCA another chance, we cling to hope. After all, they have the incentive to ensure everything goes smoothly, don't they? They can't afford the reputational damage of another family leaving because of bullying, right? I've heard of several departures, although often they're rationalized with intimations that the child has "issues" or "special needs," in a tone that doesn't make the child sound very special at all. But if the number of fleeing families keeps adding up, won't it be harder to suggest the children are the problem?

Students aren't the only ones leaving. Teacher turnover is creeping higher. Again, the school has justifications for the defections, but excuses will start to wear thin, won't they? On the last day of school, Leslie was overheard saying, "Of all my years teaching, this was the most difficult." Surely, the administration will work hard to retain their most important assets. Right?

We're relieved that this year, Hannah will be in a third-grade class separate from the Daniella and Lauren duo, but I worry for the other children placed with them. And I'm concerned about what might happen on the playground given the loose supervision there. But I want to be optimistic. I want to be able to have faith in the institution overseeing my child's well-being. I want a new beginning.

I recognize we might be suffering from a classic case of commitment bias. Now that we're here, we're questioning the alternatives, weighing the unknowns and the difficulty of uprooting our kids, and hoping we can work within the system to effect positive change. Ideally, the school can recommit to its long-standing values.

■ ▩ ■ ▨

With the decision to reenroll behind us, I focus on providing a relaxed summer for our kids. To simplify and restore. I've planned little more than growing vegetables, building forts, training and grooming Gracey, throwing spontaneous dance parties, turning recycled materials into preposterous "inventions," climbing any tree in sight, and reading stories aloud at bedtime. And we'll focus on good friends, including the ones I plan to see tonight at wine club, comprised of eight women who've evolved into my brain trust over the years. This group always creates a space where I can keep it real and access honest, insightful counsel, no matter how difficult the issue. And we've dealt with some doozies: divorce, job loss, family estrangement, sexual assault, miscarriages, and even stage 4 cancer.

I'm the youngest of the set by a few years and took time finding my mate, so I have the youngest children in the group. While we discuss kids only a portion of the time, I listen intently tonight when the women share the tribulations of parenting teens.

Tonight, one says, "How is it that my child is entering high school, and I'm learning *just now* that he has dyslexia?!" She continues, "I mean, even with eight years of private school tuitions, nothing was picked up. What the hell. And the diagnosis explains so much! But I'm pissed. We could have helped Aidan so much more if we'd intervened early! But they kept saying, 'Wait it out. Be patient. It will click for him.' Well, guess what? It never did!"

"Tell me 'bout it," agrees another. "Luckily, we found out when Ben was entering middle school. But it's still late. Now we're not only dealing with learning differences; we've got anxiety and depression piled on top. He's been assuming he's dumb. Turns out, he's not at all. Not even close. Apparently, he's what they call 2-E. Twice exceptional. He's got extremely slow processing, which covers up his incredibly high intellect in other areas."

She must see the confusion and curiosity on our faces, so she explains, "He's an extremely deep thinker, and he understands some hard concepts at a much higher level than his peers. But when he's asked to regurgitate information quickly, he doesn't perform well. The worst are timed tests. He stresses out, and his mind freezes. So even though he might understand the information, he bombs tests. His confidence is crushed. And the people around him just don't seem to understand what's going on."

"There's such a lack of understanding," says another friend. "Stella has ADHD, but she's inattentive, not hyperactive. Apparently, girls with her profile go undiagnosed. A *lot*. They aren't the ones disrupting the class, so they fly under the radar."

"The more I learn about my kids, the more I start diagnosing myself," one of the moms laughs. "I'm *sure* I have ADHD. But nobody talked about it back when we were little. I swear, I think I understand myself so much better now. I only wish somebody had told me earlier!"

I'm struck that so many families deal with these issues, and I wonder if learning differences are more common than we concede. When I ask about testing, a friend replies, "We should have done it in second grade."

Another insists, "Actually, testing at younger ages is becoming more reliable now." And she advises, "If you're gonna do it, go in knowing these aren't blood tests. There's a lot of subjectivity involved. So the results are only as good as the evaluator. And the science. There's still a lot to be learned about the ways the brain works. But if you can take the test results with a grain of salt, the information can help you learn a lot about your kid."

Before long, the wine softens the mood, and our discussion moves along. But several comments nag me, so I commit to taking personal responsibility for understanding my kids' neurological profiles. I revere educators and over the years I've seen how they're often under-resourced, so I won't pass the buck to them.

The next morning, I make a few calls and find a respected neuropsychologist who tells me she just had a cancelation. She proposes we meet in person and also set aside three mornings in July to have Hannah evaluated. The sessions are expensive, but I'm hoping they'll provide useful insights.

When I meet with the neuropsychologist, Michelle, she explains her process. I ask about school observations, which she admits are useful but won't be possible in the summer. Given Hannah's tumultuous classroom, she wonders if an observation there would have been reliable anyway. She then hands me several surveys to complete before the testing dates.

When I arrive home, I sit at the kitchen table with a warm cup of tea, open a survey, and read: "What are your child's strengths?" and "In what ways does your child struggle?" Staring beyond the window, I try to evaluate this unique child of mine.

Hannah often ignores me. I'm not sure if her actions are purposeful or if she just doesn't hear me. As a result, I don't know if punishment or patience is appropriate, so I tack arbitrarily between the two. My constant doubt in my parenting style is exasperating. And it causes disagreements with Jim, who comes from a strict "command and control" household. When I encourage him to consider softer tactics, he presses, "Do you have any idea what my father would have done if I'd ignored him like that?" I get it, but my research into high sensitivity confirmed that different kids need different approaches. I've noticed the more authoritarian I am, the more resistant and frustrating Hannah's behavior becomes. Gentler responses, when I can muster them, get better results.

Hannah is also in constant motion. I feel the need to make excuses at family dinners with friends because she's often the child who struggles to sit nicely. And Hannah has trouble respecting people's personal space. She bumps into others and stands on my feet. I wonder if she's trying to feel close to me, wants extra stability, or if she's just not aware people might need a little breathing room. Hannah's young, but people judge her already. Boys, not girls, are expected to be wiggle-worms. When boys get up from the art table, people nod. When girls do, they question what's wrong.

Hannah can also be picky about foods, like ripe bananas and avocados. She's particular about her environment too. Situations most kids enjoy—like the hectic backyard class party—are difficult for her.

When Hannah feels stressed, she tries to control her surroundings. Her desk is extremely organized, and she likes her pencils in a row. Just this spring, she impressed our dinner guests by setting that perfect table. And each night, she arranges five specific stuffed animals near her and asks me to kiss each before giving five more kisses to Hannah herself. Is this a normal bedtime routine, or is it indicative of something serious? I've wondered if Hannah has OCD, but maybe she just likes order?

Hannah is also deeply caring and empathetic. She often notices people in pain before others do and rushes to help. And she demonstrates a strong moral compass; she gets particularly upset when adults in charge neglect to discern right from wrong.

She's also a divergent thinker. She loves exploring, questioning, and evaluating the world. Some adults aren't impressed by her unique ways of thinking and encourage her to "toe the line" more. But Hannah is often undeterred as she plows ahead with her novel approaches. Fortunately, some adults respect Hannah. They're fascinated by her relentless curiosity, her ability to discuss abstract ideas, and her precocious vocabulary. They complement her profusely, but I'm hesitant to accept their praise.

I'm proud of my daughter but understand she might be more complex than most people realize. Will a neuropsychologist give me the answers I need to better understand my highly sensitive child? I hope so.

More Data, More Confusion

When I tell Hannah she'll meet with Michelle for around six hours over three days, she's not pleased.

"Why do I need to get testing? Is it because I'm stupid?"

I'm struck by how early children begin to doubt themselves. "No, Honey. Your daddy and I just believe it's helpful to understand each of your learning styles. You, Jake, and Theo. Everybody's brain is different, and we want to know how you learn best. When we understand that, we can help make learning more interesting for you."

She's skeptical, and she verifies, "Jake and Theo will get tested?"

"Yes. We'll want to understand how they like to learn too. But they're not old enough yet. This is for big kids." I'm shameless, unapologetically appealing to her ego, even though Theo probably *is* old enough to be evaluated.

"But my friends aren't getting tested."

"Actually, some are. And yes, some aren't. It's a personal decision. Our family has decided this is important. By the way, the woman you'll work with is really sweet and kind. Her name is Michelle. I think you'll like her."

Hannah looks nervous as we drive to the testing center. We have snacks and water to ensure her energy level, and, as we wait, I prompt her to talk about her favorite animals. I might look relaxed, but I'm working hard to ease her nerves. I've heard hunger and anxiety can undermine the reliability of any evaluation results.

After checking in, we wait on cushy benches. Michelle appears, and I'm relieved to see Hannah's body relax. Michelle's calm demeanor and dimpled smile are winning her over.

After the first set of evaluations, I'm surprised. Hannah looks tired, but she's also content. She enjoyed the one-on-one adult attention, and she likes that she wasn't rushed. I surmise the environment was designed to get the best out of kids.

A week later, Jim and I meet with Michelle, who gives us initial indications (and a forty-page report later confirms) that Hannah has a unique learning profile. Apparently, she has "limited short-term memory," which can cause an "impairment in math fact fluency." She also is diagnosed with "situational anxiety" and "developmental coordination disorder" (the official language to describe "sensory processing disorder" or "sensory integration disorder"). That said, she performs above average in several areas, with particularly superlative abilities in verbal reasoning and conceptual and applied math. I appreciate that the report notes some strengths (in fact, there are more strengths than weaknesses), but it's hard not to home in on words like "limited" and "impairment" and "disorder."

As I consider the totality of the report, Jim questions, "Wait, what? She has both an impairment in math and a strength in math? I don't get it."

Michelle explains there are many ways to assess and excel in various subjects. While Hannah has difficulty memorizing rote facts and recalling them quickly, she has an extraordinary capacity to understand and apply complicated math concepts. This makes sense to me. Hannah can't tell me what twelve minus five is, but she's fascinated by questions like, "What is the biggest number in the universe?" She understands that infinity is more of an idea than a specific amount, and she loves batting around the concepts behind Graham's number, the googolplex, Tree(3), and Rayo's number. I often need to research things I learned (and forgot!) decades ago so I can keep up with her.

I ask Michelle to explain sensory processing disorder. It relates, she tells us, to difficulties organizing and responding to sensory stimuli. Some children are sensory seeking; they need more feedback to their nervous system and might compensate in myriad ways, like wiggling constantly. Others are sensory avoidant and steer clear of uncomfortable sensations. For example, they might be picky about certain flavors and textures of food, or they might clasp their ears to diffuse loud noises. Complicating matters, some kids are oversensitive to some sensory input and under-sensitive to others.

"All individuals present differently," Michelle explains. "Even children with the same disorder can behave quite distinctly."

Disorder. Again, I'm struck by this use of medical language. Yes, Hannah is unique and, at times, more challenging than my other kids. But quite often, especially at home and in other calm environments, she performs capably. More than capably. People often use the word "brilliant" when they discuss her. I picture Hannah speaking with adults, setting the dinner table, caring for Gracey, and analyzing those difficult math concepts. In many ways, she's beyond her years. But now I'm looking at a report that forces me to acknowledge some arenas might not support Hannah. Worse, they might consider her incapable.

I try to imagine how Hannah might feel in her "disordered" body, and I recall the time my twenty-five-year-old self dared to bungee jump from a Swiss ski gondola hovering four hundred feet above the ground. I expected the experience to be exhilarating. Instead, it was terrifying. During the entire freefall, I stretched my limbs to their limits in desperate search of resistance, repeating to myself, "This is not natural. This is not natural." My experience with insufficient feedback lasted eight seconds. Has Hannah been living this way her entire life?

I'm pulled from my memory as Michelle circles back to the anxiety diagnosis explaining, "When a child deals with bullying, like Hannah has, anxiety is not uncommon. Her sensory integration issues are also likely contributors. She wants to perform successfully, but that can be difficult when her body feels dysregulated. For now, because Hannah's symptoms are most apparent at school, we're diagnosing her with situational anxiety. But keep your eyes open. If her symptoms become more pervasive, she might qualify for generalized anxiety disorder."

I'm overwhelmed by all that's coming at me. But of one thing I'm sure: we want to preserve Hannah's mental health. I press further so I can be prepared. "What about OCD?" I describe Hannah's perfectly aligned pencils and her bedtime routine.

She replies, "Those don't sound necessarily obsessive or compulsive. Most kids have a bedtime routine. But if Hannah's behaviors become more ritualized, we'll want to address them."

"Ritualized?"

"Yes, like she's obsessing and committed to a specific pattern, almost like it's religion to her. Rituals become problematic when they disrupt her normal functioning. If she's so committed to her routine that she can't perform basic tasks, like actually falling asleep, we'll need to intervene. But I'm not seeing that now. Are you?"

"No, she's a good sleeper," Jim says.

She must see the confusion lagging on our faces because she adds, "We've discussed several issues. Frequently, and especially for unique kids, we see a cluster phenomenon. Certain diagnoses are often associated with others, so it's not uncommon to be dealing with several things at once." She reminds us, "But each child is distinct, so we'll want to tease out what's driving each of Hannah's behaviors."

Michelle's advice to consider Hannah as an individual—her insistence that no two children are alike—makes me wonder how useful the broad labels are. Still, I appreciate that having names for Hannah's challenges can provide a shorthand to help others consider her needs. To that end, Michelle encourages us to visit Understood.org, which has a database of concise, one-page documents explaining a wide variety of issues.

Michelle then hands us a list of "accommodations" teachers can use to make Hannah's learning environment more "accessible." She recommends both priority seating (near the front of the classroom so Hannah doesn't get distracted) and alternative seating (like a wobbly stool that will allow her to rock and receive calming vestibular feedback). Tools like calculators and headphones are also proposed, as are several measures that benefit most kids, like keeping verbal instructions concise, writing information on the board, and teaching her to use planners to organize her work. Michelle also proposes extra time on tests to calm her anxiety. She then emphasizes that the accommodations are important. They are not merely indulgences. Rather, they help "level the playing field" so all kids "can access an education that suits them."

I'm immediately worried about how GCA will respond to this list of accommodations, so I decide to focus first on creating a relaxing summer break, which I hope will reduce Hannah's anxiety. And I pray that distance from second grade and a separation from her tormentors next year will also help. But before I let down my guard, Michelle advises, "If anxiety escalates, I'll recommend a therapist. Kids often call them 'talking doctors.'"

Michelle moves on to the data associated with the testing, and I buckle down. It's a lot to digest—undefined variables, reams of numbers, and seemingly contradictory charts. But the one unambiguous finding is that Hannah is not "neurotypical." Beyond that, I'm not sure which traits we should accept as Hannah's way of being and which we should try to "remediate." I want to honor who she is, but I also want to help her develop the skills she'll need to thrive.

Before we depart, Michelle offers to meet with Hannah to help her understand the evaluation results. I agree when Michelle notes she'll focus on Hannah's strengths and phrase weaknesses as "growth opportunities." The goal is to arm our child with information so she can feel empowered and self-advocate.

On our drive home, I tally the adults who enjoy Hannah's wonderful inimitability. But I can't deny the dismissive ways many peers, and even some adults, treat her when they realize she's unique. It's brutal. Is this kind of rejection just the beginning? Hannah possesses some wonderful gifts to share with the world. *Will it let her?*

I become introspective and realize I, too, am blameworthy. When I decided to have children, I pictured raucous family barbeques, baking cookies, and throwing a baseball around. But a forty-page report with multiple diagnoses (and a directive to be on the lookout for an escalation in anxiety)? *I was not prepared for this.* This last thought embarrasses me. It feels like a violation of my loyalty to my daughter.

In our meeting today, I was intent on listening and trying to understand, but here in the car, I can't help but indulge my fears. *What does this all mean? Will my child have a normal life? Will she be able to have relationships? Go to college? Get a job?*

Jim glances at me and starts to ask, "Are you . . ."

I shake my head and wave my hand, signaling I'm all right. But I'm not. Not really. Yet I sit alone in the dark corner of my distress because I don't want my concerns to overwhelm Jim. But maybe he has the same fears?

My mind wanders to last year, when Jim played toss in the backyard with Hannah. The ball often failed to find its way into her little hands. I assumed she was just too young to catch consistently. But Jim noted later, "I played every sport in the book. So did you. I assumed our genes would count for something. What if our kids aren't athletic?" He continued, "I get the sense that the hardest thing about parenting is going to be not raising our kids in our own image."

That sentence reverberates now. And I promise myself I'll sit with each of my children in their messiness and find humor in the disarray. I won't burden them with my presumptions or expectations. Instead, I'll stand by them as they stretch to be their best, truest selves. I want to commit to understanding who Hannah really is. Knowing my daughter doesn't fit a mold makes me want to legitimize her. As it turns out, science and math (and even civil rights) are on her side.

Differences Everywhere

I've been warned against using the internet to diagnose. But now that experts have directed me, I can't resist my inner researcher. I pull my chair to my computer and settle in. Almost immediately, I uncover vindicating and valuable information.

Michelle was right. Sites like Understood.org have wonderful resources. Even better, they promise we're not alone! In fact, they tell me *one out of every five* people has a learning difference or attention challenge, although most go undiagnosed. I recall scientists found the same ratio for people with high sensitivity, and I wonder if there's a correlation between it and any of the diagnoses in Hannah's report.

I try to understand the profiles of the "one-in-five" students and soon realize they are quite diverse, affected by a variety of challenges like dyslexia, ADHD, and countless others. Yet, as I dive further into the research, it looks like this lofty one-in-five ratio only initiates the story. It doesn't seem to include many *other* issues that affect learning, like sensory processing disorder (Hannah's diagnosis), even though this one challenge alone is estimated to touch one out of every six children. The one-in-five statistic also doesn't consider hearing deficiencies, speech limitations, and other physical challenges. Nor does it consider mental health concerns. I find this shocking given their potentially significant impacts on classroom performance. (In 2005, the National Institute of Health declared almost a third of adolescents will suffer from an anxiety disorder, and incidences have only increased since then.)

I consider, *What happens when we pile these statistics on top of one another?* The exact correlations, causations, and coincidences are debatable, but *on any given day*, couldn't a twenty-student class have at least five or six affected children? And *over the course of their academic careers*, won't as many as a third or half of all children be impacted? Doesn't this mean *most* families will be challenged in some way, whether we acknowledge it or not?

I push my chair away from the computer. I'm no statistician, but even I can see the implications.

Why aren't people talking about this more?

I'm relieved to understand Hannah's not alone. And yet, I'm disturbed. Are we such conforming, social beasts that we can't admit to the obvious diversity among us? Why do we continue to gag a healthy national conversation and stigmatize countless children?

No matter the site I visit, research confirms learning differences and attention challenges do not equate to a lack of intelligence. In fact, clinicians underscore that children with learning differences are more intelligent than their classroom performance suggests.

As I search, I'm astounded by the number of extremely capable people who've succeeded despite, or even *because of*, their neurological aberrations. I find several lists of famous people who are vocal about, and even proud of, their unique wiring. I also find lists of people who haven't disclosed any diagnoses but are believed to exhibit telling signs. I even find lists of dead people, historical figures who were posthumously diagnosed based on key indicators. These names matter to me because I'm seeking evidence that Hannah will be okay.

Apparently, Cher, Whoopi Goldberg, and Steven Spielberg, along with many of the world's most respected CEOs, have been diagnosed with dyslexia. And some of the most impactful individuals from our past, like Louis Pasteur, Thomas Edison, Alexander Graham Bell, and George Washington, are also believed to have had dyslexia. I also note Justin Bieber, Simone Biles, and Will Smith, among others, speak candidly about their ADHD. And, lately, more and more public figures are forthcoming about their challenges with anxiety, including Adele, Missy Elliot, Ariana Grande, Michael Phelps, and Oprah Winfrey, to name just a few. I also find a list of some of the most influential names known to humanity, each of which is believed to have had what people refer to as "high-functioning" autism (formerly Asperger's syndrome). It includes names like Albert Einstein, Charles Darwin, Marie Curie, Emily Dickenson, Sir Isaac Newton, Beethoven, Andy Warhol, Mozart, Alan Turing, and more. Every single one proves that kids who learn differently can thrive.

I then recall how just last week, a parent of one of Hannah's classmates told a group of moms that she believes her son is "Aspergergian." She described how focused he gets on his areas of interest and how he plans to build a robotics company. He also has perfect pitch. Later that day, another mom noted, "That kid is smart," and said she advised her own son to ask him for help in math.

But at the end of the conversation, a different mom whispered to me conspiratorially, "He doesn't fit here. He should go to a special school." I was thrown. This woman donates time to our local nonprofit that supports children with learning differences. How could someone so intimate with the issue be so intolerant? Is she simply raising money so she can check the box that says she's a good person, never mind the way she regards those she's supporting? Or maybe she engages with the organization to confirm her own kids are more capable by comparison?

I take another look at the list of people with autism and think this mom shouldn't be so quick to underestimate that little boy.

As I read more about public figures with unique brain wiring, I become enamored, in particular, with those who discuss their challenges openly. They're forcing the rest of us to reconsider stigmas so that future generations might not be so incapacitated by them. *What a gift!*

I then try to imagine our world without the people on the lists in front of me. It's practically impossible. What would life today be like without the contributions of Albert Einstein, Alan Turing, or even Oprah Winfrey? I think I'd rather not know.

I'm relieved to find proof that unique people *can* function in and contribute to society, if only we let them. But my reassurance chills as I consider all the people whose gifts were dismissed over the course of history. For every young Sir Isaac Newton, how many others were demeaned and ostracized just for being different? How many capable people were told they were "weird"? "Lazy"? Or "crazy"? The pain of dismissal must have been crushing. And the loss of their contributions to society, devastating.

I then realize something even more tragic. Not only are we casting aside the exceptional, we're dismissing millions of wonderful, interesting children who are not necessarily destined for greatness, yet are wholly human and deserving of dignity— who have a right to compassion and respect, just like anyone else.

And I am to blame just as much as anyone else. The pit in my stomach reminds me of my youth and the ways my friends and I regarded, or disregarded, our classmates who didn't fit in.

I feel it now: the consequences of our actions are not only unfortunate; they are unconscionable. I promise myself that I will never, ever call another human being "weird" or "strange" or "crazy." I will look for each individual's strengths and appreciate their unique ways of being. I refuse to participate in a system that demeans certain people just for their inability to fit in a contrived, arbitrary box. Nobody deserves second-class citizenship.

I think back to that meeting when Richard told me he loves my children. My response was, "I don't need you to love my children. I need you to see them." I now understand what I was trying to convey at a deeper level. Too many children operate in environments that don't allow for their differences. The consequences are demeaning and debilitating. Loving my child doesn't entail treating her like everybody else and ignoring her unique attributes and needs. Loving my child requires acknowledging her distinct characteristics and ensuring the environment supports them. In kinder ecosystems, the culture would even value them.

I See You

In the hottest days of summer, I allow myself long breaks from research. One particularly humid day, Jim and I take the kids out for ice cream to beat the oppressive heat.

As our family finishes our cones, we're entertained by a little boy trying to figure out how to drop a coin into a machine that will distribute a plastic egg with a tiny toy inside. He's probably about three years old and chatters incessantly. When he finally turns the lever sufficiently, an egg pops out, and he yells, "Yellooow! I got yellllooooowwwww!" He has won the lottery in his mind, and my whole family smiles at his joy.

"YELLow! YELLow! YELL-OWWWWWW!"

I turn to his mom and say, "I wish it was that easy for all of us to be so happy."

Her shoulders slump in exhaustion as she closes her eyes. "Just wait," she utters. "In about three minutes, he'll be crying about something completely irrelevant."

I notice the boy with the yellow egg has an older brother and a baby sibling in a stroller. The father smiles, but it's the mom who draws my attention. She's depleted.

I know I should keep to myself, but I can't resist. "Is he highly sensitive?" I ask.

She looks surprised and then nods. "Almost anything sets him off. Good or bad. I used to be that mother who judged other moms in the grocery line when they couldn't keep their kids under control. And then I had *him* . . ."

I see you, Sister. I think, *Maybe you have a canary too.*

She queries, "How did you know?"

"His excitement over the egg. And I see how hard you're working. You're a good mom." I know this is presumptuous, but I feel she needs to hear it and that people probably don't extend this kind of gift to her very often.

Her eyes reach mine, and, without speaking, she conveys, *Thank you for seeing me.*

I then follow my family out of the ice cream shop. And even though I know canaries don't lay yellow eggs, I smile at the symbolism of her son's exhilarating treasure.

Smart Girls

The little boy and his yellow egg stay with me as I move through my days. I take special notice of unique children doing quirky things, and I want to understand them better. So in pharmacies, coffee shops, and parks, I watch other little kids, maybe as much as I watch my own.

At Jake's drop-off one day, a boy with glasses starts telling me about a house he's building in his room for his hamster. The boy speaks with such enthusiasm that I have trouble following his explanations, but it's clear this is no regular hamster nest he's talking about. I hear words like "slides" and "prisms" and "trap doors," and I'm sure it's a marvelous creation.

Apparently, two kids nearby are also struggling to follow this glorious amalgamation of ideas, and one asks the other, "What's he saying?" He seems fascinated at the prospect of building a home for a creature in one's very own bedroom.

The other onlooker responds, "I dunno. That's weird. He's dumb." And with that, the two stride away.

I hope the hamster owner didn't overhear, but a quick glance confirms he did. His head drops and his mouth shuts, halting the stream of fascinating ideas.

Dismayed to realize this probably happens regularly, I become fascinated with the concept of intelligence and how some people qualify while others don't. Clearly, even first graders have strong opinions on the topic.

So I pull out the IQ test Hannah completed as part of her work-up (the Wechsler Intelligence Scale for Children), and I see it measures capabilities in ten areas, which are averaged in pairs to get five sub-scores, and then averaged again to get the final intelligence quotient. While the ten original scores might offer a window into a child's unique capacities, I've never heard anybody talk about them outside of my neuropsychologist's office. Instead, people generally refer to—focus on—the one big composite number.

As I review the data, I can see how the number crunching actually chips away at—or maybe even sledgehammers—any semblance of individuality, any nuanced understanding of the test taker's particular strengths and weaknesses. For example, the process of averaging can cause someone who registers at the fiftieth percentile in all areas to be equated to another with ridiculously high marks in some sections and very low ones in others. Said another way, a true "genius" in a specific area could get the same IQ score as someone whose underlying scores demonstrate no particular strengths or weaknesses at all. And a fascinating first-grader with a brilliantly creative mind can be considered "dumb" when his ideas flow faster than his brain's ability to organize them.

I consider this in light of a fascinating book by renowned education researcher Todd Rose. In *The End of Average*, Rose details the perils of averaging, especially when analyzing heavily nuanced issues. And what could be more complex than the human brain? Throughout his writing, Rose demonstrates how "when it comes to understanding individuals, the average is most likely to give incorrect and misleading results." While averages can show a middle point, frequently, no single individual actually sits at that point. And by focusing on the average, we miss the wide variety of traits that are present and important to understand. In the end, Rose shows that when we have designed something—a workplace, a classroom, or even a fighter jet—around an average, we have actually "designed it to fit no one."

I look again at the test variables and realize that maybe even more interesting than the information measured is the information excluded: attributes known to be meaningful drivers of success and brain power. Countless researchers have demonstrated the importance of things like emotional intelligence, street smarts (common sense), judgment, creativity (divergent thinking), grit, a knack for making connections among seemingly disparate ideas, an awareness of spatial relations, linguistic capabilities (including communication skills), musical aptitude, and the ability to override biased preconceptions. While skeptics might consider some of these characteristics "soft," many scientists disagree. Neurology has proven that *all* perceptions, instincts, evaluations, judgments, and reasonings are, in fact, cognitively based. So, how did only a few measures get included on a test that's entrusted to provide a fair, broad-sweeping assessment of people's intelligence?

In reading, I learn that almost forty years ago, Dr. Howard Gardner developed a theory of multiple intelligences, which promotes a more comprehensive understanding of intellectual capacity. He advised against presuming people can be ranked along a single scale of intelligence. Instead, he encouraged us to see one another more holistically by acknowledging the broad range of "autonomous" intelligences. After all, who's to decide which manifestations of smarts are more valuable? And why would we want to favor some capabilities—and people—in the first place?

I start rethinking my assumptions about intellect entirely. And the more I read, the more I see the IQ test as an artificial construct that, when relied upon too heavily, suffocates our understanding of neurology *and* our appreciation of one another's individuality.

I find many problematic aspects. For example, standardized tests favor speed. Yet for decades, scientists like Benjamin Bloom have shown that speed is not a good indicator of scholastic ability. I've always wondered why people would favor speed of processing over depth of understanding, yet that's exactly what most standardized tests do.

Standardized tests are also unreliable when anxiety is at play. And they are biased toward certain students depending on their socioeconomic background, prior education, and language fluency. I find it shocking that institutions still demand these tests given the apparent civil rights implications.

And, evidently, standardized tests are at odds with the current neuroscience on growth mindsets and neuroplasticity. While scientists once believed cognitive abilities were fixed, research proves that brains continue to reorganize synaptic connections throughout our lifespans, especially in response to learning and experience. Unfortunately, standardized tests only assess a limited set of capacities at one point in time, so they are not designed to capture one of the most remarkable characteristics of our brains: their plasticity.

Confused by our society's long-standing adherence to standardized testing and an arbitrary definition of intelligence, I wonder how we began to rely on them in the first place. Several books, like Carol Dweck's *Mindset* and Scott Barry Kaufman's *Ungifted*, suggest that even the father of the IQ test himself, Alfred Binet, did not believe his evaluation captured the rich diversity of intelligence, nor did it measure cerebral development over one's lifetime. In fact, Binet claimed that using the composite IQ to determine overall intelligence was a betrayal of the test's purpose. Yet, over a century later, that's exactly what we're doing.

My annoyance converts to disgust when I learn that Binet's tests in France were adapted for use in the United States by people like Henry Goddard and Lewis Terman, well-known eugenicists who sought to segregate schools and identify the "feeble-minded" among us. Goddard went so far as to integrate labels like "idiot" and "imbecile" and "moron" to categorize test takers. I knew IQ evaluations were eventually used to condemn people to institutionalization and sterilization. I just didn't realize that the actual *origins* of IQ testing in the United States had eugenic underpinnings.

The more I read, the more it seems we would benefit from reconsidering our current, often politically motivated, measures of intelligence, which were developed during the second industrial revolution when standardization and Taylorism were all the rage. The goal was to feed people into assembly lines, not help them evolve into their best selves. Ideally, a new understanding would appreciate the broad diversity of human intellect and emphasize its evolving capacity. A reasonable definition would also be intolerant of any discriminatory bias.

Until now, I took standardized test results at face value. Going forward, I'll be skeptical when people ignore the intricacies of the underlying data. And I'll be concerned when I hear anybody refer to a child's weakness without also considering strengths. For example, "Your son doesn't decode well. He has dyslexia, and we recommend tutoring for his disability," versus "Your son has dyslexia, which we can see in his low coding scores and slow reading rate. But look here. He also has impressive aptitudes in areas often associated with dyslexia, like three-dimensional thinking and pattern recognition. Let's leverage those to enhance his overall cognitive output!" I, myself, have never been inspired to work hard for people who harp on my shortcomings and ignore my capabilities. Why should we expect kids to be any different?

I also will raise an eyebrow when I hear people label one child as smarter than another without copping to the diverse forms of intelligence, many of which are neglected in common testing. After all, no one has a monopoly on smarts. And we all have weaknesses. I once heard someone say about a Nobel

Laureate, "The guy can barely communicate with other human beings, and he's lucky to find his way home some days!" Even highly lauded people have deficiencies.

I will perhaps be most annoyed when people regard intelligence as a fixed trait without considering the possibility of neural growth. Currently, we praise people who demonstrate aptitude at the outset. But wouldn't it be more interesting to document when someone enhances brain capacity, no matter the starting point? Shouldn't we be praising *that*? Isn't human effort and deliberate development more impressive than stagnant capacity (no matter how high)?

■　▩　■　▩

Later that week, with lots of new research under my belt, I gather my clan, and we head to the park to meet one of our favorite families. The two oldest children are peas in a pod, but the similarities are not apparent to some. Hannah and Ava are both eight, but due to a rare genetic aberration, Ava functions closer to what might be expected of a three-year-old. Nonetheless, Hannah adores Ava. Actually, we all do, but the two girls have a special connection. They listen to music, play, and enjoy their own form of communication. Hannah doesn't mind that Ava can't articulate words and has flailing limbs. Instead, she delights in everything Ava does.

As we approach our friends clustered around Ava's wheelchair, we notice a new tool on her lap. It's a digital touchscreen with "buttons" labeled with colorful icons to help her communicate. We watch her select a food button, and up pops pictures of her favorite things to eat. She presses one, and an automated voice declares what she wants.

When Hannah sees Ava plugging away, she declares, "Ava's so smart!"

My instinct reacts, *Well, no* . . . But I reel back, embarrassed by my quick judgment. Hannah sees the world, and other children, without the expectations and bias that encumber adults. She values Ava as an individual, not by where she falls in comparison to others. Hannah appreciates her friend's unique capacities: her infectious joy, her love of music, her kindness, and so much more. She doesn't reduce Ava to some arbitrary metric (like IQ). She doesn't harp on what Ava can't do. Instead, she delights in what Ava can do. Right now, she's identifying Ava's capacity to stretch and grow her brain, to demonstrate neuroplasticity, just as I should have. I've been doing the research, after all. Shouldn't I be able to apply it?

I flush with pride. My girl's reminding me that the world is more than the sum dots along a bell-shaped curve. Today, Hannah watches her dear friend achieve something we all thought was impossible. *She's speaking!* So Hannah stands firm, "Ava is smart!"

I can't help but acknowledge, "Yes, she is, sweet girl." *And so are you.*

Typical Versus Diverse

When I share Hannah's assessment of Ava's intellect with a friend, she suggests I investigate the concept of neurodiversity. Apparently, while digging away in my rabbit hole researching the results of Hannah's neuropsych report, I overlooked an important tunnel. With instructions and a headlamp, I set off to explore a new realm.

So far, our journey has been shrouded in obscurity. We seem to be burrowing in a parallel universe hidden just below the Earth's surface. Entrances are difficult to find, and paths are revealed through hushed whispers and vague nods of the head. Few people speak publicly about this subterranean world, causing us to feel daunted, disoriented, and isolated. Yet, the labyrinth becomes habitable as we find individuals unhindered by stigma. Each time somebody nudges us toward relevant information, I'm grateful to watch new portions of our burrow illuminate. Often, the light reveals thoughtful people and intriguing perspectives.

Unfortunately, however, we regularly encounter obstacles as well. Today, I search for the term "neurodiversity," and Merriam-Webster.com insists: *The word you've entered isn't in the dictionary.**

---

*Merriam-Webster finally did add "neurodiversity" to its dictionary during the publication of this book. Hopefully, it won't take as long to add other words that help us understand and appreciate one another.

I try again at Dictionary.com and find the word is known and defined as: *the variation and differences in neurological structure and function that exist among human beings, especially when viewed as being normal and natural rather than pathological.*

I like this explanation. It legitimizes my child and all people who don't fit a mold. And it's consistent with scientists' warnings about averages, especially when studying complex subjects.

I consider how often I've heard the term "neurotypical" over the past few weeks, usually in the context of explaining our family's deviations from it. I now wonder if the "neurotypical" standard should be employed with such high frequency. After all, very few—perhaps no—brains are typical in totality. Every single brain has unique characteristics, including those of twins. But when we sort children along bell-shaped curves, differences become deficiencies. And even twins are ranked against one another.

I wonder if the word "neurodiverse" should be at least as common in our lexicon as "neurotypical." I do like the idea of a diverse community more than a typical one. It speaks to a more interesting world. But as I continue my quest, I'm deflated to see that use of the word "neurodiversity" is mostly confined to discussions about autism spectrum disorder. Doesn't the very definition suggest a broader application? Selfishly, I don't want the ASD community to have a monopoly on this validating terminology.

I look again at Dictionary.com's definition and can't help but home in on the final word: "pathological." It's a big concept with profound implications. Are we, in fact, pathologizing children's differences rather than recognizing them as normal variations inherent to humanity? Are we so opposed to individual nuances that we employ the language of disease and injury to describe them?

Over the past weeks, my research into the world of learning differences has been infused with words like disorder, deficiency, dysfunction, and disability. Each case study slots kids into concerning categories: *Michael has a visual processing disorder; Chloe has a reading comprehension deficit; Joey's learning is affected by a central nervous system dysfunction; Mary has dyscalculia, a math disability.*

And once the labels are assigned, they seem to supersede all others. It would be one thing if diagnoses were used simply to help identify specific impairments and support people's weaknesses. But the consequence is far greater. In everyday life, I've seen diagnoses effectively become overarching descriptors of the individual as a whole. People look past all capabilities and instead focus on, even aggrandize, the "dis."

I wonder, *Why are we defined most by what we can do least?* That doesn't make sense. If we must choose one attribute, shouldn't we then be defined most by the things we can *do* most? By the things we *are* most? Kind, articulate, fast, perceptive, loyal, funny, brave . . . whatever . . . anything, really, besides our biggest weakness. Even better, shouldn't we strive to acknowledge the complex, interwoven, deep amalgamation of our humanity rather than highlight one trait?

Maybe our instinct to accentuate weakness is a result of word derivation. While Merriam-Webster.com officially defines "disability" as a *condition that impairs, interferes with, or limits a person's ability*, the dictionary takes a more austere stance on "dis." The prefix doesn't indicate that something is *limited, below,* or *less than*. Rather, it means the *opposite* or *absence of* or even simply *not*. As a result, the term "disabled" seems to translate literally into "the opposite of abled" or "not abled."

But does anyone really believe that a young child with a learning disability is "not" able to learn? Or that an individual with any sort of impairment is the "opposite of" abled?

Words are powerful. They are used regularly to demean and "other" people. I consider how even on a standalone basis, the word "dis" denotes how we treat others with *disrespect or contempt* and *insult* or *criticize*. Is this really the association we want to make, the aura we want to cast, with young learners? With anyone?

I become increasingly concerned when I realize how liberally people use the language of pathology in the education world. If one in five children have a learning difference and we consider each one "disabled," we are effectively pathologizing *twenty percent* of the population. And we are doing so while children are developing their self-perceptions and identities, vulnerable endeavors with potentially lifelong impacts.

I consider the wide variety of people affected. Scientists estimate that one in seven have dyslexia; one in nine live with attention challenges like ADHD; one in six, like Hannah, have trouble with sensory processing; one in ten experience dyspraxia, which affects fine and gross motor skills; one out of every twenty struggle with auditory processing; and one in twenty also present a speech impairment by first grade. The list goes on . . . and on. It's staggering to think of all the kids who are being told they're "abnormal" when, quite often, they are simply different.

The most common learning challenge kids face is dyslexia, which is officially referred to as a "specific learning disorder with impairment in reading." I wonder, *Is it really a disorder?*

The dictionary's website says a "disorder" is *an abnormal physical or mental condition.* But dyslexia is common, affecting one in every seven people. Also, dyslexia is not correlated with lower intelligence. Instead, by definition, the diagnosis is assigned when students' aptitudes are higher than their classroom performance suggests. Further, dyslexia is regularly associated with several strengths, like creativity, divergent reasoning, three-dimensional thinking, pattern recognition, and strong interpersonal skills. Some of the world's most successful business leaders—like Richard Branson, John Chambers, and Charles Schwab—are dyslexic and have noted the ways these related capabilities help them lead.

I don't deny that dyslexia causes difficulties in language-based learning, which children deserve to have addressed. But what, exactly, are we trying to accomplish when we focus on children's weaknesses without acknowledging their strengths? When we label them "disordered"?

Is it any wonder research shows that twenty-nine percent of children diagnosed with a "specific learning disorder" also suffer from anxiety? Or that forty-five percent of children believed to have "learning disabilities" report being bullied?

What are we doing to our children?

I find the tendency to pathologize especially disturbing when I consider the research on neurodiversity (which documents the natural variation among brains) and neuroplasticity (which shows brain function continues to develop throughout one's lifespan, especially in response to learning and experience). Pigeonholing students with rigid labels when we know brains are distinct and their capacities aren't fixed seems terribly short-sighted. Again, I'm not suggesting we shouldn't address weaknesses. I just think we should reconsider and reframe the methods we use to do so.

As I read on, I become fascinated when people discuss how they regularly feel more disabled by the ways society treats them than by their impairments or aberrations. The social model of disability holds that people's activities and well-being are often restricted by the environment and views of what's normal. I consider this concept within the context of various learning diagnoses, like ADHD, which was granted a double-whammy of pathology: attention-*deficit*/hyperactivity *disorder*. My research reveals that, in fact, many people with ADHD often don't feel deficient or disordered until they are forced into certain rigid contexts, like traditional classrooms with hard chairs and expectations to stare at whiteboards for long periods of time. But in modern, flexible, adaptive, accepting environments, these children can be quite successful.

As a result, several advocates encourage us to distinguish between conditions that are debilitating in almost any setting and those that present problems primarily in specific contexts. For example, bipolar disorder can be devastating anywhere and is worthy of serious medical attention. By contrast, many people with autism can feel quite capable in unprejudiced environments that consider the individual strengths and needs of everyone rather than just those of the dominant group. In cases like this, accommodation and support can be more effective than pathology and diagnosis.

I've started to share the results of Hannah's neuropsych report with the professionals around her—clinicians, educators, school administrators, and others charged with helping her evolve into her best self. Some treat her with respect, recognizing both her challenges and her aptitudes as they endeavor to support the "whole child." These people often pursue a "strength-based" approach to leverage Hannah's many interests and capabilities so they can enhance her "growth opportunities." I especially appreciate when they work with me to consider how to enhance the environment to be more accommodating to *all* children.

But I feel wary around the others, those with deficit mindsets who let diagnoses overshadow Hannah's many wonderful abilities. Many *sound* supportive at first and inspire hope for my family. But their subsequent actions and judgments can belie their words. I'm especially confused when learning specialists reveal deficit mindsets and focus on weaknesses. I wonder why anybody, especially the experts, would flatten a child this way. Maybe some find it easier to blame the child rather than turn the spotlight to reevaluate the environment and systems? Perhaps other people emphasize problems—and thereby augment hysteria—so parents might pay for more services. After all, if certain characteristics are deemed "abnormal," parents will feel more compelled to "fix" them.

I know from my own experience that if children are made to feel insufficient and parents fear for their futures, the whole family might become distressed, even anxious. Many of the clinics that diagnose learning disabilities also provide mental health services. So the "dis-es"—the disorders, dysfunctions, deficiencies, and disabilities—can be good for business. But why augment anxiety? As an economic matter, the extraordinary demand for psychology services is currently unmet. Why drum up more?

In his book, *Neurodiversity in the Classroom*, Thomas Armstrong suggests, "Instead of regarding [certain] students as suffering from deficit, disease, or dysfunction, neurodiversity suggests that we speak about their strengths. Neurodiversity urges us to discuss brain diversity using the same kind of discourse that we employ when we talk about biodiversity and cultural diversity. We don't pathologize a calla lily by saying that it has a 'petal deficit disorder.' We simply appreciate its unique beauty." He argues that we similarly ought not pathologize children who have different ways of being. We should appreciate the inherent beauty and value they bring to the world.

This sounds like a worthy goal.

■ ▨ ■ ▨

I'm so intrigued by the concept of neurodiversity and the language of pathology that I ask a friend to introduce me to a board member of a national organization that advocates for students with learning differences. I'm thrilled to have the opportunity to pick her brain, but when we meet over coffee, it takes me only a few minutes to shove my foot into the back of my throat.

I express concern over children who learn differently being considered disabled, and she warns me, "Be careful. You don't want to sound ableist."

Oh, shit. In my drive to support one group of people, apparently, I've dismissed another. I feel flush and compelled to shut down. I'm ashamed I might be prejudiced or ignorant, or even a bad person.

But the words of one of my favorite social scientists, Brené Brown, ring in my ear: "People are opting out of vital conversations about diversity and inclusivity because they fear looking wrong, saying something wrong, or being wrong. Choosing our own comfort over hard conversations . . . moves us away from meaningful and lasting change."

So I stay engaged. And the woman across from me acknowledges over her mug, "It's hard. But we need to remember that some people take deep pride in their association with the Disabled community. And they don't want the word 'disability' to be considered bad. Many want to *own* the term to decrease its stigma. They've worked hard to gain rights through legislation—civil rights others take for granted—and we don't want to do anything to take those away."

"I agree!" And my mind is reeling. There's so much to consider. I'm on a quest to honor all individuality, after all, and I don't want to demean *anyone*.

I wonder if, in order to avoid being ablest, I should submit to the pathology that labels my daughter "disabled," even if I don't consider her disabled. And even if she doesn't see herself as disabled. She is so capable in so many ways! But is signing up for this construct the only way we can demonstrate our support of civil rights for all?

I then recall the motto of the disability movement: "Nothing about us without us." And I feel adamant Hannah deserves this kind of respect as well. She should have the opportunity to shape her own identity.

I ask the woman, "What if we let individuals decide for themselves if they identify with the term 'disabled'? Our current approach, where designations and labels are assigned by third parties from on-high seems pretty arrogant. And it strips people of agency. Shouldn't individuals have a say in how they present themselves to the world?"

She agrees, "I think that's part of the answer: self-determination." But then she pushes back. "Diagnoses are just really important because they provide civil rights."

I ask, "Are we conflating two things? Must people be identified as 'disabled' before they are allowed reasonable access to common resources and treated humanely? Right now, we have a system that demands diagnoses as preconditions for enabling inclusion. People must visit doctors or engage court systems in order to access basic rights. Can't we instead acknowledge and even appreciate differences from the outset and build systems that enable *all* people to participate in society? And then, separately, let individuals determine their own identities? Why must these two things be intertwined?"

She sighs, "Unfortunately, that's just the way the world works." She insists that as long as people view community assets as a fixed sum, those in control and those who see no personal need for change will resist a more reasonable distribution. And they'll lean back on historic, albeit arbitrary and contrived, standards for determining who's worthy and what's "normal."

I find this depressing. Clearly, all our lives would be enhanced if we appreciated the wide variety of people's strengths and enabled more individuals to contribute to our communities, both socially and economically. Why fight over a slice of pie when we can bake a larger, richer dessert?

In his fascinating book *NeuroTribes*, Steve Silberman reminds us, "Inclusion is not about doing something nice for disabled people; it's about making sure that everyone has the best chance to succeed." Specific to neurodiversity, he insists, "We have to learn to think more intelligently about people who think differently."

I take that as a challenge. I know I'm only just beginning to understand the complexity of these issues, but I'm determined to learn more.

A Fresh Start

As we face the new school year, we're thrilled to learn that Hannah is paired with a well-loved teacher, Megan. But last year she was an assistant; this will be her first time leading a class. Hannah is complex, and she has responded well to experienced educators like Leslie, who saw Hannah's individuality and embraced it. We cross our fingers and hope this enthusiastic young teacher can do the same.

When we walk into the third-grade classroom for our back-to-school parent conference, Megan tours us around the room. It's adorned with crisp, fresh wall decorations, reflective of her status as a new teacher. While she speaks capably, she appears nervous. I try to put her at ease, noting, "This classroom is so organized! Hannah will love this!" I mean it. Hannah responds to structured environments, and with her separation from the two girls who bullied her last year, she might get a real do-over. I start to relax as my hope rises.

Megan beckons us toward miniature chairs, and we sit askew as she introduces the upcoming curriculum. She asks us to provide any pertinent background information while her teaching assistant, Sonia, sits quietly beside her.

Jim and I share an abbreviated neuropsych report, including the recommended "accommodations," like preferred seating in front of the classroom and alternate seating that rocks or wiggles to provide sensory feedback. I'm hesitant to share this list because I don't want teachers to think Hannah is high-maintenance or to resent her before the school year even starts. But I know my daughter needs the tools to focus, listen, and learn. Fortunately, Megan and Sonia smile and nod receptively. Before we leave, I mention that I'm hopeful Hannah's anxiety will ease in a classroom without the girls who targeted her last year.

Megan questions, "Hannah was bullied?"

I'm astounded. "Nobody updated you on the dynamics of this class?"

Megan and Sonia's shared glance confirms nobody prepared them. *Ugh.* This means I won't get the opportunity to start the year simply as Hannah's mom. I already need to inform and advocate. But if I want my child to have a fighting chance, I have no choice.

■　▨　■　▨

The morning of the first day of school, Hannah wraps one arm around Grace while she twirls her hair with her spare hand and murmurs, "Mommy, can you walk me into the classroom?" Her eyes fixate on the floor. I'm struck that even nuzzled next to her canine companion, Hannah is fidgeting with her hair. She still needs to self-soothe.

"Of course! I'm excited to see it. Most parents will walk their kids in today. And it's totally normal if you're a little nervous. I felt the same way each time I started a new grade."

When we arrive at school, Jim and I divide and conquer: he leads Jake and Theo to Jake's classroom while Hannah clings to my fingers. When we reach her room, Hannah stalls. I sense she's contending with an invisible force field emanating from the door. I attack it first to demonstrate she'll be okay, and she trails through. Beyond the barrier, Hannah relaxes a bit. We search for her desk, and I'm reassured to find it at the front of the room. I consider this placement an encouraging gesture of goodwill.

"Mom, look!" she says smiling, pointing at Amanda and Aisha. She's thrilled to spy her two favorite friends' desks placed on either side of hers.

We're on a roll! She actually looks excited to be here.

I feel optimistic but then re-tense as I peak under the desk and spy a standard chair. Surveying the room, I tally five wobbly stools along the back wall near a large mat and bookshelves. I consider that, perhaps, all kids start in regular chairs but are given the opportunity to swap as necessary. Maybe Megan doesn't want to single any child out on the first day.

Hannah directs my attention back to her desk. "Mom, what am I supposed to do with that?" I peer down and see a checklist that includes things like sharpening pencils, finding cubbies, and choosing books from the class library. Nothing looks challenging, but Hannah is nervous to be tasked so quickly.

"Look, Honey. It's all fun stuff to help you get oriented! Maybe Amanda, Aisha, and you can work on this together!" The girls smile and bound off.

Megan uses the opportunity to sidle up to me, and I'm quick to say, "Thank you so much for placing her in front of the room. It'll be so helpful for Hannah."

"Of course!" she affirms.

I compliment her room again, and then I stammer, "I was just wondering . . . if it looks like Hannah's wiggling a lot in her chair, can she use one of those stools in the back?"

"Oh, definitely," she promises.

I'm grateful, and I offer to pull together some parents to source additional stools if more kids require them. I acknowledge, "I know budgets don't always cover all classroom needs."

"Thanks so much! I appreciate it!"

Hannah returns with her friends, giggling as they investigate their new desks and delighting in one another's company. Sensing the opportunity to escape, I lean down, kiss Hannah on the cheek, and say, "Have a great day, hon! It looks like you're set for a great year!"

She surveys her surroundings, nods, and returns to her friends.

After bursting out the front door of the school, I resist the urge to jump and cheer. *Maybe we did it! Maybe Hannah gets to have a good school year!*

I'm beyond relieved.

■　■　■　■

Over the next few days, Hannah continues to ask me to escort her to class while Jake rushes ahead on his own. But with each passing day, Hannah is less anxious. A week into school, as she finishes brushing her teeth before bed, she remarks, "I'm excited to go to school tomorrow!" I had forgotten. It was something she used to say regularly. But her enthusiasm waned last year, until that awful morning when she curled up in my bed and refused to go. The contrast between then and now is remarkable. *My daughter is back!* She *wants* to like school, and now she's able. I'm thrilled.

With Hannah feeling more self-assured, I encourage her independence and eventually make regular use of the carpool lane. Her safer classroom enables her to rise to new challenges. And I gain a little more freedom. *Hallelujah.* It's so much easier to parent without bullying and anxiety undermining our efforts.

Each day, after tumbling in the car to join Theo, Gracey, and me, my two oldest kids interrupt one another to review their school days. But over the course of a few weeks, Hannah grows quieter. She looks exhausted and withdrawn.

One day about two months into the school year, Hannah collapses into her seat as the door shuts behind her. She looks not just tired, but upset.

"Honey, are you okay?"

"There was a lot of mat time today," she whines. "And now my head hurts."

"What's mat time?"

She explains how they have to sit on the floor for long periods. "Like when the teacher's reading a story. Or teaching about math."

"You do math on the floor?"

When she confirms they do, my frustration rises. The doctor was very specific about Hannah's need for support while sitting.

Two out of five days the following week, Hannah melts down as soon as we pull out of the school parking lot. A week later, it's three out of five days. She's twirling her hair more, and she again starts pleading with me to walk her into school.

Please, no! I was just getting the hang of the drop-off line. And enjoying it! So I decide to investigate.

The following Monday, I park my car and walk the kids into school. Jake scurries to his classroom while Theo and I escort Hannah to hers. Fortunately, Megan looks unoccupied.

Hannah clings to me, but I encourage her to show Theo around the classroom so I can chat with her teacher alone.

Megan is polite, but I detect an air of annoyance. So I get to the point by asking if she has noticed anything different with Hannah lately. "Does she seem okay?"

She insists Hannah is doing "really well." She acknowledges Hannah can get off track but "listens when redirected." She tells me Hannah's engaged in their US presidents project, but I already know this. And I didn't come here to talk about presidents, so I probe, "You haven't noticed her getting tired or falling apart during the day? It sounds like she's especially having trouble working on the mat without back support."

"No. Not at all. Things are great!"

I wonder if Hannah's putting on a game-face in the class-room, or if Megan's right and there's really no issue. We seem to be experiencing two very different girls.

The next afternoon, after Hannah and Jake climb in the car,

Theo declares, "Mommy, today is October seventh!" He's proud to be learning about the calendar in school.

I tell him, "Some people think seven is a lucky number. Maybe it's our lucky day?!"

Hannah explodes, "I hate seven! Seven is terrible!" She's absolutely furious.

I try to reclaim peace, but she refuses. Instead, she yells, "I hate odd numbers!"

What am I supposed to do with that? I want to tell her to *chill out*. But instead I say, "Hannah, Babe, yes, seven is an odd number. Is there a reason you don't like odd numbers?"

She yells at the top of her lungs, "They're awful!"

The whole car drops into silence. Nobody knows how to react to this war on digits.

Then Hannah admits sheepishly, "My teacher won't let me use the wobbly stool on odd days. And I can't sit on the hard floor! We have to stay there forever, and my body doesn't work that way!"

I'm glad she can articulate her needs but frustrated to hear this arbitrary rule that no one has informed us about. When I ask Hannah why she can't use a stool on odd days, she explains that the other half of the class has priority then. Her half, ten children, is only allowed to *take turns* on the five stools during even days, meaning she doesn't have access over *half* the time.

I ask if she's sure, and she yells, "Yes! And the mat hurts! It's rock hard! And there's nothing to lean against! So I ran out of the room to move my legs and the teacher got mad." She bursts into tears again.

I want to hug her, but how am I supposed to console a distraught child and drive safely at the same time? As soon as we get home, I calm Hannah and then dash off a quick email:

Hi, Megan. Hannah is really enjoying her presidents project and has been practicing her presentation at home.

But she's also been enormously tired at the end of the day. It seems the mat time is draining her. Are you seeing the same thing? As you probably recall from her neuro-psych report, they recommended alternative seating to help Hannah regulate her nervous system and concentrate. I remember you saying she could have access to a wobbly stool if she needs one, but evidently there is a schedule for this? Or is Hannah misunderstanding?

I almost delete the technical language because I don't want to sound arrogant. But I decide to keep it to signal I'm not trying to be difficult. I'm trying to follow the expert's guidelines.

Megan answers later that evening:

Yes, Hannah is very enthusiastic about President Taft. She was excited to learn that he kept a cow on the White House lawn! As for stools, yes, Hannah has access. Thank you for checking in. Sincerely, Megan

I type back:

Thanks for assuring this! Hannah is so much more attentive if she can use a stool. I'll be sure to remind her to grab one if she's feeling unsettled. Thanks again for all you do! Kind regards, Kayla

The next morning, I review emails before preparing breakfast and see Megan responded:

Hi, Kayla. Please feel free to remind Hannah that she can use the stools on even days. Thank you so much, Megan

So Hannah was right.

My blood pressure starts to rise. And since we're getting nowhere on email, I shoot one last message to request a meeting in person.

Megan answers quickly, suggesting we get together at the end of the week.

When I drive the kids to school the next day, Jake rejoices, "Yeah! We get hamburgers for hot lunch today!" Wednesdays are always his favorite meal days.

"I hate lunch!" Hannah shouts.

Again? I think. *What is with the outsized reactions? Must everything be difficult?* Instead of voicing my frustration, I say, "Hannah, you love hamburgers. What's bothering you?"

"I like hamburgers, but I don't like lunchtime. I have to sit with Daniella and Lauren."

My eyes dart to the rearview mirror. "What?" The school *promised* to separate Hannah from these girls. Maybe there was a one-off mix-up? "How many children are at your lunch table?"

"Four. On Monday I was assigned to sit with Daniella and Lauren and a boy until Thanksgiving!"

Why is everything so hard at this school? I feel like I'm constantly banging my head against a wall. Each year I need to help teachers understand my child. And even when I provide a neuropsych report with recommended accommodations (most of which incur no additional costs), and I'm promised Hannah will be separated from the children who torment her, I *still* need to advocate for her well into the school year.

WTF.

After dropping off the kids, I notice the car behind me belongs to a mother with third- and second-grade boys. Lily has shared with me that her younger son has been hit on several occasions by a girl in his class. His confidence is now shot, and he's become disruptive. The school is aware her son has an ADHD diagnosis and suggested an increase in his prescription, but nobody seems to have addressed the girl's aggression. Maybe the school thinks ADHD is a bigger problem than physical abuse? Or that boys can't be bullied by girls? In any case, Lily looks miserable whenever I see her. And I've seen how other parents ignore her. Speaking up for her child made her a prime candidate for judgment—and ostracism.

I can relate. I'm desperate for understanding, so I direct my smartphone to call Lily. Not only does she empathize with bullying issues, but since her older son is in third grade, she's familiar with the Daniella/Lauren dynamic. We chat for a bit until I eventually mention our predicament.

She says, "I'm not surprised. They've been disrupting the class all year. I can't believe a new teacher was put in charge. She has absolutely no control. If only Mrs. A hadn't left last year!" It's true. Several of the more experienced teachers have retired lately, so the entire third-grade staff is fairly green. Lily then confides, "Parents are angry. They want either a different teacher or to have those two girls separated."

I'm beyond discouraged. It doesn't seem fair to blame the new teacher for this long-standing issue. And I'm annoyed the school hasn't been more intentional about addressing the poor behavior. The consequences could be significant for Hannah. I lament, "Richard promised to keep those two away from Hannah. How is she supposed to get her confidence back if she's forced to sit with the kids who tease her?"

"I know. And it's not getting better," Lily commiserates. "I've hardly seen either girls' parents all year. Daniella's parents' divorce is ugly, and Lauren's parents are MIA."

I think back to last year, when I spoke with Lauren's mom about the body-shaming episode. She ended up pawning responsibility to her nanny. It sounds like little has changed.

The confirmation that we're not the only family having trouble makes me feel less alone. But I'm still upset the administration isn't intervening effectively. I guess it's now up to the parents and the staff.

My meeting with Hannah's teacher Megan on Friday can't come soon enough.

Fairly

On Friday afternoon, I head to school an hour before pickup to meet Megan while the students attend PE. We offer niceties and dance around one another before she finally questions, "Was there something you wanted to discuss?"

Sonia looks up from the stack of egg cartons she collected from parents earlier in the week for an art project.

I choose my words carefully. "I'm a little concerned that Hannah's feeling overwhelmed. You mentioned you don't see her exhaustion, but I sense she's working really hard to please you during the day." I know Megan will be more receptive if she doesn't feel threatened, so I make sure to say, "Hannah likes you so much and wants your approval." But then I explain, "Once she gets in my car, she collapses into a heap of tears. You couldn't know this since she doesn't show this side to you, but I'm wondering if we can work together to find a solution that might help Hannah."

Sonia nods, and Megan asserts, "Absolutely! I want the best for all my students."

"There is something specific we can do," I say. "You mentioned at the beginning of the year you'd be able to accommodate Hannah with a wiggly stool to help her manage her sensory processing issues. I understand that she's only getting access on odd days, and I'm hoping that she can be allowed regular access to a stool so she can have it when she needs it."

Megan asserts, "Hannah has a stool much of the time. But I need to ensure all kids get a turn."

Sonia's eyes drop to the floor.

And I'm exasperated. How can Megan feel so comfortable withholding a tool that a PhD determined Hannah needs? I'm sure she wouldn't keep a wheelchair from a child. But maybe she doesn't believe a problem exists if she can't readily see it.

I question, "Oh. Several of your kids have sensory processing disorders?" While I've been hesitant to use language like this liberally, I'm hoping it will get her attention.

"Well, I'm not really sure that's a thing. An official diagnosis, I mean." Sonia adjusts the egg cartons for a second time while Megan continues, "I don't think we're doing Hannah any favors by singling her out and giving her more access to toys than the others. I want to be fair."

My frustration unreels. She considers the stool a "toy." And she says she wants to be "fair," as if the best way to do that is to treat the students as though they're all the same. In fact, she's withholding a crucial resource my child needs to learn, but not all children do.

I glance at Sonia, still shuffling the cartons, and wonder what would happen if they were delivered with actual, fertilized eggs at the beginning of the school year. It's not hard to imagine based on what we've experienced so far. I can see it all quite clearly, actually.

I envision that within several days, a few eggs crack open and eaglets poke through. My imagination becomes even more vivid as Megan stands proud. After all, under her care, majestic birds just hatched in her classroom! She speaks to the eagles with a delighted tone. She's awed by their majestic wings. She even forms small groups to practice the tricks in which the eagles excel. She calls this "accelerated work." Megan's pleasure is clearly visceral, never mind the fact that she had little control over which eggs were delivered to her room in the first place.

But then the other birds peck through their shells—like hummingbirds and owls and flamingos. They're tolerated, yes. They're even encouraged to work with the eagles. But Megan doesn't take the same pride in their development. After all, they're not as strong nor as solid as her grand pets. These other birds require a different, more cumbersome form of attention. The hummingbirds, for example, are so busy. They won't stop fluttering their wings! *Those birds need some damn chill pills*, she thinks. And the owls, the poor owls. They might see well at night, but their ability to read in this classroom is only average. Too bad their eyes weren't designed appropriately. And those quirky flamingos. They're eye-catching, for sure, but they're disabled, you see, standing on just one leg.

Some teachers would be impressed that the flamingos, on just one leg, can do many of the things the other birds can do. And they can do some things the eagles can't. But for this teacher, the flamingos' particular beauty and competence is of little consequence. They are no eagles, after all. Fortunately, this school believes in equality, so they're allowed to coexist.

I consider the broad array of eggs that were delivered to Megan's classroom on the first day of school, and I'm discouraged. She has already demonstrated she won't alter her environment to accommodate the various needs and strengths. All birds will be offered the same nutrients, expected to perform the same basic tasks, and allowed to share the same perches. They will be treated "fairly."

By now Megan must realize one of the eggs delivered to her stoop held a canary. I'm here today trying to discuss what a canary might need—how we can help her thrive. I'd love to point out how a canary's song and acute awareness might even benefit the classroom. But this teacher isn't interested. She doesn't demonstrate the slightest understanding of the research on "high sensitivity" nor the enormous impact she could make if she created a welcome setting for her canaries. Instead, she stands before me looking annoyed. To confirm as much, Megan peers at Sonia and rolls her eyes halfway around their sockets. She doesn't complete the revolution because she intends to be gracious. Instead, she plants a rigid smile on her clenched jaw, signaling, ever so slightly, her mind is made up.

The message couldn't be clearer: It would be a disservice to coddle the pesky canary who chirps too much. She will be denied a stand that suits her. The eagles need a turn with them, too, after all! They're fun to play with! And we must be fair.

Soon the canaries will figure it out. They'll stop chirping altogether. And this teacher will be relieved. *Finally, the damned canaries shut up! Now if only this mother would do the same!*

Unfortunately for Megan, I'm not as submissive as she hopes. I mean to care for the canaries and all the other species in the room. And I'm incensed she thinks she knows more about sensory processing issues than the neuropsychologist who wrote Hannah's report. The doctor is twice Megan's age with significantly more experience and education. Even if Megan doesn't believe in the diagnosis, one look at Hannah's bodily behavior, the way she wiggles in a chair, for example, would tell her that Hannah's needs are different from many of her peers'. Megan's arrogance is breathtaking.

But I keep my cool. I need to be careful. I won't upset Megan because, ultimately, I need her support. If I annoy her, she might release her frustration on Hannah, the easier target. Hannah's already struggling in the classroom, and the last thing we need is for her teacher to judge her even more.

So I try to appeal to Megan's interests, "I appreciate your concern, and I realize the stool is fun for a lot of kids." I tread slowly as I attempt to reframe the situation, "But it isn't a *toy* for Hannah. It's a *tool* to help her body regulate so she can concentrate. When she's able to calm her nervous system, she can participate more readily in your class. The stool helps her body feel at ease so she can focus on her mind and be more receptive to your efforts and less disruptive to the classroom."

"I understand, but I need to consider all the children. And let's be honest, people aren't going to be handing out stools wherever Hannah goes. She's going to need to learn to deal in the real world. And, for now, we'll *definitely* need to teach her not to run from the classroom when she gets frustrated."

And there they are. Confirmed. Her true colors. She sounded so supportive at the beginning of the year, but when I need her understanding and compassion the most, she's downright stingy.

I don't know what to say. She thinks her job is to make Hannah toe the line, to suck it up. She believes treating children equally entails treating them as though they are all the same. And she's sure she's being fair, kind even. After all, she's allowing lesser birds to cohabitate with her eagles.

I sigh and press on. If the stool is a dead end, maybe I can make headway elsewhere. I remind her, "Richard promised us last year that Hannah would be split from Daniella and Lauren. That's worked so far, but now it sounds like they're assigned to the same lunch table?"

Megan's quicker to her defense. "That's only at lunchtime, and Sonia is there monitoring."

"So Hannah is forced to sit with the children who taunt her?"

"Well, I think it's good to give them the opportunity to smooth things over. We can't separate them forever. And Sonia is always nearby."

Sonia looks up, but she remains mute.

Hannah hasn't reported any actual bullying at the lunch table in the past week, just her apprehension sitting near her tormentors. So I'm limited in what I can say. "What happens if Sonia needs to help another child?" I ask. "She can't watch all twenty at the same time. Or is it forty with both classes? Because, in my experience, these kids aren't dumb. They choose their moments when teachers are focused on something else. Watching that many kids is a lot to ask of one teacher."

Sonia nods almost imperceptibly, but the motion halts when Megan asserts, "I will remind Sonia to keep her eyes out."

I sigh again. This meeting has turned into a complete bust. On my way out, I consider making one last plea, but Megan beats me to the punch. "By the way, Kayla, I appreciate all the support you're giving Hannah at home, but it's probably best to let her do her homework on her own."

I'm shocked, almost into silence. Somehow I find the voice to say, "What? Of course she does her own work."

Megan initiates another half eye-roll. "It just seems that the assignments coming from home are much more proficient than what I'm seeing in the classroom."

Holy shit. Does she really think I have the time or interest in completing third-grade material? I've helped Hannah understand instructions, yes, and I've refocused her when she gets distracted, but do her work *for* her? I hold my tongue, knowing any defensiveness will most likely be perceived as guilt. I also sense her mind is fixed.

So I respond, "Thanks for your time today, Megan. I'll make sure Hannah continues to complete her own homework."

What else can I say?

Getting Educated
on Education

On my way home, I phone Hannah's neuropsychologist, Michelle. During our last meeting, she offered to meet with Hannah's teachers. I didn't take her up on her suggestion because I wanted to respect the teachers' time, but it seems I miscalculated. A report listing accommodations is useless if the teacher is unwilling to implement them. And my own advocacy is failing. Worse, it seems I've permanently risked any goodwill, respect, or leverage I might have had. I am now, I fear, officially one of "those" overprotective, meddling, helicopter parents.

When I explain the situation to Michelle, including the fact that a critical tool she recommended was dismissed as a "toy," I hear a frustrated sigh.

"Yes," she confirms. "I've heard similar stories from other grades. I lent a rocking chair and some stress balls to a classroom, and the same turn-taking thing happened there, too."

Michelle again offers to attend a meeting at GCA to try to pull together Team Hannah, but I'm doubtful. I explain, "I'd love to think that'll work, but Hannah's teacher seems to believe she's got it all figured out. She even accused me of doing Hannah's homework."

"Really." She's almost laughing.

115

I don't think it's funny, and I don't care that I sound defensive when I answer, "Yes. She actually thinks I'm doing it. And I swear, I'm not. I know better than to do my kids' work. They won't learn that way. I get it."

"Well, okay. But think about it. Hannah has a quiet place to study at home, right?"

"Yeah."

"And if she needs help with instructions, you explain them, right?"

"Well, I try."

"Right," she responds. And then she helps me see: "Do you think Hannah has a similarly quiet place to work, without interruption, at school? Or are there kids running around? Loud noises? Insecurity about her seating options? Multistep instructions that might be confusing for her? And other things that can make her anxious?"

"She's been complaining about having to sit on the hard floor a lot," I report.

"Yes! And that's really taxing on her vestibular system. So, of course she's able to work better at home. But the teacher can't acknowledge her classroom management might be affecting Hannah's achievement. If she did, she might need to implement our accommodations more intentionally. So she blames you for the difference in performance between school and home."

"She really thinks I'm doing Hannah's work?"

"Isn't that what she said?"

I'm indignant. "How ridiculous is that?"

"Well, you and I know that," she says, "but this isn't the first time I've seen this. Environment matters so much. To be honest, I don't blame Hannah. I couldn't get any work done on a hard floor with a lot of distractions. But then, I'm classically inattentive. Of course, I didn't know until I learned about it in my own textbooks!"

My hope plummets. "But why can't this teacher support Hannah's differences? Why is she so intolerant? And punitive?"

Michelle responds with words I won't be able shake for days: "Most teachers aren't taught about learning differences."

I don't believe her. "They aren't taught different kids learn differently?"

Michelle insists, "Well, superficially they've heard the message, but you can get a master's in education without ever taking even one class focused on learning differences. So, naturally, the general understanding is a bit, uh, superficial. It's no fault of the teachers. It's the training. The system."

"There's nothing about neurodiversity? How about neuroplasticity?"

"Same thing."

No wonder this is so hard. Still, I feel defensive. "But Hannah's last two head teachers were great. They were kind and nuanced in their teaching. Last year was rough because of the bullying, but I sensed they wanted to help her and were just handcuffed by the Head of School."

"I'm not saying there aren't amazing teachers out there. There are. But chances are they learned about learning differences on the job. Or maybe they have their own unique kids at home." Michelle continues, "It's also important to consider that many students are smart and observant, like Hannah, and they can mask their learning differences. So some teachers might not believe they're there. But after a while, as the schoolwork becomes more challenging, it becomes harder for kids to compensate. As a result, accommodations are crucial for enabling them to remain strong learners. Without the accommodations, students fall behind, no matter how experienced or caring the instructor is."

Michelle sighs. "And this year, you have an inexperienced teacher. From what I've seen, she doesn't get much support from the administration. So, she maintains control by forcing everyone to fall in line. While she might have heard the word 'neurodiversity' in one of her classes, chances are the discussion was fleeting and gave no real strategies to help her manage the typical diversity of a classroom."

So the one-in-five (or more) remain unseen. What can be done?

■　▦　■　▦

The next day I head off on another research expedition.

I understand the fallacies of ranking educational institutions, as if one school is the best fit for all kids. Still, I'm curious to learn which graduate programs of education are deemed the best in the country so I can see how they prepare new teachers. My analysis is informal and wouldn't pass any peer-reviewed process, but the results are jarring all the same.

Unfortunately, Michelle is right.

After searching the websites of the five institutions considered field leaders, I notice that the term "neurodiversity" is nearly nonexistent. I'm amazed. The institutions that should be most aware of the concept are ignoring it. On the rare occasions that learning differences are mentioned, they're called "disabilities" and put under the umbrella of "special education." (Several schools neglect these topics entirely.) And the very few class offerings that focus on learning differences usually aren't required at all. So even though all children in a special education classroom and at least twenty percent of children in a general education classroom ostensibly have differences that affect learning, most aspiring teachers aren't given the information necessary to recognize and teach to various learning styles.

I realize, *Wow. Michelle was right.*

And apparently, our government doesn't seem to get it either. An impressive publication by Understood For All and NCLD called "Forward Together" notes that only ten states in the entire country require teacher candidates to meet standards for learning differences. As a result, "the vast majority" of educators feel "underprepared and unsupported" in teaching students with learning differences. (In fact, just seventeen percent "feel very well prepared" in their efforts to address even "mild to moderate" learning differences.)

In my first deep dive into the research, I was concerned about the ways we treat students. Now I'm worried about our teachers. How can we expect educators to foster the next generation if we don't provide access to the relevant knowledge and tools?

I remember a conversation I had with a psychologist who told me she thinks teachers are dealing with their own marginalization and demoralization. She wasn't referring just to low pay. She actually used the word "trauma" before asking, "Are we setting them up for failure and then blaming them for the outcomes?"

As I continue to read "Forward Together" and other related studies, I get confirmation that the lack of training hurts the entire ecosystem. Apparently, one-third of educators believe learning and attention issues are signs of laziness. No wonder Megan is so annoyed and critical! She doesn't understand how much harder Hannah has to work than children who happen to respond to traditional teaching techniques. And the report reveals that a quarter of educators believe ADHD comes from bad parenting. Ostensibly, this philosophy extends to other conditions as well. If parents are to blame for their kids' learning challenges, Megan probably feels we're sabotaging her efforts. That would be terribly frustrating and demoralizing for her. It's debilitating for us as well, as the stance undermines our credibility. Twenty-five percent of teachers also believe learning challenges can be outgrown. So, kids are left, abandoned really, to "wait it out."

Teachers and kids aren't the only ones affected. I have a friend who confided in me that her husband begged her not to talk about their child's struggles. She explained, "He's worried if we admit to Josie's differences, people will judge her. They'll judge *us*." She pleaded, "Please don't tell anybody what I said."

So, now, the entire family remains misunderstood, and isolated. It's heartbreaking because the consequences can be significant.

My previous studies informed me that unique learners are some of the most likely targets of bullying. My research today tells me that kids with learning differences also demonstrate higher incidences of substance abuse, delinquency, school drop-out, and mental health problems. Once set in motion, the trend continues. As adults, these individuals are apparently more likely to contend with unemployment and incarceration as well.

When I read this last outcome, my heart jolts. *Incarceration?* Several books taught me the devastating consequences of race-based injustice. And I've read studies describing the ways we imprison, rather than treat, people with mental health challenges. It's all so abhorrent.

And now I'm confused. The pain experienced by children who learn and think differently is so obviously distinct from the agony felt by families contending with racism or mental illness. It feels wrong to consider them in tandem. But I also can't simply dismiss the bias experienced by the neurodiverse as less consequential and move on. If I, as a mother of a neurodiverse child, ignore what's happening, will *anyone* care? A sudden maternal instinct demands I protect my child. None of this is okay.

And even as I recognize that bias and discrimination play out differently for various communities and each one deserves its own platform, I consider that there is intersectionality here. Neurodiversity can affect racial minorities and the mentally ill too.

So I try to find information on how learning differences might impact various cohorts, but I have difficulty finding granularity in the studies. One scientist says minorities are overrepresented in special education classrooms, noting diagnoses are used to further marginalize and segregate people. (Apparently, misdiagnoses are especially common when children suffering from traumatic stress are assumed to have ADHD or oppositional defiant disorder. Meaning, the kids who need the most support can be the ones who are most misunderstood and neglected.) Another researcher says it's the privileged communities that have higher rates of diagnoses. She holds that well-heeled families have the capacity to fight for more resources for their children. I can't find enough rigorous studies to verify what's happening, but it seems to me that both might be true. Diagnoses can be used both to ostracize children and to support them.

I continue my investigation into the implications of not addressing learning differences effectively, and I find the statistics jaw-dropping. Studies reveal that up to forty-three percent of juvenile delinquents have an identified "special education disability." Who knows how many were misdiagnosed or remain undiagnosed, but I'd bet pretty much all of them had very real needs disregarded. Unfortunately, the consequences only worsen with time. Research documents that *over half* of all individuals with learning differences are involved with the criminal system within just eight years of leaving high school. And studies reveal that about half—*half!*—of adults in US prisons have dyslexia, compared to fourteen percent in the general population. Imagine what would happen if more kinds of learning differences were included in the statistics!

I step back and ask myself, *Are we essentially criminalizing learning differences?*

I started my studies in an effort to support my child. But this problem now feels so much bigger than my family. It's hard to deny that, in so many ways, penitentiaries essentially have become a repository for the people society didn't want to acknowledge—or didn't make an effort to understand and support—earlier in life.

I imagine the people languishing in America's prisons as they once were: young children with full futures ahead of them. If we are intellectually honest with ourselves, can we deny that we failed them the moment we didn't allow for their unique attributes, struggles, and histories? When we didn't treat them fairly, thoughtfully, and with civility?

The inhumanity is depressing.

And incredibly expensive.

The Prison Policy Initiative estimates that incarceration in the United States costs a staggering $182 billion per year, much of which is funded by our taxes. When I weigh this astounding expense and then add the emotional *and* economic losses represented by each individual who could have been a productive member of society (what economists call "opportunity costs"), my heart breaks. What might each individual have contributed had we supported children's basic needs from the outset? After all, I would much rather fund children's potential in school than their demise throughout the criminal legal system.

If only we could find another way. A starting point seems relatively simple: appreciate each other's differences, believe in one another's desire to be good and do well, and allow for reasonable opportunities for individuals to work and make all this possible. And then, of course, we must implement the tools and systems to support these values.

I realize a new approach would require a complete shift in philosophy—one that truly values individuality.

I wonder, *Is our society really ready to do that?*

Naive or not, I'd like to think so. And I acknowledge that I need to start with myself. So I recommit to supporting efforts that promote a kinder, fairer future for *all* of us, even as I admit that I still have a lot of learning to do.

Inside Information

Two days after my visit to the classroom, Hannah's assistant teacher Sonia finds me on the playground where I'm encouraging my kids to let off some steam before we head home. I've never seen Sonia in the yard at this hour, so I'm surprised when she approaches.

"Kayla!" She greets me with a smile.

"Hi, Sonia!" I return her enthusiasm, relieved to be treated with genuine warmth.

She continues, more seriously now, "I just wanted you to know that yesterday, Daniella and Lauren teased Hannah again at lunchtime."

I note the word "again" and remain quiet, hoping to learn more.

"They were teasing her about the way she talks. You know, her big vocabulary. So, I got involved." She starts speaking more slowly. "I, um, overheard your conversation the other morning and wanted to follow up. I'm doing my best to watch over them."

"I know you are. Thank you, and I really meant that. But you said this happened before?"

"Yes, well, it was different. They like to talk to Hannah about spiders."

Oh, no. Hannah hates spiders. *How did they know?*

Sonia continues, "They like to tell Hannah they see spiders on her chair. Or in her sandwich. But I'm on it. I promise her there are no spiders anywhere."

"Why is she even sitting with them?" I can't help asking.

She shakes her head and sighs audibly but is clearly hesitant to say more. Maybe she's worried she's already overstepped her bounds with the conversation we're having. But I'm grateful. This is one of the few proactive efforts anybody at the school has made to keep me informed.

"Look," she begins, "I'm not sure if I should say this, but Megan is going through a divorce. I think she's having a hard time."

I wasn't even aware she was married. Her appearance suggests she isn't even thirty, so I hadn't made any assumptions about her marital status.

"Well, I just thought I'd let you know . . . so you can be aware that however Megan may come across, it might be uh . . . about something other than you. Or Hannah." She's stammering now. "I can't say much more."

I appreciate the information. Megan *is* behaving differently now than she did at the beginning of the year. I realize Sonia might be affected as well, so I ask, "How's the year going for you?"

"All right. It's a busy class!" The word "busy" feels like a euphemism for "difficult."

"If there's anything I can do, will you let me know?" I venture. "Obviously, parents can't be there during the day, but we want to be supportive." She nods, so I continue. "I'm curious about something. I know Hannah learns differently. And she's highly sensitive. Do you think she fits here?"

"Here? At this school?" She thinks then confirms, "Yes." She elaborates, "There are kids who require *much* more attention than Hannah. I obviously can't speak about them, but if you're worried about Hannah, don't be. I mean, yes, she struggles with transitions and often needs me to repeat instructions. But she's not the only one. And when she gets overwhelmed, she sometimes escapes to the corner, where our classroom library is. Things like that. But she's a really great girl. So sweet. With her, I try to use my ABCs."

"Your what?"

"Well, if I see a *behavior* that's out of line, before I jump to enforcing a *consequence*, I first look for the *antecedent*. And in Hannah's case, it's usually that she's confused or unsettled or even nervous. At least that's what I've noticed."

"I see her stress building. Do you?"

"Actually, yes," she says. "I don't know if this is the cause, but Megan's no longer designating assigned seats. She says she wants the children to learn to be flexible. But Hannah gets upset if she can't get the seat closest to the front of the room. She considers it her spot."

I restrain myself from interjecting, *It should be her spot. Her accommodations list specifies the need for a desk near the front of the room!* But I don't interrupt.

"So now transitions seem harder for her. And focus too. For example, if the kids are working on the mat in the library area, but Hannah knows the next lesson will be at the desks, she has trouble finishing the task at hand because she's so focused on racing to a certain desk. And if someone beats her to it . . ."

"She gets upset," I finish. And then Megan probably considers her "unflexible." My head aches, as if to acknowledge the extent to which I've been banging it against a wall.

Sonia consoles me. "I'll try to help Hannah get her seat. She does seem to be less distracted when she's at the front of the room."

"Thanks, Sonia. I really appreciate that."

"Not at all. But um . . . Can you do me a favor?"

"Yes. Anything. What do you need?"

"Would you mind keeping this conversation between us? I mean, I really care about Hannah. And I thought you should have some background on what's happening. But I'm not sure people would appreciate an assistant teacher speaking directly to a parent."

"I get it. I promise to keep this between us."

"And I promise, I'll keep watching the girls."

She smiles weakly and walks away.

I'm grateful for Sonia's candor, but I'm deflated by what she's shared with me. All the promises and accommodations we'd been assured at the beginning of the year have been thrown out the window. No wonder Hannah's so exasperated.

The Lion in the Room

O ver the coming weeks, Jim and I notice more fears about spiders, even in unfathomable places, like our refrigerator. And Hannah starts gnawing on her twisted hair to the point that, after some school days, the ends look as though they were dunked in a pool.

One night, as the kids fiddle on the floor, Jim towers over them and urges me toward him. When I approach, he points toward a quarter-sized bald spot on the top of Hannah's head. She has the most effervescent mop of curls, with soft corkscrews bounding in all directions. A bald patch on Hannah is paradoxical.

Not wanting to alarm the children, I signal shock with my eyes. *Is Hannah so stressed that her hair is literally falling out?*

Fortunately, Jake has a pediatrician appointment two days later, so I decide to bring Hannah along. I email the doctor in advance, and we agree she'll pretend to give the kids lice checks to avoid making Hannah self-conscious.

After viewing her scalp through a magnifying glass, the doctor distracts the children with toys while murmuring her assessment, "trauma," meaning Hannah's hair is not falling out; she's pulling it out. She writes the diagnosis on her pad of paper: *trichotillomania* then lists the names of three psychologists.

My mind reels to six months ago when I first started crisis counseling. I'd felt called upon to help *others*. I was supposed to be a *giver*, not the needy receiver. *What the hell just happened?*

Was I so arrogant that I assumed issues like these only affect other families? Yes, I knew Hannah had situational anxiety, but it now seems to have advanced to an entirely different beast. Why hadn't I done more to prevent this? Was my head in the sand? Or was I triaging the greatest need, unable to keep my eye on everything? The turn of events is humbling.

After settling my kids at home, I email the three psychologists. One tells me her practice is full, but I'm able to make appointments to interview the other two the following week.

I'm still feeling restless and insecure about my ability to support Hannah. I don't even know how to pronounce her diagnosis, so I look it up online. The information confirms that trickletolo-whatever is often induced by anxiety, which drives irresistible urges to pull hair from one's own scalp, eyebrows, or other parts of the body.

I also learn that anxiety is distinct from stress or fear. Yet, the three words are often used interchangeably, causing their functional nuances to be misunderstood.

Apparently, stress is a normal, even functional, response to a challenge, like a large school project or a disagreement with a friend. We all face stress at one time or another, and it can make us more alert and motivate us to tackle the problem at hand. Fortunately, feelings of stress subside once the difficulty has been addressed. Experts advise parents to help children learn to work through reasonable amounts of stress rather than avoid it as small challenges can help build the resilience and confidence to tackle greater problems in the future.

Too great a challenge, however, can induce anxiety rather than stress. While anxiety might exhibit many of the same physical reactions as stress, clinical anxiety isn't functional, and it doesn't dissipate when the stressor is removed or overcome.

Instead, it's characterized by persistent feelings of distress, apprehension, or dread.

I learn anxiety is also distinct from fear. Fear is an emotional response to a *real* or *reasonably perceived* threat, while clinical anxiety produces excessive concern over the anticipation of an *unknown* or even an *unlikely* threat. Anxiety becomes a disorder when it inhibits normal day-to-day functioning, like sleeping, eating, and interacting with others.

I wonder if Hannah is stressed, fearful, or anxious. She's functioning—going to school, eating, and sleeping—but I sense she's on a precipice. Sonia tells me Hannah escapes to the class library, and she even fled the room once. Is this a child's version of "flight," as in "fight or flight"? And Hannah tells me her mind "freezes"—it goes blank—so she can't think or do her work when she's worried about where she can sit. This also seems to be a sign of anxiety.

As I mull all of this over, books advise using a nonjudgmental, "no-fault approach." Just as we wouldn't blame children who have asthma or type 1 diabetes, we shouldn't blame children who have anxiety. Individuals who suffer from anxiety are not acting out or misbehaving willfully. They are responding to actual, physiological challenges in their brains.

The literature also resets my perspective by assuring me Hannah's behavior reflects neither poor judgment nor low intelligence. The reading is dense, with lots of unfamiliar vocabulary, but basically, I learn that Hannah's otherwise very capable "rational brain" (including the neocortex, which manages reason) is present, but it's being overridden by her "emotional brain" (including the limbic system, which houses the "fear center"). The books explain that the limbic system, and the amygdala, in particular, triggers a release of stress hormones and nerve impulses that induce the bodily functions we associate with anxiety, like increases in heart rates, respiratory rates, blood pressure, muscle tension, sweating, and tunnel vision. And these cause people to fight, take flight, or freeze.

To this point, whenever Hannah expressed concern, I used logic to dismiss it. I explained more than once that I've never, ever, seen a spider in a fridge, and I became frustrated, annoyed even, when Hannah still refused to get herself a glass of milk. But of all people, I should have known better. Once a week, I volunteer as a crisis counselor. And each time, I do what I was trained to do: validate. I can't help but ask myself, *Why do I show empathy toward complete strangers but neglect to truly see my own daughter?*

This realization is humbling and forces me to interpret our situation more clearly. Hannah is not being irrational or stupid. She is trying to tell me that her body feels the same way it would if a venomous spider actually was poised to attack her. The physical response is very real to her. What she needs is understanding and compassion, not dismissiveness and judgment. I vow to slow down and be more patient.

I'm astounded when the literature, like Helen Riess's book *The Empathy Effect*, explain that the amygdala can respond to threats (real or perceived) in a mere fifty milliseconds. By contrast, the prefrontal cortex—the reasoning part of the brain—can take ten times as long, around five hundred milliseconds, to kick into gear. As a result, the body can instinctually *respond* to threats *before we are even conscious of them* and before we can form a rational plan. In other words, if this were a track event, Hannah's amygdala would be able to cross the finish line before her reasoning center could get off the starting blocks.

Dang. We have some serious training to do if we want to even the race.

■ ▦ ■ ▨

After Jim and I meet with the psychologists, we choose the one who has a broad range of skills, beyond just "play" therapy. Hannah is a complex, articulate girl, and she doesn't like being treated as though she's younger or less mature than she is.

Hannah is tentative about meeting her new "talking doctor," but Joanna is skilled at easing her nerves. Over the following few weeks, Joanna teaches Hannah to distinguish between her "thinking brain" and her "worry brain," but Hannah and I adapt the latter term to "worry bug" so we can put whatever's troubling her in its place with less-threatening imagery. Joanna also teaches mental exercises designed to distract Hannah from her worrisome thoughts and force her to reengage her intellect instead. The therapist instructs me to facilitate, so I learn to ask Hannah to list ten colors, then ten objects in outer space, then ten US presidents. The effort forces her to slow down and *think* rather than react instinctively. She's also taught to use diaphragmatic breathing exercises—to exhale more slowly and deeply than she inhales—which are proven to slow heart rates. And Hannah learns to rank her anxiety on a scale of one to ten using a "worry meter." This tool helps her determine which fears are most debilitating and which techniques deescalate them best. The rankings also force me to take Hannah seriously. Too often, I don't recognize when her anxiety is triggered, but when she tells me that she's "at a four," I know to start paying attention.

Naturally, as Hannah buckles down with her psychologist, I'm compelled to do my own work. I meet with a psychiatrist who works in Joanna's practice. About three minutes into our discussion, Dr. Lee uses an old-fashioned projector to flash images of two brains on her office wall. She explains that one shows average levels of amygdalic activity, while the other is highly anxious. She points to the second brain and says that mine might look similar if a lion walked in the room, but people suffering from anxiety can experience this heightened state regularly.

Until this point, pictures of brains always looked similar to me—like masses of gooey slugs. But I'm intrigued by how shockingly distinct the two images on the screen are. Here is incontrovertible proof that people with anxiety are neither hypochondriacal nor self-indulgent. Their brains are literally functioning differently.

I feel compelled to gather every anxious child in the world and protect them from their beasts. How can people live this way? Growing up is hard enough. I can't imagine having to do so while cohabitating with a predator.

Dr. Lee explains that while one's amygdala might over-activate due to ineffective neural wiring (an internal trigger), anxiety can also arise in response to our surroundings (external triggers). As a result, homes and schools play significant roles in children's well-being. Dr. Lee references trauma expert Bessel van der Kolk's book, *The Body Keeps the Score*, which explains how our neurology literally changes in response to unhealthy environments. I'd read about neural plasticity and the brain's ability to grow, but now is the first I'm hearing that plasticity can be counterproductive. When people experience anxiety, the neural pathways that trigger the "fight or flight" response can become more entrenched. As a result, anxiety attacks today can elevate the likelihood of more frequent and stronger reactions in the future.

It's clear we need to address Hannah's mental health now, before her brain normalizes, or even amplifies, her suffering. I worry, *What if we've waited too long?* I've clung to the hope that Hannah will outgrow her distress, but the doctor insists anxiety can be chronic and often comes in spikes. While one might be lulled between episodes into hoping the body has resolved the issue on its own, that hope is often false. Denying problems often only exacerbates them.

Our early therapy sessions are more like classes for me as Dr. Lee helps me understand Hannah's condition—and I'm like a sponge soaking it all in. The geek in me is fascinated when she explains that our genes' DNA sequence is not the only element that affects their behavior. Experience and environment can "flip" the expression of specific genes on or off, and the flipped expression can then pass to offspring. This science of epigenetics is still in its infancy, but it's alarming to consider that Hannah's children could inherit her increased propensity toward anxiety. I must act now.

Dr. Lee acknowledges the destructive ways many people address anxiety, like substance abuse or self-harm. Fortunately, other methods exist, many of which leverage neuroplasticity constructively. Dr. Lee tells me the most clinically proven options known today include cognitive behavioral therapy (CBT) and medication.

Her words make me bristle. I'm resistant to popping pills into my third grader, so I make a mental note to follow up with Hannah's psychologist.

After our sessions, I always follow up on whatever topics might have surfaced by reading more online and ordering any relevant books. I discover how CBT employs conscious thought to confront an overactive amygdala. A key component of CBT includes "exposure therapy," which gradually introduces patients to their anxiety triggers. For example, Hannah might first be shown a picture of a friendly-looking cartoon spider. Then she might be asked to draw a spider (engaging her own physicality in the process). Then she might be shown photographs of actual spiders. Eventually, she might even be introduced, purposefully, to a real live spider, which she could smoosh if she wanted. After each stage, Hannah would be asked to reevaluate the outcome so that her brain could confirm she is still okay, even after confronting her fear. That recognition might become ingrained to help her create a new reality and be less anxious the next time she faces a similar experience.

I then read about dialectical behavior therapy (DBT), which integrates CBT with mindfulness. The word "dialectical" recognizes that the therapy involves two seemingly contradictory efforts: using cognition to *change* feelings and mindfulness to *acknowledge* the reality of those feelings. Evidently, acceptance helps limit shame and decrease further stress.

Desperate for information about what I can do as a parent, I read on. Published psychologists, like Tamar E. Chansky and Bridget Flynn Walker, advise parents not to play into irrational fears. They say if parents try to protect kids from their triggers or if they share their kids' fears, the children won't learn to cope with them. Instead, we're to model calm in order to signal that everything will be okay.

I then learn about all kinds of therapies—eye movement desensitization and reprocessing (EMDR), internal family systems (IFS), neurofeedback, psychomotor therapy, Feldenkrais, and craniosacral therapy. Knowing that Western medicine is slow to offer non-pharma options, I try not to be intimidated by the unfamiliar names. Several researchers also promote familiar alternatives like yoga, chanting, singing, listening to music, dance, martial arts, acting, bodywork, therapeutic massage, and acupuncture. And, as my own family has experienced, even comfort from a support animal (like Gracey!) can help.

When I see "writing" on the list of therapies, I smile. It's one of the activities texters in crisis have told me they use to quell their distress. Years ago, I would have doubted such a common activity could be considered a treatment, but my own recent experience says otherwise. Journaling during this time has allowed me to connect research with my personal experience without any naysayers gaslighting me.

At the end of our next session, I tell Joanna that Dr. Lee introduced the idea of medication. She sees I'm resistant, but she sides with Dr. Lee. She explains that medication isn't a failure. Rather, it's a practical method for addressing a serious problem. She says that, just like the prescriptions people use to manage diabetes, asthma, and high blood pressure, anxiety medication can be a godsend for people with mental health issues. Sometimes, it's only necessary for a short period of time, just to "get over the hump" of distress and allow the thinking brain to engage regularly again. And sometimes it's used for longer periods. In either case, the medication helps people live without feeling like lions are poised to strike.

Jim and I agree to keep working with Joanna and to hold off on the medication for now. But if Hannah continues to feel hunted, we acknowledge that medication might be a humane option. She's already suffered so much.

Descartes's Legacy

Jim and I love spending time with a dynamic couple that happens to be well-versed in the field of neurology. After spending the week trying to understand anxiety, we're looking forward to seeing them at a little bistro. Their conversation is always thought-provoking, and tonight's banter is no exception.

Not long into the evening, one of our dinner companions asserts, "If I could go back in time and kill two people, the first would be Adolf Hitler."

His ideas are usually more novel, so we nod and wait.

"The second would be René Descartes."

I think, *Now, that's more like him.* But I'm not sure what to say. I'm not even sure I recall what Descartes did. "Wasn't he a scientist? Or mathematician?"

Our friend smiles and declares, "Both! He also created the concept of mind-body dualism. Descartes believed the majority of the body belongs in one category, but the mind goes in another. In other words, the *body* is a *physical* entity, so when a problem arises, we can use science and medicine to address it. But for Descartes, the *mind* is entirely separate from the body, somewhat ethereal. So people experiencing mental illnesses are basically just crazy."

His comment hits the gut. He is essentially acknowledging that some people might consider my daughter "crazy." But our friend's words are also vindicating. His tone reverberates with scorn for people who demean others in this way.

Long after dinner, I reflect on the stigma surrounding mental health. I consider the many brave souls over the course of history who sought help but were subsequently misunderstood, mistreated, and dehumanized. Many were even institutionalized, deemed possessed by the devil, labeled as witches, castrated, or executed. And three hundred seventy years after Descartes's death, we're still suffering from his dualism. We *still* treat mental health as though it's separate from physical health. We *still* stigmatize and marginalize people. We *still* don't provide appropriate medical care. We *still* throw people suffering from mental health issues in jail. And Hannah is *still* at risk of being mistreated by those around her.

I'm starting to believe that people with mental illness are not crazy. Instead, the way we treat them is crazy.

I want to protect Hannah from this ignorance, so I delve back into my research. I'm astounded by the shallowness of the average person's—including my own—understanding of mental health issues. For example, we commonly note that feelings emanate from the heart, even though scientists have documented that feelings result from signals running among neurons that produce various neurochemicals in our *brains*. Even now, people generally believe the *mind* is ephemeral and transcendent, somehow separate from the body. Yet scientists have documented that most functions attributed to the mind—thinking, feeling, perception, consciousness, judgment, language, and memory, for example—occur within the *brain*. I ask myself, *Is mental health really any different from brain health, a subset of neurology?*

I wonder why we continue to distinguish between the mind and the brain. Maybe people believe brain-based behaviors are deliberate while others aren't? But nobody's going to convince me that people suffering from bipolar disorder choose their volatile mood swings, or that women coping with postpartum depression are acting willfully, or that Hannah wants to be taunted by spiders.

I share my concerns with a friend, and she confides that her family is also battling mental health issues: her son is self-harming through cutting.

I freeze, unsure of what to say. He's ten.

I assumed cutting was an epidemic among teenage girls, not elementary school boys. And I thought it was driven by contagion, when girls talk about their behaviors among one another.

"How'd he get the idea?" I ask. "Who told him about cutting?"

"Nobody," she responds. "He did it on his own. He said that there was just so much pain on the inside, he needed to get it out. He has such deep feelings of inadequacy."

Her comments are incongruous. Her son is a *great kid*—smart, talented, and caring. From the outside, most people would never know he could feel so insufficient and depressed. But it seems his many wonderful capacities aren't immediately apparent to him.

I then admit my ignorance about male self-cutting, and my friend enlightens me, "Yeah, the stereotypes are misleading. My nephew is bulimic. People assume boys can't have eating disorders, but they do. And when people dismiss a whole gender, it only adds to kids' isolation and low self-esteem."

I realize I did this *just now*, so I apologize. "Oh, I'm so sorry. I should have been more thoughtful." And I vow to try harder.

Knowing this child is walking through the halls of GCA hiding his self-inflicted wounds haunts me. How many other children carry anxiety or depression or trauma around school? Too many kids seem to be suffering in secret. There must be something we can do!

I take my concerns to a board member I know well and withhold the child's name as I share what I've learned. But she cuts me off as she probes, "Is it Teddy? That kid has *prob*lems."

I'm not referring to Teddy. And now I'm definitely not revealing the child's name. Anger swells, and I grasp to contain it, reminding myself that those who know better, do better.

Then and there, I decide to create a presentation that summarizes all I've learned about mental health, neurodiversity, and bullying and shows how the issues intertwine. I'll distill the information that took me months to gather into a tidy package that can be read in a matter of minutes. I want to believe any missteps at GCA are due to ignorance rather than intentional neglect or ill will. I want to help my friend's boy and all other children in need. In fact, I'm so concerned that I drive myself to finish the presentation in just a few evenings.

Upon completion, I ask the assistant Head of School, Paula, to meet. I know her socially—we met on a hike with mutual friends—so she seems like a safe place to start.

When we get together a few days later, I show her my work and offer to find independent experts who can support our community and help our kids.

Paula's tone is pleasant but dismissive. "The staff doesn't need extra assistance," she says. "We've got it under control." Then, perhaps in an effort to throw me a bone, she wonders aloud if my materials could be included in an upcoming series to educate *parents*. But she's adamant that any references to bullying should be "unpacked" from the presentation as it might be "confusing" to families.

Usually, when I see Paula outside of school, she's agreeable. But today, she's flexing her muscle to remind me that she's in charge and doesn't want my assistance. She also seems to be implying that the parents are the problem here.

I take note. Any mission to support children clearly will need to be pursued delicately.

Presidents

Hannah has been rehearsing her impersonation of President Taft for days. She's allowed to use index cards, but she doesn't need them. She memorized every word. And today is finally the day she gets to present.

"Mom, it won't stay!" Hannah struggles to hang a pocket watch from the vest of her makeshift three-piece suit so she can emulate the twenty-seventh president. I catch the chain around a button, straighten her fake mustache, and give her a fist bump. I then spin around to see who else might need help. I signed up to help with costumes, but I have an ulterior motive: getting an inside view of the class dynamics and protecting Hannah if necessary. Normally, I would encourage her independence, but the administration's ambiguous stance on bullying makes me apprehensive, especially during events like this. Assemblies with distracted teachers are perfect opportunities for kids looking to test boundaries.

Hannah is eager, like the other girls, but she's also timid. Her peers giggle and point and shriek at one another as they begin to resemble men fifty years their senior. I smile too. They *do* look both ridiculous and fabulous at the same time.

After ensuring the girls are clad presidentially, I head to the auditorium and plop down next to Jim. The other parents are buzzing, excited to see their little statesmen.

The presentation proceeds chronologically over three days (so parents don't have to sit through all forty-four presidents and the president-elect). With forty children in the class, a few dignitaries don't make the grade: Martin Van Buren, William Henry Harrison, Millard Fillmore, and Rutherford B. Hayes. On this second day, Andrew Johnson kicks us off, and Jim and I settle in to wait for President Taft's rise to power (and the stage).

When a little Teddy Roosevelt descends clutching a stuffed bear, the stage remains empty. A few, long minutes later, a diminutive Woodrow Wilson enters guarding his Nobel peace prize. Jim and I share nervous glances. What happened to Taft?

Hannah labored over her presentation. She now knows Taft is the only person to hold both the office of president and chief justice of the United States. She also learned that, prior to becoming president, Taft was governor-general of the Philippines and the US secretary of war. She knows he lost his second-term election when former president and fellow Republican Teddy Roosevelt joined the race, splitting the vote of their party and handing the election to Democrat Woodrow Wilson. But the audience isn't going to learn any of that today.

What happened?

Jim and I ignore inquisitive glances of parents. I don't have any answers.

After the final presentation, Hannah's teacher makes her way toward us. Megan whispers, "I touched her back to prompt her to go, but she stiffened so quickly that I didn't push her. It was such a strong reaction, I didn't want to make things worse." She looks apologetic and worried that I might be mad at her.

I respond, "Thank you for being so sensitive. And for reading the situation." I'm truly grateful for her compassion.

After whispering the update to Jim, I go in search of Taft.

I finally find Hannah in the girls' bathroom, cowering like a dog who's been caught nabbing meat off the kitchen counter.

I approach as casually as possible, but the moment she sees me, she bursts into tears. "I'm so sorry, Mama. Are you mad at me?"

"No! Honey, of course not!"

Hannah nods and explains, "I just couldn't do it. I was too scared."

She relaxes a little upon seeing I'm not upset. But I can tell she's still sad and maybe even embarrassed she couldn't perform alongside her classmates.

I concede, "Public speaking is scary. For everyone. I get it."

She whimpers, "I just didn't want to do it today. Is that bad?"

"No, Sweetie. You did the important part. You worked hard, and you learned so much! If you want to present later, to just your class, I'm sure you can. Or maybe you can present with the next bunch tomorrow. But for now, let's focus on all you did do: you prepared and you learned." Because of my reading, I know I'm supposed to push her to meet new challenges, but not so much that I induce anxiety.

"Are the teachers mad at me?" She's terrified she disappointed them.

"Not at all! Your teacher was the one who told me she didn't want to force you. She gets that different kids need to do different things at different times." I'm not totally sure I believe this, given Megan's intolerance at our last meeting. But today, I'll give her the benefit of the doubt.

■ ▨ ■ ▨

After helping Hannah choose a snack, I crash on a sofa and attempt to release the stress of the day. But instead of feeling calm, my mind races back to my own third-grade studies of presidents. I can almost hear my teacher as she asserted, "FDR would be unelectable today." She told us how Roosevelt went to great lengths to prevent the public from seeing his wheelchair, but that wouldn't be possible today.

This memory rankles me. I head to my computer and search: "Presidents with disabilities." A list pops up with more names than I expect, probably because it classifies all learning differences as disabilities. I see many notable names, like Abraham Lincoln (who had depression and Marfan syndrome, a tissue disorder), Woodrow Wilson (who had dyslexia and partial paralysis), and Franklin Delano Roosevelt (who was also partially paralyzed). I also note that as many as nine out of forty-five presidents (twenty percent!) are known or believed to have been dyslexic.

I review the list and realize that no president since FDR (or since the widespread use of television) has had a visible impairment. I would have assumed that technology would have enabled us to advance our human ideals, but it seems that, in this case, it has led to more covert, and perhaps more insidious, methods of discrimination. For all our championing of diversity and inclusion, for all our efforts to become a more civil society, I wonder, *Have we moved backward in some ways?*

Breaking the Code

I'm giddy heading to the coast with a few GCA girlfriends. November isn't exactly a balmy time to visit the shore, but I'm thrilled I won't be responsible for anybody else's well-being for a few days. The forecast suggests clear skies and chilly air, perfect for relaxing by a fire. Even more enticing: two nights of glorious, uninterrupted rest.

As soon as we arrive, we head for the spa, where the sleek minimalist decor does nothing to detract from the luxury. I've been dreaming of this. And yet, the moment I settle under the crisp, white sheet on the massage bed, my guilt creeps in. *What am I doing here?* The thought of a "treatment" makes me feel frivolous and undeserving. My guilt reminds me I have more important matters to attend to. I'm a fraud here.

But I decide to indulge anyway. I want to belong. I want to celebrate friendships and feel independent. And I wouldn't mind getting rid of those damned knots that have formed up and down my spine over the past few months. So, I remind myself that martyrdom is useless and self-care is good.

After our massages, my neck has a bit more mobility than usual. I pray it lasts and turn my attention to my friends, who are wrapped in plush robes and laugh as they snuggle into chairs to lunch by a fire. My sense of exhaustion and inadequacy doesn't match their exuberance and confidence. Yet, I will myself to play along. I know there's a "Code." My job is to contribute to the comradery and fun, to the veneer that everything is okay here. I cannot be the downer on the girls' weekend, so I plop myself into the one remaining seat and smile.

Later that afternoon, we break into smaller groups. Some choose to explore the small shops nearby, but Ellen suggests a hike along the coastline through the trees. This is more my style: the dusty path, the crashing waves nearby, and the light filtered through the dense trees. The simplicity and ruggedness are consistent with who I am right now.

As we set out, I'm determined to keep my cool and not burden my companion with my concerns. *Everything is okay here.* We're amused by some squirrels playing tag up a tree and by a bird trying to lift off with an abandoned sandwich twice its size.

Ellen soon asks, "How are you?" It's usually such an innocuous question, but today it feels loaded. What do I say?

I remind myself that if I create too much fuss, I'll be regarded as "one of them," the mothers who don't abide by the Code. The labels cast toward the women who don't present an aloof sense of calm are endless: "high-maintenance," "helicopter," "unhinged," maybe even a bit "crazy."

I am tired of the drama in my life, so I remind myself, *Play along. Hold your piece.* But, apparently, I'm so desperate for support that my own admonition isn't enough to keep me from walking through Ellen's open door. My truth escapes. "We're still dealing with bullying, unfortunately. It's been really hard." My words are at the surface in a neutral tone, but underneath I'm pleading, *Please hear me. Care. Please care.* Given my friend's strong standing at the school, she's in a position to support Hannah. And even if she's not willing to take action on campus, a simple consoling word here in the woods could make me feel so much less alone.

She responds, "Oh."

Is that a flat, don't-tell-me more, "Oh"? Or is it a prompt, asking me to say more? Probably the prior, but I press on. I could use any sort of affirmation right now. "We've tried so hard with the school. But they won't acknowledge what's happening. So Hannah's completely on her own."

"Huh."

Maybe she'll be moved to engage if she realizes bullying affects the entire ecosystem? I explain, "The girls who target her are being so disruptive that parents want the new teacher fired. So the whole class is struggling."

"Hmmm. Really?"

Again, I hope, *Please care. Please say, "I know what a tough time you've been going through. This is just wrong. How can I help?"*

But she's not going to give me the gift of her validation today. She's now peering the other way, looking as though she wishes she was with anyone else . . . any*where* else. As she gazes into the distance, she offers, "You know, Kayla. You might not want to rock the boat on this one." And then she marches on.

Her demeanor suggests she's done me a favor. She feels good about extending herself to advise a friend. She has stooped to remind me about the Code and pushed me back in line.

But instead of falling in place, I step back, literally dropping a few steps behind.

Did she just advise me not to rock the boat?

I agree. It's rocking. The waters at school feel turbulent, especially for my little girl and the other kids targeted with bullying. But is Ellen suggesting *I'm* the one creating the swells? If I point to the crashing waves, does that mean I caused them?

I wonder if she understands that we're not talking about a single child on a dingy here. We're talking about a large vessel. Many children and families are affected. Maybe if she sees the extent of the problem, she'll reconsider her suggestion that I created it. So I explain, "I know at least ten other families—more, actually—who are having similar experiences. And the administration stonewalls them too."

"Oh really? That hasn't been my experience. Richard usually responds to me."

Huh.

Apparently, she believes that if she hasn't witnessed something personally, it must not be happening at all. Her unique point of view enables her to deny mine. Not even a group of families can sway her. She won't stand up for us. After all, if she did, she might rock the boat.

I look around, amazed that Ellen and I are unable to have a candid conversation. We are secluded in the woods with nobody to overhear us. Nobody for miles. But she won't lower her guard and consider what I'm saying. Maybe she's concerned I might tell others if she expresses support. Maybe she doesn't want her name associated with people on the fringe of the school community, so she negates our experience to avoid being related to it.

I decide not to let her off the hook. "*You* might not be experiencing this, but a lot of families are really upset."

She, too, digs in. "Yeah, but who are they? Some of the crazy parents?"

I flip from exasperation to anger. *Who is she to decide who's sane and who's not? Whose story is rational and worthy?*

I know the names she puts in the "crazy" category. Every class has a few parents known to be meddlesome and abrasive. Some speak arrogantly about their "deeply gifted" child and are condescending to teachers. There's no lack of entitlement in private schools. But not *all* parents are like that. Some simply speak up when they feel genuine concern for the well-being of the community. But in so doing, they, too, are cast as "problem parents."

I find the ease by which Ellen categorizes these parents as crazy to be indicative of a larger problem—at our school, certainly, but more broadly too. GCA's social structure, its eagerness to slot parents into certain groups, and its readiness to label someone as a "helicopter parent" have been weaponized to the point that I'm nervous to advocate for my child and other children who are being victimized.

This doesn't seem right. If an adult witnesses one child being cruel to another, shouldn't the adult step forward to help define an acceptable code of conduct, one consistent with the community's values? Yet, as I've seen with Hannah, parents are largely unwilling to get involved. Instead, they often labor to distinguish themselves from the helicopters with dismissive comments, like "Oh, the kids will figure it out on their own," or "That's just what girls do!" and the classic, "Boys will be boys!"

It seems to me that we've gone too far. I believe we should distinguish between parenting *so much* that we obstruct our kids' independence and parenting *so little* that we abdicate our responsibility to raise good citizens.

I reconsider Ellen's inference that the families troubled by bullying aren't credible. In fact, the ones I was referring to don't sit on her "crazy" list. I realize they have probably remained off the list, however, by expressing their concerns very selectively, if at all.

I'm embarrassed as I compare myself to them and acknowledge my effort today probably only hurt my case. I said too much to Ellen. I broke the Code. I am probably now officially a "crazy person," someone to be tolerated but not believed.

I contemplate all that my family needs to do to stay in good standing at GCA, and I wonder if we really belong anyway. It seems the only way to be respected there is to deny Hannah's very essence and our authentic experience. Yes, my husband and I are sometimes invited to school-related cocktail parties and other social outings, but when it matters most, we stand alone.

With this understanding, I abide by the Code for the rest of the weekend. I am here with friends, but I am completely alone.

■ ▩ ■ ▨

Four days later, I wait in a sterile room for a routine physical exam. I've been "good." I've abided by the Code for almost a week now, even though my ache for my daughter and the desire to live honestly still lurk below the surface.

My doctor enters and asks, "How are you?"

Maybe the thin, insufficient green gown inspires me to own my obvious vulnerability. And I don't have to worry about school politics here, so I admit, "Okay. We're dealing with some bullying at school, but you know, standard stuff." I don't expect much. I figure my words are candid, but my tone is blasé enough to give her the opportunity to move on to the next topic.

But my doctor disregards her chart to lock eyes. "I'm so sorry. There's no excuse for parents who don't take responsibility for their children's behavior." I'm shocked by her directness, and the fact that she jumped ahead in the story. Her intensity tells me I hit a nerve.

"Yeah, it's tough." I want to sound competent, so I explain, "We're trying to use this as a way to help our daughter build agency and the confidence to believe she can manage conflicts. But it's hard. She's only eight." I then venture, "Actually, what's been most surprising isn't that kids bully or that their parents protect them. I wasn't prepared for the *other* adults, the ones who are in a position to help but won't. My own friends, even."

My doctor's face betrays her. I've never seen a metamorphosis so instantaneous—the whites of her eyes just shot to dark pink. Nothing about the professional environment, the lab coat, or the reading glasses can mask her pain. "The judgment is awful. They just isolate you," she concedes. Her emotions are raw, so close to the surface, that they divulged her truth when I startled her with my own. I return her empathy, hoping to assure her that she's not alone.

And then we get on with the business of my checkup.

When I leave her office, I'm struck by having just witnessed a smart, professional woman acknowledge her child's pain and also indulge her own. Are we allowed to do that? The victims here are the minors, the direct targets of the aggressive behavior, right? I had been suffocating my own feelings of betrayal to prioritize the kids who are suffering so much. But I recall a friend once suggesting, "Maybe identifying and moving through our pain can free us to be more present for our children. And we can model for our kids that we are worthy of self-care so that they can know they are too."

I tried to "self-care" at the girls' weekend by getting a massage and lunching by a fire. But that didn't work. I can see now that I was covering up the pain. Maybe I need to sit in it.

Later that evening, I draw a bath. I lower myself into the warm water, hoping it will extract the stress from my clenched back as I just let myself be. But as the water turns tepid, too many ideas still bound through my head. So I towel off and once again turn to my computer. This time, however, rather than pursue strict research, I scour articles and chat rooms where mothers pour their hearts out and seek comfort in community. I finally feel understood as I listen to their voices:

They think that because my son is different, he doesn't deserve kindness like everyone else. They treat us like we have some sort of contagious disease.

My poor other kids! I have no time left over for them. They deserve so much more from me.

The isolation put me in a dark place. I had to put my child on anti-depressants, and then myself.

I'm so alone. My husband works all day while I deal with the school and stay strong for my daughter. When he comes home, he doesn't want to talk about it. It's not that he doesn't care. We just handle the stress in such different ways that it's affecting our marriage.

I recognize the posts' common threads of loneliness and depression. Ironically, when parents need community, empathy, and help the most, they are denied on all counts. So we must somehow summon the strength required to bear this heavy load on our own.

The anecdotal evidence suggests many of us do this through alternate, or masked, personalities. If we show too much emotion, we're considered melodramatic. If we reveal anger, others pull away. So, we must display composure and serenity on the outside when we're exhausted, miserable, and livid on the inside. Basically, when we feel our weakest, parents must give the acting performances of our lives to project everything we are not. Yet, we do so because our children need us to.

I wish there was another way. I would like for friends to see my anguish, to help me release it, and perhaps even to help me carry it. I think the whole community might benefit if we worked together. But most people lean out. It's not *their* problem, after all. A few do offer guarded support by saying things like, "You're a mama bear." I know they're trying to be kind; they're acknowledging an instinctual need to protect my children. But I'm under no illusions. By comparing me to a wild, aggressive force in nature, haven't my peers just found another way to dehumanize me?

What if, instead of pulling away, denying one another's unique experiences, and justifying the status quo, we leaned in and asked, "That sounds so difficult. Can you tell me more about it? How can I support you best right now?"

Not My Experience

I continue to ponder how I can establish a real community for my children and myself. I want more than internet chat rooms. So when the mother of one of Jake's friends asks me to join her on a walk after drop-off, I accept. Lexi and I have spoken several times, and I like her. She's smart and thoughtful, and her son is a wonderful mix of mischievous and kind. A walk with her could be a nice escape and maybe even a way to build ties that would benefit my children.

About halfway through our walk, Lexi hints at her own struggle at school. She speaks judiciously as she tells me some families are concerned about a specific teacher who has demonstrated racial biases, like accusing the dark-skinned students—but not the white kids—of stealing when something goes missing. Just last week, a child was blamed for taking the teacher's desk keys, which were later found in her tote bag.

Lexi knows this because she recently hosted a dinner for the families of color at school, and, at one point, several parents shared their experiences. Apparently, the issue with this teacher has been going on a few years with no investigations or changes. Lexi learned that several parents had requested that their child be moved mid-year to the other class in the grade, but the administration pushed back, reminding the parents that, "in the best interest of the students," the two classes needed to maintain approximate diversity.

"So the school's underlying concern is not the behavior of the teacher but a dedication to numbers and appearances," she sighs.

I wish I could say I was surprised.

Lexi goes on to explain that a few parents warned her and other mothers with younger children to request a specific teacher *before* class assignments are made each summer. While not guaranteed, these appeals are honored more often than are pleas to move children mid-year.

I'm annoyed as I realize the school is institutionalizing the racism by fostering a system to work around the issue rather than confront it directly. Simply shuffling a few kids on the roster won't solve the problem. I suggest, "Maybe the parents need to take their concerns to the board? Not just Richard's office?" I know all too well the gaslighting that occurs there.

She says, "People are hesitant to speak. They're worried they'll be considered 'an angry Black person.'"

I consider Lexi's words the rest of the day. There are only a few families of color in each grade, and I don't know all of them. But I do know several, including one of the mothers whose child has been mistreated. She's thoughtful and brilliant—literally trained as a rocket scientist—and her husband is a respected lawyer. Yet, now, when it matters most, they can't use their obvious competencies to speak up without risking legitimacy. And apparently, many of their peers don't feel comfortable doing so either.

I know Lexi and other families of color are coping with issues far more complex and insidious than mine. They have long histories of painful discrimination to overcome, not just the experiences at this one school. Hannah's situation is quite distinct, and it would be ridiculous to put her on the same platform as those dealing with racial injustice. I won't. Yet, I can't help but notice that while we have separate situations, one similar *tactic* is being used to silence a wide variety of people, albeit to different degrees.

I was taught that if people want to correct an injustice, they need to say something. They need to *do* something. But I'm noticing that far too many are degraded when they do. Parents of color know they'll be characterized as "angry," cast as scary and worthy of resistance. Parents of bullied kids are labeled "hypersensitive" or "crazy" and therefore irrelevant. Parents supporting students with learning differences, the neurodiverse, are considered indulgent and presumptuous. *Who are they to demand their kids have access to special tools? That would take away resources from others! Why should the rest of us be put out?* Despite the wide variety of challenges, when it comes to helping their kids, too many parents are forced to tread delicately, privately, slowly—in a way that ultimately enables the status quo and keeps children and families "in their place."

Sitting at my desk that night, I look at the clock. It's 8:58 p.m., not too late to call. I pick up my phone, and when she answers, I blurt, "Lex, what can I do?" I tell her I've been thinking about our conversation all day. "I'm here in any way you need. I know I can't tell anyone's story for them, but I can stand by you. Your one voice *should* be enough. It's enough to convince me. But maybe there's strength in numbers?" I want to take action, and I can't imagine anybody wants to be on the wrong side of this. So we start to brainstorm.

■ ▧ ■ ▨

A week later, over coffee with Ellen and Heather, I plunge in. "I heard recently that several students of color are dealing with racist behavior from a specific teacher." I describe the situation, believing the information will incite them in a way that my reports about bullying have not. And Ellen's on the school's board, so she can do something about it.

But Ellen surprises me when she replies, "Oh, that can't be true."

And then Heather adds, "Maybe they misunderstood."

I'm shocked into silence.

Yes, they've shown themselves to be less than supportive of my situation, but I have been guarded around them as I tried to respect the Code. Generally, however, I know these women to be good, decent people. They *care* about civil rights. I was *sure* they would be concerned about the possibility of racist behavior at our school. I thought they might even propose a plan of action. I suppose, if I'm being honest with myself, I hoped this issue of race would finally galvanize them to help children in need, if not mine, then at least someone else's. But they just reflexively dismissed my report, and their body language tells me they're done discussing it.

I rack my brain for ways to convince them. But as I prepare my plea, I reassess. And then I see it: I've already lost power with them. The respect I once enjoyed disintegrated the moment I spoke up for Hannah. Anything I say now will only fuel their judgment.

After a bit, I make a cheap excuse and slide out the back door.

I'm dejected but also incensed. This insidious acceptance of injustice feels surreal. How can so much pain and maltreatment be so normalized? I was initially drowning in Hannah's experience, but a broader pattern continues to reveal itself. Several families are overwhelmed by the consequences of bullying. And we, along with many others, are also banging our heads against walls trying to facilitate understandings of learning differences, attention challenges, and anxiety. And multiple families are dealing with the fallout of racism. Others surely have different concerns. Each of these challenges is distinct and worthy of its own platform, *for sure*, but as I mull them over, I continue to identify common threads. We are all fearful of the consequences of advocating for our children. And when we *do* try to share our experiences, others don't listen. They even dismiss our concerns out of hand. The rejection is consistent:

"Oh," they say, "that can't be true." (Even though they weren't witnesses, so how could they possibly know?)

Or, "That hasn't been my experience." (As if one person's reality negates another's.)

Or, "Are you sure?" (Suggesting the speaker might be irrational.)

Or, "That kid has *problems*." (Meaning: The child is to blame, not the environment or the adults judging him.)

Or, "She must be having a bad day. She's not like that." (After all, it's easier to make excuses than to consider uncomfortable complexities.)

I want to scream at my peers. These are not stupid people. They know injustice exists. But they are reluctant to admit it lives *here*, in the crevices among the stones they stand on. So they look away as the blight festers.

I keep asking myself, *How can people do this so easily? How can generally nice people lack so much empathy?*

I'm so upset that I decide to investigate the phenomenon intellectually. (My emotional response will just weigh me down more). So once again, I turn to the research.

Empathy and Compassion

The science of caring is fascinating, and it helps me understand how people who are generally quite lovely can be so callous at times.

I'm surprised to read that the word "empathy" was only introduced into the English language at the beginning of the twentieth century. I consider, *Maybe this explains why the learnings haven't been embedded into our culture yet.*

Apparently, empathy research proliferated after World Word II, when young Holocaust survivors grappled to comprehend the ways their neighbors, and the world in general, failed to respond to their suffering.

The readings teach me that empathy is more complex than I previously understood; there are, in fact, three distinct types. The first is cognitive or "thinking" empathy, which occurs when one is able to identify what others feel. The second is affective or "feeling" empathy, which causes one to experience personal distress over the pain of another. And the third is the empathic response, when one is driven to demonstrate a compassionate act. So while people might understand or even feel for others, they might not necessarily help them.

I soon recognize that the research on empathy is consistent with my earlier explorations into mental health. While people generally assume empathy comes from the heart, scientists have demonstrated that its roots are, in fact, neurological. Researchers documented that specific areas of the brain not only fire to make certain body parts move; certain portions activate when we observe *others'* actions and experiences. These "mirror neurons" are closely related to the limbic system and the almighty amygdala, that crucial part of our "fear center." I already knew the amygdala fires when we sense assaults to our own well-being. Now I'm learning that it triggers when we witness the discomfort of *others*. This has important implications because when the amygdala drives us to "fight" or to take "flight" or to "freeze," the rational parts of our brains are impeded and we are less able to assist others.

I consider, *Maybe my peers aren't insensitive, obtuse, or cruel after all.* Maybe they are so upset to see my child's pain that their brains inhibit their abilities to demonstrate empathy for her. This seemingly convoluted reasoning brings me peace. I like believing that people, especially those I consider to be friends, aren't intentionally coldhearted.

Evidently, my compatriots are in good company. "Empathy overload" affects many of our communities' most indispensable professionals, like medical providers, social workers, therapists, teachers, police and public safety officers, and humanitarians. People who work in these vocations can experience "compassion fatigue" and become emotionally paralyzed after witnessing extraordinary suffering. They might even endure "secondary trauma," the emotional duress caused by indirect exposure to others' anguish. As a result, researchers call upon employers to teach their caregivers how to balance cognitive and affective empathy so they can remain capable of responding with compassion.

I've asked myself many times why some GCA teachers are reluctant to help Hannah, why they refuse to acknowledge the bullying and intervene. Perhaps they're dealing with empathy overload and secondary trauma. After all, they, too, are likely affected by the unsupportive environment. And it seems they've been given little guidance on how to manage challenges like bullying, learning differences, and anxiety. When they witness pain, perhaps they feel too disturbed and ill-equipped to help, so they turn away, leaving kids like Hannah to fend for themselves.

And it's even easier to dismiss individuals in need if they're obviously distinct, as Hannah is. I'm shocked when I read several books and reports by the likes of Robert Sapolsky, Helen Riess, Tiffany Ito, and Geoffrey Urland and learn just how quickly our subconscious works to distinguish those around us. Apparently, humans make determinations about others' status in a mere forty milliseconds; we register racial differences within one hundred and twenty milliseconds; and we identify gender at around one hundred and fifty milliseconds. Not long after, the amygdala, our fear center, can begin to respond to these differences (often within fifty to one hundred milliseconds!). Unfortunately, the reasoning, impulse-controlling portion of the brain, the prefrontal cortex, only gets engaged after about five hundred milliseconds. As a result, we can respond to differences before we are even aware we have identified them.

The reading reminds me that, early in evolution, an ability to discern unique traits helped competing clans identify threats quickly. But today, the ramifications are depressing. The instinct drives us to "other" people and withhold empathy.

All of this research helps me understand how people can feel so comfortable with their mistreatment of my daughter. They judge her and react to their perceptions before they've even realized they've done so! The data also explains, but obviously doesn't justify, how my friends instinctively dismissed the possibility of racial prejudice at school. And I bet that, to this day, they don't even realize what they did.

The neural reaction times underlying human behavior are fascinating to me, but I learn they aren't the only phenomenon impeding empathy. Another obstacle is normative social influence, which drives people to conform so they can be accepted by others. Apparently, the amygdala not only activates when we identify threats in our environment and when we relate to others' experiences. It also fires if we consider going against group opinion. Again, our subconscious galvanizes quickly, registering if the group has picked a different response from ours in a mere two hundred milliseconds and initiating that stress response—the release of hormones and nerve impulses that make our hearts race and our palms sweat (among other uncomfortable sensations). By contrast, brains reward kowtowing and consensus with a dopamine rush—a reward for imitating others that we can actually feel. As if all this weren't enough, I learn that the hippocampus, the brain region engaged in learning and memory, can then activate to *revise* any recollection of our original opinion so we can actually believe facts we once didn't. This helps me understand how people come to believe the lies they tell. It also explains how my close friends feel so comfortable refusing to hear my lone voice, even in the privacy of the woods.

The science of empathy doesn't stop there. I'm fascinated by several studies that reveal how individuals will even act against their own judgment and moral codes to gain social acceptance. *This is powerful stuff!*

In 1951, Solomon Asch, one of the social scientists influenced by World War II, ran a series of tests in which people were asked a simple question: Which line on a card matched the length of another line on an adjacent card? The task was so easy that subjects got the answer right about ninety-nine percent of the time when they didn't have an audience. But something curious happened in group settings. When an individual heard several people—actually associates with pre-assigned scripts in the experiment—give the same wrong answer, the test subject frequently followed suit and answered incorrectly. In fact, over twelve trials, about seventy-five percent of the subjects conformed to the wrong answer at least once. Most stated later that they didn't really believe their responses, but they didn't want to look "peculiar" by giving a unique answer. Several insisted they actually believed their obviously wrong answer, suggesting to me that the hippocampus might have rewritten their memories, allowing the test subjects to stand by their stances more easily.

In the context of Asch's study, I now understand how people at GCA might deny their better judgment simply to fit in. Do they really want to side with me, a "peculiar" lone wolf, and risk losing their position in the community?

I find another study particularly fascinating and relevant. In the early 1960s, Stanley Milgram—a Jewish scientist who was born the year Hitler was appointed chancellor of Germany—investigated the psychology of obedience. His disturbing studies found that even everyday people would intentionally electrically shock others if instructed to do so by an official, especially if they were nudged to value the scientific process.

Psychiatrists predicted almost all test subjects would refuse to administer north of one hundred and fifty volts and that only one out of a thousand would flip the switch to deliver a potentially fatal four hundred and fifty volts. In fact, the outcomes were much more disturbing. *All* subjects stayed engaged until they thought they delivered at least three hundred volts, and an astounding *sixty-five percent* made the move to administer the maximum shock possible. (Fortunately, the experiment was designed so that while subjects believed they were delivering real shocks, the cries they heard were, in fact, recorded.)

Let me be honest. As I read these studies, I tell myself that I would have been an exception. But almost every single analysis of the studies tells me I am wrong. The researchers did not recruit people known to be deviants. They enrolled everyday people. It would be self-serving, and even disingenuous, to presume that I might have behaved any differently. As a result, this study, too, helps me understand the distressing extent to which people, even those who believe themselves to be good and kind, will hurt others given certain circumstances.

While I find several additional factors that impede compassion, fortunately, I also read about individuals who *do* help people in need. Two of the early pioneers of empathy research, Holocaust survivor Samuel Oliner and his wife Pearl, found that the people who risked their lives to help others during World War II were more likely than average to appreciate the benefits of community and feel personal responsibility for the welfare of others. These values were often instilled by parents who role modeled "tolerance, care, and empathy toward their children and toward people different from themselves" from an early age.

I realize this means we can probably teach children to be more empathetic. In fact, several scientists have been so moved by research findings that they have founded entire institutes to train people how to be more compassionate. These efforts are especially effective when students learn how our cognitive wiring works so that they can override the amygdala and other unfortunate influences that can lead us astray. Experts warn, however, that simple awareness is not enough. Empathy training can even be counterproductive if it causes people to feel "morally credentialed," and therefore off-the-hook for staying vigilant. As a result, this is a lifelong process.

I wonder why we all aren't taught how to be attentive to others from the earliest stages in life. The knowledge could enhance every human interaction and every single relationship we ever have.

Ticks

A warm spell passes through, and the school uses the opportunity to reschedule a field trip that was canceled two months ago. The second and third grades are visiting a working farm today, and Jake and Hannah are ecstatic. Jake is particularly pleased to be associated with the "big kids." I expect he'll latch onto Hannah, Aisha, and Amanda for the entire day.

In the afternoon, Theo and I collect the bigger kids, and I'm amazed to be wearing short sleeves in December. It was thirty-five degrees just last week!

Jake hops in the car, bubbling with excitement, and Hannah follows in silence. Jake babbles, listing the animals he saw. "I even milked a cow! Do you know they can't make milk when it gets too hot or too cold? Same with chickens!"

I smile as I question, "Chickens make milk? Cool!"

"Moooom! Eggs, silly." He's proud to be enlightening me.

Hannah still hasn't said a word, so I peer into the rearview mirror and see she's using one hand to thrust her ponytail in her mouth while her other strokes her forearm. She's soothing herself, and I wonder why she's not more upbeat. Spending the day bounding around a farm—away from a hard floor mat and rigid expectations—should be an exhilarating break for her.

When we arrive home, Hannah whispers, "Can you come to the bathroom with me?" Once there, she reports, "I'm scared. Can you give me a tick check?"

"Uh, sure. Why?"

"The lady who led the tour told us we need to do tick checks."

"Okay, that sounds like a good idea."

"She said ticks will bite us and then we'll die. So check every-where! Okay, Mom?" She's almost hyperventilating now.

"Whoa, Hon. Yes, it's good to make sure you didn't get bitten. But even if you did, you're not going to die." *How did we go from a sweet field trip to death?* Hannah and Jake are acting like they went to opposite sides of the world today.

Hannah ignores me. Her voice rising, she insists, "Mom, the lady was really mean. She said it a lot of times. We need to do this NOW! Hurry! Jake too!" Her distress is alarming.

"Okay, wait. Let's slow down. Everything is fine. Can you take a few deep breaths?"

I coach her to exhale deeper and longer than she inhales, but Hannah refuses to follow my instructions. My frustration grows. Not only is she freaking out about ticks—which *can* be dangerous but are unlikely to kill her if addressed promptly— she's unable to follow basic directions that will *help* her. *I mean, how hard is it to exhale?*

I model the exercise, but Hannah has none of it. "Mom, the check!"

"Okay, okay." I brace myself. I want to scream but resist. "Let's breathe while I look. Sound good?" I lift her arms, search-ing for bugs I doubt I'll find, all the while breathing audibly, hoping she'll follow suit. She doesn't, so I rack my brain for other tools the psychologist recommended. My mind freezes under the stress, but I finally recall an option. "Hannah, I can see you're worried." Her face leaves no doubt, so I ask, "On a scale of one to ten, how worried are you? What's your number?" I remember that just grading the anxiety can help her engage her prefrontal cortex, the rational, thinking part of her brain.

"A seven, Mom! A seven!"

I've never heard her rank anything higher than a five before.

I was initially annoyed by her hysteria, but her anguished face and seven rating bring me to her reality, where she perceives, and actually feels, imminent danger. She's petrified. I recall this scale is not only designed to help her; it also forces me into her world.

I give Hannah a cursory check, but she's not placated. She directs me to examine every last crevice. Between her toes. Behind her ears. Throughout her hair. She wants to leave no hiding place unprobed.

As I inspect, I remember other tools to distract her "worry bug" and reengage her "thinking brain."

"Hannah, What's your favorite color, Honey?"

"Huh?"

"You heard me." I feel impatient, but I will myself to slow down. "What's your favorite color?"

"Uh, purple. Well, light purple. Lavender."

"That's right. You like soft, calm colors, right? What are some other colors you like?"

She looks confused but lists a few. I then introduce a few new categories, and, slowly, she relaxes.

When we finally depart the bathroom a half-hour later, I'm ready to scream at the docent who terrified my daughter. Was it necessary to tell these kids they could die? This might have been the first time my eight-year-old ever considered her own death. *What the hell was that woman thinking?*

Over the next few days, the need for tick checks increases. Hannah starts to demand them every few hours, even if she hasn't stepped outside. And she starts resisting leaving the house at all, especially if it means traversing through long grass. This is debilitating because running, playing, and jumping in the yard normally help to ease her stress and anxiety. Hannah even insists on tick exams for her beloved Gracey, which is a caring gesture but leaves me depleted of time and energy.

I contact Hannah's therapist, who says it's time for cognitive behavioral therapy. She also reminds me not to indulge the fear and to maintain a regular schedule. Joanna warns that if I check Hannah compulsively, the "worry bug" vying to control her brain wins and will demand even more attention next time. So Hannah and I enter a little dance: she tries to convince me to do more checks, and I try to withhold them without letting her feel abandoned. It's a delicate, nuanced choreography.

I learn that arrangements made in advance are more effective than demands made in the heat of the moment. She and I agree to one tick check a day, but only if she's been in the grass. I tell her I don't want to work with her worry bug. I want to work with *her* and her thinking brain. She acquiesces begrudgingly.

After a few weeks, I'm proud of us. We're making progress, especially since Hannah implements the tools she learns at her now biweekly psychology sessions—the frequency increased to address the heightened need. I often need to prompt her, but Hannah is motivated; she'll do almost anything to avoid the terror her anxiety imposes. So while we were once performing ten tick checks per day, we've now inched our way down to a few. It's not as low as I'd insisted, but we're working on it.

But then we fall back hard. At pickup a few days later, I search the gaggle of kids for my daughter. Finally, I spy Hannah, and her eyes pierce me. Her hair is twisted and stuffed in her mouth, the way a hungry seal might guard a freshly caught fish. This can't be good.

Hannah scurries into the car and snatches the door handle to slam it behind her. When I climb in, she releases the mass from her mouth and wails, "Mom! It was scary!"

"What do you mean, Sweetie? What happened?" I say, working to remain calm. Having Theo home with a babysitter and Jake away on a playdate helps.

But as I pull away from the school, her demeanor tells me I can't keep driving. So I search for a space on the side of the road and park as Hannah gasps for breath. Her face is now streaked with tears, both wet and dry.

Between gulps, she recounts, "At recess . . . Lauren and Daniella said . . . ticks were all over me . . . They kept . . . touching my back. They said the ticks were . . . biting me! They wouldn't stop!"

"What do you mean they wouldn't stop? Where were the teachers?"

"I don't know! But they wouldn't stop! For like twenty minutes!"

"Twenty minutes?" Hannah doesn't wear a watch. And it's probably impossible to keep track of time when her brain is going haywire.

But she insists, "A LONG TIME, Mom! Like almost the whole recess!"

Wow. So maybe it was a long time. "And there were no teachers around to help you?"

"No!" She gasps for breath. "And they wouldn't stop. Well, Daniella did." She inhales again. "For a few minutes."

"And Lauren?"

"She kept running around me, *laugh*ing at me, touching my back, pinching me, telling me I had ticks! They were *stuck* to me!" She continues, "And then Daniella started again."

I'm frustrated to realize Daniella might have listened to her conscience, but the environment sucked her back in. "Where was everyone else? Were your friends there?"

"Amanda was, I think."

"Did she help?"

"No."

I guess I shouldn't be surprised. The school hasn't built a culture that encourages students to be upstanders. So kids lower their heads to avoid being targeted themselves. Even good, sweet friends bow out.

"And it was a one hundred!" she screams.

"What do you mean 'one hundred'? One hundred ticks?"

"No! My number! It was one hundred out of ten! *One hundred!* I kept turning around to make them stop, but they made me go in circles. When I yelled at one to stop, the other one went behind me and touched me and told me there were more ticks!"

One hundred? Is she telling me this was a full-blown anxiety attack? She has never before given a number over seven. And that was when she was told ticks could kill her. When she thought she might die. And now she's telling me she was at one hundred.

Oh.

My.

God.

I can just picture the scene: Hannah twisting in circles, begging them to stop, which only fueled their taunts. She probably looked strange, contorted, out of control, even weird as she spun around in fear.

And they were laughing.

Hannah's unraveling was their entertainment.

Holy shit.

■　■　■　■

Later that night, I receive calls from two moms. Both are near tears telling me their children witnessed the incident but didn't know what to do. Both women say their kids are crying. It was traumatic for them to observe the episode. I can't imagine how an anxiety attack, if that's what Hannah experienced, looked to eight-year-olds. One parent tells me the girls used spikey holly leaves to prick Hannah, to make her feel like she really was being bitten. I wonder how the girls could have known about this new phobia, but then I realize Hannah must have expressed her fear of ticks at some point and they seized upon it, just as they did with spiders. The intentionality is hard to process.

When Jim returns home from work, I relay the details. He fumes, "Those bastards." His word choice suggests he isn't addressing the girls. He's furious at the adults who allowed this to happen. I feel the same way. I suppose I could be angry at the girls, but they are broken cogs in a defective machine. Where are the damn engineers to fix this wreckage?

Jim helps me draft an email documenting Hannah's account and the description the two mothers relayed. We demand apologies and consequences. We copy Hannah's teachers, Richard, Paula, and the school psychologist. And then we wait.

Given our social ties and mutual friends, I'm not surprised when the assistant head of school responds first:

Sorry to hear this. Busy packing the family for our trip to Florida. I hope everything goes well. I'll see you in the New Year! Paula

I don't think I've ever heard a louder mic-drop. She believes her work is done here. And I feel utterly betrayed. Just a few weeks ago, I spent an hour on the phone with her brainstorming ways to help her children cope with the death of their dog, and now she responds in my time of need with the equivalent of a shoulder shrug and a "Check ya later!" Once again, I feel sucker-punched by a failure of kindness. It's amazing how this inaction feels like a direct assault.

We receive another email, this time from Megan:

I wasn't on the playground at the time. Let me regroup with the team to see what happened and get back to you.

We hear nothing from Richard, nor the school psychologist, who's also the director of social and emotional learning and in charge of teaching the kids how to be kind.

I call Lexi for advice and relay the entire story.

"Fucking unbelievable," she says. And then she sighs and continues, "Just the other day, I was talking to Paula. She's got this idealized vision in her head about the school. She even said, 'I've drunk the Kool-Aid.'"

"Paula said that?" I'm incredulous. Does she realize she's admitting to drinking poison willfully? What makes somebody do that so consciously? I lament, "I thought Paula was a friend. Or at least friend*ly*."

"I think you're about to find out who your real friends are," Lexi says.

The words sting. This whole situation should be easy:

Child is bullied.

Peers say, "That's unacceptable," and advocate to keep children can safe.

School engages to support all students.

End of story.

But it seems things aren't going to be so simple.

After I get off the phone with Lexi, I call my closest friend, Monica, who's not associated with the school. I need compassion and objective honesty, and I know I can count on her for both. She delivers the first when she says, "I'm sorry. Your family doesn't deserve this. It's just wrong on so many levels." And she addresses the second when she continues, "I know you've tried to get help from some friends there. But not everybody's going to have the strength to support you." She reminds me that she too "had to learn to see people's true colors" and "not paint red flags pink." She says, "I would love to have a few words with the people looking the other way. It wouldn't be pretty. As parents, they should be ashamed. But Kayla, maybe it's time to be more selective about who you share your story with, who you reach out to." There's no inflection at the end of her sentence. It isn't a question.

■　■　■　■

The next day, I wake up and, still, there's no reply from Richard nor the psychologist. I can't believe they think this incident isn't worthy of attention. Am I not understanding things correctly?

170

Or is this more gaslighting? Some crafty Jedi-mind-trick where they ignore problems and maintain, "Everything is okay here," even when everything is *not* okay? Richard acts as though his will alone should be sufficient to change our minds and our experiences. But it's not. We've been trying to solve this problem for months now, and things are only getting worse.

What are we going to do?

The Holidays

Our neighborhood is awash with bright holiday decorations, yet I feel little joy. I'm supposed to attend a ladies' holiday luncheon hosted by Heather today, but I'm dreading it. I don't think I have the energy to partake in any sort of merriness, especially after yesterday's events. But I worry that if I cancel, I'll feed the narrative that I'm overly emotional and not "pulled together."

I scan the online invitation and see that a dear friend, Julie, is included. She's actually the only non-GCA mom on the list. I call to fill her in, believing that if at least one person at the event knows what my family is going through and has my back, I'll be able to abide by the Code alongside everyone else.

I then head to my closet and throw on a red dress. It's one of my favorites, but when I check my image in the mirror, I'm disgusted. The woman staring back at me is a traitor. She appears festive and carefree, which is treasonous given all I know about her. She makes me want to vomit. I consider disrobing and staying home, but that would set off a distress signal. And I feel too vulnerable to let the GCA ladies know just how precarious my family's situation is, how badly I feel. They might look the other way again, and I couldn't bear another rejection right now. So I wear the uniform they expect and head out the door.

When I arrive at the restaurant, I spy my hostess and her other guests nestling into chairs. Fortunately, Julie saved a seat at her side, and I plop down next to her. The women banter over kale salads, but I find myself unable to engage. The whole event feels so extraordinarily vapid.

Then one of the women says, "So, I was just asked to be president of the PTA. Do you think I should do it?" Her question is clearly rhetorical. Her beaming face conveys her pride and the likelihood that she's already accepted the invitation.

But Heather urges her anyway. "Yes, definitely! That's so great!" And she adds coyly, "I was just nominated to the board!"

She nods at Ellen, who's already a trustee, so this can't be news to her.

The congratulations are effusive.

As I look around, I realize each GCA mom at the table has been invited into the school's inner circle. Everyone, that is, except me. I have supported the school as much as any one of them. Arguably, I have as much, and perhaps more, relevant experience given my pre-motherhood career in management consulting and my current nonprofit work in education. But none of that seems to matter. I sink into myself, feeling like the only girl not invited to the prom, forcing a smile as they discuss their scintillating plans.

My discomfort stews until disbelief engulfs me. Are these women this insensitive? Do they not realize I'm being dismissed as they revel in their inclusion *right in front of me*? Do they not care how it might feel to witness them championing the glories of the school that allows my child to be mistreated?

Heather even encourages Julie to send her kids to GCA. "It's such a fabulous place! You should come! I'll write you a letter." She speaks like it's a country club our friend would be lucky to join. The suggestion kicks me in the gut.

How obtuse can they be?

Then someone asks Ellen, "Wasn't Greg Crawford invited onto the board too?"

Ellen nods, and my stomach plummets. The day after Lauren instigated my daughter's anxiety attack, her father is invited onto the board? Aren't trustees and their families supposed to exemplify the institution's values?

What the hell?

"I have to use the ladies' room," I blurt as I flee the table. For the second time today, I think I might throw up.

Julie trails behind me. By the time we arrive in the bathroom, I'm no longer going to be sick, but I feel pummeled, dazed, trying to understand what just happened. "Did I hear that right?" I ask her.

"Yes." Julie's tone is morose. I'm thankful I don't have to explain how I'm feeling. She, unfortunately, gets it. In fact, she has experienced betrayal far worse than mine. Decades before, in her mid-teens, she was groomed and sexually abused by her priest. He was transferred without conceding any wrongdoing, and he ended up leading a church with an even larger congregation. That her assaulter advanced while she was expected to just "get over it" was debilitating.

"Julie, do you mind me asking? Back then, what did you need? How should they have handled it?" I'm a bit nervous I might reopen a wound for her, but she's spoken to me about her experience before. And I'm willing to bet she has insights. Over the years I've noticed that people too often assume that individuals who've suffered are somehow compromised—that their opinions are unreliable because they are "damaged goods"—but I disagree. I find survivors are often uniquely informed and keenly perceptive. Sometimes, the awful experiences can give people understandings that others don't have.

Julie doesn't flinch as she explains, "I needed someone in a position of power to come to me proactively and say, 'What happened to you is not okay. We don't condone it. I am so sorry for what you've been forced to go through. It was wrong.'" Her face is firm, maybe steeled after years of considering the very question I just asked her. I wonder if anyone else has bothered?

174

She looks steady, but I hug her anyway and insist, "It was wrong. They were cowards for not saying so and for not supporting you." But I know I'm not the person she is aching to hear this from. She's already heard my opinion several times over the years.

She shrugs her shoulders and laments, "Well, it's nothing we're going to solve here in the bathroom." And then she rises, signaling she wants to move on, or at least back into the dining room.

But I'm still not ready, so I ask, "Would you mind making an excuse for me? Just tell them I needed to run home to deal with a blown water heater or something? Give them my apologies." I don't have any more energy for this charade.

She reads my mind and says, "I get it. Go. I'll call you as soon as I leave. We'll get through this."

I hug her feeling struck by that "we." It might be the kindest word I've heard in a year.

■　▩　■　▩

Before bed that night, I take one last look at my email. I can't help but hope Richard made time to reply. He didn't. And neither has anyone else.

Upset and emboldened, I email Megan again, copying the others. I edit my message a few times, striking words that reveal the depth of my feelings so I can appear "civil."

Megan, we are curious to know if there is any follow-up from the incident the other day. We are hopeful that Hannah will not need to wait until after the winter break to receive apologies from the children who taunted her and that someone will confirm the measures you are taking to ensure GCA does not tolerate bullying behavior. GCA's mission is to teach, but learning is impossible when kids feel threatened.

I hate that I have to ask for an update. Why am I the one leading this process?

When Megan responds later that night, she, too, copies the others and writes:

With all the holiday activities, life has been hectic. But I want you to know that I spoke with all children involved (the two girls who targeted Hannah and the witnesses). I also reached out to the parents of both girls and encouraged them to speak with their children about how this type of targeted behavior can never happen again. I used that word: targeted. I will check in with Hannah tomorrow to make sure she feels okay. Each child will be expected to apologize, and we are designing appropriate consequences. Those might have to happen in the New Year because of the holiday break. We will monitor the situation to ensure this does not happen again.

I want it to be enough. I really do. But it's not. For almost a year, we've been fighting this battle. Hannah—and our entire family—needs so much more.

So I cling to the fact that at least Megan documented her assessment. And the others are now on official notice. Maybe this is what they need to take the situation seriously.

Thank the Lord there's only one more day before winter break. I'll be at the school for the holiday performance, and I won't let Hannah out of my sight. Then, we'll escape. After these past few intolerable days, a few weeks of vacation feel like an absolute godsend.

A Break

I hope the winter break will calm Hannah's anxiety, but her symptoms take off. She chews her hair incessantly. She resists going outside, especially to areas that aren't paved. Suddenly, she refuses to drink water. After probing, I learn that she overheard a news report on mercury poisoning in a completely different state, so she's now worried our own water might be contaminated as well. When she realizes all animals and crops rely on water, she avoids meals altogether, offering any other excuse she can muster.

Some nights it takes three hours to help Hannah fall asleep, as she's convinced a spider nest lurks under her bed. Other times she's sure a baby tiger resides in her closet. (I recall the psychiatrist describing how anxious people feel as though they're living with a lion.) And when one of Jim's childhood friends visits the house, Hannah asks, "Mom, do you think he has a communicable disease?" Her anxiety apparently doesn't override her precocious vocabulary.

Essentially, Hannah is now resisting leaving the house, drinking, eating, sleeping, and meeting new people. She is nonfunctional. There's no denying we've plummeted to a new level.

The whole family is impacted. Jim and I are exhausted taking turns trying to help her fall asleep. Once we think we finally have all three kids in bed, Hannah runs down the hall, escaping spiders, tigers, ticks, or whatever other demon petrifies her that evening. As one of us leads her back to her room to start the lengthy anti-anxiety routine *all over again*, one of her brothers rushes out proclaiming, "I heard noises. What's happening? I can't sleep!" And so they fall like dominoes—each child waking another, and Jim and I spend hours on the verge of screaming, "Stay in your fucking beds!"

The more exhausted the children are, the more sleep eludes them. The next morning, they are irritable and groggy. They argue and tussle with one another, and tears are common. Jim's and my daily activities (work, chores, and everything else) flounder, as does our relationship. We struggle to summon enough presence to function through our ongoing fatigue.

Some holiday.

When things get really bad, and especially when Jim is unavailable to help, I cancel my evening crisis counseling sessions. I can't risk having my children escape from bed to interrupt me while I try to help anonymous texters choose life over death.

And guilt skyrockets—not just about our inability to honor commitments. We're haunted by the implications of ignoring Hannah's siblings while we triage the most apparent need. Jake and Theo deserve so much more! Guilt even infiltrates our relationships with Hannah. Logically, I know yelling won't help, but how many times do I need to explain that there are no spider nests under her bed? My exhaustion challenges my tolerance and wins more often than I'd like to admit.

The entire situation is infuriating. Hannah's worried mind resists reason and facts, the primary tools I use to solve most everything. So I lose my temper, and then I recoil in my failure. I was not made for this.

Hannah was not made for this either. At her essence, she's a thoughtful, highly analytical, playful child, but her amygdala is holding the rest of her hostage.

After more grueling nights, it's apparent our tools aren't working. The worry bug laughs at lists, anxiety meters, and breathing exercises. CBT too. So on our next appointment with the psychologist, Jim and I finally agree to start medication. We see no other options. We decide we'll use pharmaceuticals on a short-term basis until Hannah can reengage her thinking brain. Joanna invites Dr. Lee to join our meeting, and I'm relieved when she strives to understand Hannah's specific case and individualize her treatment. She asks Joanna thoughtful questions about Hannah's progress in therapy. She also orders blood tests, which she says can help ascertain if any of her anxious behaviors are driven by undiagnosed conditions or previous infections. And she recommends a DNA test to identify specific genetic variations that might be more responsive to certain medications or make Hannah more susceptible to various side effects. After experiencing so much rejection, we're grateful to have a team that doesn't dismiss our reality and instead initiates a full-court press.

■ ▩ ■ ▨

On the night that Hannah places the first pill on her tongue, I suppress my disappointment over the many failures that led us to this moment. Yes, Hannah is sensitive, and maybe even prone to anxiety, but the assaults on her dignity, her very core, certainly haven't helped. I'm particularly disgusted by the complicity of the adults involved.

I kiss the top of Hannah's head and wish her goodnight, but her sweet curls don't comfort me like usual. I'm undone by the cruelty and insensitivity of the world around us. Why don't people care? How can they prize the fiction of GCA's reputation, their precious appearance of status, more than the truth? More than the mental health of a little girl? Make that *many* boys and girls. I wonder if the children will carry the stain, the consequences of the mistreatment, throughout their lives? And I wonder if the parents of the other devalued and debased children feel as alone as we do? Have they climbed into a dark hole, like I have?

I sink deeper.

But then I remind myself that I don't have the luxury of wallowing in self-pity. I have obligations. I am responsible for others. For dependents. I must pull myself out and find a way to move forward. I focus on a small comfort: we don't have to get up early tomorrow. It's still winter break.

But the next morning I don't sleep in. In fact, I awaken early, feeling unexpectedly and wholly serene. It's the calmest I've felt in two years. I dreamt we enrolled Hannah in our local public school, and everything was okay. In my dreams, the effects of the larger class sizes were miniscule compared to the threats lurking at GCA. Maybe Hannah would benefit from a fresh start. Especially since we have little confidence anything will change where she is now.

When Jim rises, I share my dream, and he says, "Okay. Let's do it." But as the day wears on, my fears of enrolling Hannah in a large, chaotic environment reignite. I call several doctors and therapists for advice. They divulge things like, "That school has a known reputation for bullying, which will take time and intention to change," and, "I have a number of patients struggling there with similar issues."

Why didn't they tell us these things before? I guess they didn't want to become entwined in local school politics. And, let's not kid ourselves; they probably hope for referrals from the school. Yet their reluctance to speak candidly until I presented my case is unsettling. Hannah needed these experts to enlighten us *before* we ended up in this fiasco.

Unfortunately, now that we're ready to go, we can't extract ourselves easily. The advisors agree we should change schools, but they also say things like, "Hannah's highly sensitive. We need to be thoughtful about how this is done." And, "You won't want to switch her multiple times. It's important to get the next move right." And, "Hannah needs to be part of the process so she doesn't feel further stripped of power. Of any semblance of control." They encourage me to do my research and to even consider schools requiring a significant commute and extra expense. So I resolve to spend the spring finding the best fit for our family, and then we'll leave GCA forever.

A Glimpse

The meds seem to calm Hannah, but I'm not sure if the response is psychosomatic, due to wishful thinking, or an actual medical outcome. We are "leveling up," increasing the dose bit-by-bit to monitor efficacy and side effects. Fortunately, we haven't hit any obstacles. I know we're lucky in this regard. Other parents have anguished over this process. I remain hopeful that the new year—the meds, a determination to search for a new school, and even (in the interim) any meaningful efforts on the part of GCA—will herald a new beginning for Hannah.

My children return to school after our turbulent, unsatisfying break, and Megan emails to say the girls who taunted Hannah were punished. She explains she chose a "logical" consequence. Since the school has "no protocols for situations like this," she determined independently that the two girls should be forced to spend the first recess of the new year sitting on a bench at the side of the playground, near where they bullied Hannah.

After school, I ask Hannah how she feels about this outcome. She shrugs and says, "I didn't know. Nobody told me . . . I saw Lauren and Daniella sitting together at recess. They were playing clapping games and pointing at kids and laughing. It didn't look like a punishment." She adds, reaching for her ponytail, "I thought the school is okay with everything."

My heart drops, especially as I consider what Julie said about her own abuse—that she needed someone to recognize that what had happened was wrong. She needed an irrefutable acknowledgement that her well-being mattered. I hug Hannah and promise, "Sweetie, people care about you. Nobody thinks what happened is okay." But I can't help but remind myself that we have heard *nothing* from Richard—not a single word.

Since Megan doesn't seem to be getting any direction on managing bullying behavior and because her stance toward Hannah has tacked between annoyance and concern, I can't trust her to keep Hannah safe. So, I seek out Sonia on the playground after school. When she notices me, her face softens, and I'm reassured that she's more than a teaching assistant; she's a partner. She has proven that intuition and compassion can outweigh experience.

Sonia promises to keep her eye out for Hannah. In fact, she tells me she started skipping her breaks to eat lunch on the playground and keep watch. She also reports the administration *is* aware parents are concerned. Maybe they are starting to see that the school's reputation is on shaky ground. That educating *global citizens* could be exposed as one big sham if they don't address the issues authentically. In any case, I feel safer knowing Sonia's on the lookout.

■　▩　■　▨

The next evening, I get an email from a learning and development specialist. I had forgotten that about a month ago, long before the tick incident, I had arranged for him to visit GCA tomorrow to observe Hannah. He was recommended by the school after I told them I was wondering if Hannah was in the right grade. Her social difficulties made me question if she should be in a lower grade, while her strong verbal and conceptual math skills made me think she could benefit from more challenging material. I wanted this expert to help me figure it out.

Now I think the school culture is the overriding issue, but I'm still curious to hear what he might say after his visit.

He follows up the next day stating that he can't make any determinations on grade-readiness given the impact of the recent social dynamics at school. But he emails me a copy of a letter he just sent to Richard that expresses concern about bullying and recommends various prevention programs.

After our previous experience with third-party specialists being hesitant to call out a school for fear of losing business, I'm grateful. This is exactly the kind of support kids and families need!

I pray that this documentation from an independent expert, one recommended by the school itself, finally motivates people to take to action.

■ ▧ ■ ▩

We soon receive requests for commitments and deposits for the following academic year, and we ignore them. Through the grapevine we learn that several families are withdrawing, to the point where Richard requests individual meetings with those planning to leave. Jim and I get emails and then phone calls from Richard, even on weekends. We let them go straight to voicemail. Maybe we should be happy that the head of school is finally reaching out, but the fact that he still hasn't addressed our pre-holiday email is gnawing at us like a festering wound. In his messages, Richard expresses concern for our children and promises GCA is a "wonderful place" for them. He begs us to meet him in his office. We don't believe a word.

To confirm my intuition, I email the learning specialist and ask if he received a response to his letter about bullying prevention. He confirms:

No. But I wasn't exactly expecting them to follow up with me, per se. That said, sometimes letters like mine can push schools to act when they were previously resistant.

Richard calls again, and Jim's so annoyed at being bothered on a Saturday that he finally picks up. With me standing by his side, my husband tells Richard that his interest in our children sounds insincere. If he really cared, he would have contacted us after learning about the tick fiasco that induced Hannah's anxiety attack. Instead, he waited until he realized we're not reenrolling, when our kids represent a loss of revenue. We tell him we'll come to his office only if he acknowledges Hannah has been bullied.

He does not.

Over the next few weeks, Richard convinces more than half of the departing families to stay. But we've heard his shtick before. We know that real change won't come until he can cop to reality.

■　▩　■　▩

We experience a few uneventful weeks and are grateful. But each time we get too comfortable, a new incident rocks our world. On one day, Sonia reports a total of three. She explains that a child (not Daniella or Lauren) smashed holly berries in Hannah's cubby. Fortunately, Sonia found the mess before Hannah did. I'm grateful because I know Hannah's scared the wild berries at the playground's edge are poisonous. The boy who smashed the berries was once a sweet, timid child who dealt with his own anxiety by being a strict rule-follower. But now that the environment has normalized meanness, even one of the most compliant students evidently feels comfortable taunting others. Sonia explains that she forced the boy to clean the cubby before Hannah noticed the mess, but as she oversaw the effort, Daniella and Lauren walked by and snickered. One taunted Sonia, "Do you even *like* Hannah?" while the other laughed. Sonia was astonished that the young children expressed their disregard so freely to her, an adult. She also worried their sneers undermined her efforts to correct the boy who defaced Hannah's cubby. And in the final incident of the day, the school psychologist noticed Hannah standing in line among her classmates, pointed, and sneered, "Ewwww. Her hair's sopping wet. Disgusting! Somebody needs to get that ponytail out of her mouth! The germs could get everyone sick!"

Sonia was stunned an adult would deride a student in front of peers. She tells me she's not sure the extent to which Hannah is aware of any of these incidents—they all happened behind her back—but she suggests I keep my eye on her.

I barely know what to say. The fact that the woman who should understand anxiety (and its associated behaviors) more than anyone else demeaned Hannah so publicly makes my head want to explode. The incident will surely feed Hannah's classmates' disregard for her. And then I recall that this director joined Richard in not responding to our emails regarding Hannah's anxiety attack. I guess I shouldn't be surprised. I want to scream at her, but it's becoming clear that the fault doesn't lie with one person. We're experiencing an institutional breakdown. And we're no longer tallying failures of kindness. These are more like derelictions of duty. The absence of professionalism and humanity feels as inexcusable as it does depressing.

I thank Sonia for helping Hannah throughout the day and for sharing the information with me. I'm sure there's some risk attached to her actions.

After school, I make an extra effort to be present for my children. We play a board game, I remind the big kids to read, and life seems to move along normally. I start dinner, waiting for Hannah to collapse in some way, but she doesn't. I guess Sonia buffered her from a potentially devastating day. My kids' sense of calm feels surreal against the depth of the transgressions.

As I evaluate the discrepancy between Hannah's dreadful day and the tranquility her naiveté affords, I receive a text alert. Apparently, volume has gone through the roof at the crisis center, and they need all available counselors to pitch in. Occasionally, an unanticipated influx of demand floods the service, usually after a troubling news report or a suicide-related message goes viral on social media.

Hannah hasn't resisted sleep for a few weeks, so after the kids go to bed, I ask Jim to cover for me while I sign in to the counseling service. Hopefully, I'll be able to support at least one or two people before I go to bed tonight. I feel helpless at school, and I want to know I can have a constructive impact somewhere.

As I prepare to hit the button that tells the system I'm ready to be paired with a texter, I notice the colossal red number on the top of the screen. It's the tally of the people needing support right now, and it's ten times larger than I've ever seen.

Oh, no. We're in for a big night.

I scan the list of counselor names cascading down the left side of my screen. Some are pseudonyms and most attach handles like @EmpathyWarrior and @HereToHelp. I look at the fifteen names on my screen, and I scroll down to find fifteen more. And then fifteen more again. I'm reviewing their notes to decode the tenor of the evening. What's behind tonight's spike? How are counselors responding? Is there anything I need to know to get through the evening?

I scroll down multiple times, and then I lose my breath. I'm overcome by just how many people are working. Every single name represents a person who gave up a Friday evening with friends or family to connect with someone at risk. I scroll more. And more. I'm no longer reading their notes. I'm trying to grasp the totality of the effort.

It strikes me that even just one name is proof of the existence of humanity. Yet before me is a multitude coming together to support individuals they will *never even meet*. The names scream at me, "People *do* care. They *do* show up." Just because compassion is elusive at my children's school doesn't mean it doesn't exist.

I inhale as relief washes over me.

I'm just where I need to be tonight.

The Manifesto

I'm in a sort of suspended space, ready to begin an earnest search for a new school for the fall but also hanging in the balance. Hopefully, I'll find a home for our entire family, but with three children, I might separate the kids to honor their individuality. I know I'm fortunate in this sense. Too many families don't have access to options and struggle relentlessly.

The thought of joining a new school community and beginning again feels as tiring as it does unjust. I'd like to believe we're worthy of belonging. We've been strong supporters of GCA over many years, and we've invested in relationships here. Was it all a waste?

The truth is, part of me doesn't want to leave. If GCA only did what it says it does, it would be an amazing place! But I need to accept the fact that it doesn't. Hannah no longer feels safe here, and it would probably take years for her to regain trust. Me too.

So I commit to moving on. But the fact that other children are still bullied and disregarded at GCA lingers like a bad taste in my mouth. I hear about them through the grapevine regularly. I feel traitorous fleeing without using any last bit of influence I might have to help them. But, *How can I?* And, *Haven't I already tried?*

I consider the document I prepared months ago to help faculty understand and respond to neurodiversity, mental health issues, and bullying. I realize now that I created the presentation as much to empower the school as to process *my own* thinking during that frenzied, frightening time. We felt we were fighting to understand and help our daughter while blindfolded and gagged. But now, I feel more assured as I've seen the research play out around me.

Unfortunately, assistant head of school Paula was unwilling to distribute the information to staff, and she was even less willing to touch the topic of bullying. She said it needed to be "unpacked" from learning differences and anxiety, but now it's crystal clear that they can be, and almost always are, heavily intertwined. I scoff as I recall Paula suggesting the facts might be too "confusing" to parents, as if their brains are too fragile. This parent body is sophisticated, and the research is both compelling and useful. I wonder, *What if I presented my case in a different way?* Might people listen so that children can be helped?

I consider that I might have been too reserved before. I tried to appear composed to avoid being dismissed as a histrionic, meddlesome mother. I presented data and facts. But maybe I needed to include something more. And then it occurs to me, *If I don't show them my humanity, how can I expect to see theirs?*

I also wonder if I should target a different audience. I've been getting nowhere with the administration. I realize the board isn't responsible for GCA's day-to-day operations, but it *is* responsible for ensuring its values and mission are preserved. It also has the right, the obligation even, to replace the head of school if he doesn't uphold either. For the most part, trustees are parents—the exact people Paula thought couldn't process the research. I wonder, *Are they my last resort? Or my best chance?*

Then I recall that I *did* reach out to a few specific board members, and they dismissed me. But maybe contacting individuals was a mistake. Maybe if I approached the board as a whole and pointed to trustees' *professional* obligations . . . maybe then they'd take me seriously.

I decide both that I need to speak with feeling, not just show data, *and* I need to target a new audience (the trustees who are designated to uphold the school's mission, not the administrators who enabled this mess).

So I string together a set of nights at my computer after the house is quiet, and I start a new document: a letter. I try to appeal to trustees' compassion (assuming it's available) and their reasoning (in case it's not). I thought it would be hard to document all I know and feel, but the words flow. Writing this letter is cathartic.

While I feel relieved to reclaim agency and release my truths into the open, I also feel uneasy. Every word is a disclosure, an exposure of my core. I'm terrified I'll be rejected. *Again.* I'm not sure I can handle the shame in that. It's one thing to humble one-self to ask for assistance. It's another thing entirely to be denied.

I pray the readers will hear my message and treat it with the same care I put into it. But my insecurity taunts me with some very real possibilities:

What if my story doesn't resonate? I'll be as candid and authentic as possible.

What if they don't believe the evidence? I'll disclose more.

What if they don't think the concepts apply to this situation? I'll provide specific examples.

What if they lack empathy for other people's kids? I'll show how it affects their own.

What if they don't even respond? That might be the most devastating of all.

When I'm done, I give a draft to Jim, and he says, "Honey, I think we just need to let this go. Let's get our kids out of that damn school and not look back. I'm so done with that place!"

I can see his anguish, and I get it. But I'm different. From the depths of my soul, I know I can't turn my back. I've spent too many evenings wishing others had helped us. Ideally, parents in a position of power would have been the ones to step in—those with no personal stake but who still cared for others. I can't count the times I lamented, *If just one of them had spoken up and helped the school find a better way, our family would have avoided so much pain.* But they didn't, and I'm adamant I need to be different. I'll advocate for people in the way I wish someone had for us. Almost every single grade has stories of bullying, confirming to me this is a systemic issue, not a one-off aberration that only affects Hannah.

I don't consider just the children who continue to be bullied at GCA. I'm haunted by the families who fled before us in search of a kinder home for their children—those who departed quietly, defeated and ashamed. I wish people hadn't cut them down and had instead valued them and encouraged their stories. I want to live in a community that holds people in rather than casts people out.

But my husband is exhausted. He advises again to "let it go," and I do something I've done only a few times in all our years together. I yell at him. "I will *not be complicit!* I *will not!* Kids are *hurting* there. They're self-harming. And the number of children—*children!*—on anti-depressants is alarming. We have friends who *need* somebody to *do* something!"

Jim, ever stoic, doesn't react to my outburst. Instead he insists, "Then they can leave too. Why shouldn't others just follow in our footsteps? And the families who left before us?"

"Some have limited options," I explain. "And even *if* there is another school alternative, they still feel stuck, scared if they uproot their kids, they'll induce even more anxiety. So they choose to believe what Richard tells them. That everything will be okay. That the problems aren't that serious. *But we know the truth.*" I throw the letter down on the table next to him.

He whispers, "I'm just tired of all this crap. And I don't want to give them reason to come after us."

"But this letter isn't about us. I hardly even mention our family. I'm speaking for the *other* families. Somebody needs to hear them."

Jim gives me a long look. He hates conflict, but I know he doesn't want to be complicit either. He nods. And then we sit down and edit the letter together.

When we're done, Jim once again voices his fear that the school could become litigious if we don't bow our heads and leave quietly. Administrators surely won't appreciate us going over their heads. So, we decide to share our letter with one of Jim's friends, who's a lawyer, just in case he has some relevant advice.

After his friend reads our letter, he asks, "Are you sure you don't want to lodge a complaint? You have a viable case. Very. We have a specialist in education law in my practice. This is right up his alley."

I lock this stallion in his gate. "No, I don't have the energy for a lawsuit. We've already lost too much precious time with our children. And we're not litigious people. We just want to appeal to their sense of humanity. But we also want to make sure this letter doesn't give them grounds to sue us."

"Hah! They should be more scared of you than you are of them. You have a First Amendment right to speak." He continues, "And you can claim real damages," and he lists several. He's clearly chomping at the bit.

But I'm adamant. "No, I just want to compel them to do the right thing. I want to help the kids we'll leave behind."

Jim's friend sighs. "Okay, then. But your letter's too long. It needs to be two pages or less, or nobody will read it."

I sigh also. "I tried to write a shorter one, but it sounded professional and threatening. It takes time to share feelings and convince others to care. But I get this is long. Do you think they'll bother to read it? Or will they just dismiss it as an irrational manifesto?"

He responds with one word: "Manifesto."

I consider mustering the emotional fortitude to rewrite the letter, but I'm depleted. I acquiesce when he offers to pare it down for me.

He turns around his version in just a few days. I want to be pleased to be done with this. But I hate it. His letter sounds aggressive and litigious. Yet, I'm worn and doubting my judgment. Everyone else prefers the new version. So I wonder if I'm too far inside my own head. Am I too emotional to be rational?

That evening I poll one more person—a law professor I've known for years through my volunteer work who teaches classes on persuasion, language, and public speaking. She responds diplomatically:

I see the value in each letter. The shorter version is indeed concise and more likely to be read in its entirety. If I received that letter, I would assume you intend to pursue legal action. The longer letter sounds more like you. It's not from a lawyer. It's your voice, your conviction. I suppose it depends on which message you intend to send.

I show her email to Jim, and he responds, "She's right. The short letter sounds aggressive. Yours is sensitive and thoughtful. Let's do you."

I smile. I'm more comfortable sending feelings than a venom-filled arrow. After all, I'm trying to bring them to their feet, not their knees.

I address the email to GCA's board chair, Priscilla Lansing, and send copies to each of the twenty trustees. The letter begins:

We are reaching out to you because we are concerned about many of the children at the Global Citizens Academy.

We explain how trustees are in a unique position to help, and we continue:

Even though we are leaving, we are still hopeful that we can support the school to ensure its commitment to its founding values and help it prosper long into the future. Unfortunately, the school's reputation is currently threatened by an unhealthy environment.

Our letter goes on to describe the concerns expressed to us by the families dealing with bullying, racism, and mistreatment of their children's learning and mental health challenges. It includes quotes from education experts and data from researchers, but mostly its intention is to reveal the human toll. We explain parents' fear of retaliation and of being labeled as "troublemakers." We describe their dejection after their concerns were dismissed. Rather than receiving support from the school, many parents felt "kicked while they were down." We remind them that the school's mission and values statements promote kindness and community, for *everyone.*

The letter ends with a plea:

It's too late for our family. But will you help others?

We then hover over our draft and review one last time. But we look at each other and agree not to hit send, not just yet.

I think, for the umpteenth time, *Maybe we should just fall in line, right behind the parents who left the school before us.* A silent departure would be so much easier. Shameful, but easier.

The Center Divide

I show the letter to a few close friends with skin in the game. They tell me they're proud of me for sticking up for others, and I breathe a little easier with their endorsement.

Then Lexi confides, "I've been thinking, maybe we should share our stories with a reporter. At least ten families have left the school in the past few years because of bullying. And there's the racism. If we could speak off the record, I think a lot of people might talk. Since the school won't listen, let's expose the false marketing of their rainbows and unicorns." Her eyes brighten as she instructs me, "Imagine the headline: 'Local Private School: Breeding Ground for Bullying and Racist Behavior.'"

Oh, wow. That could be devastating for GCA. Part of me thinks the school deserves a public exposé, but I want to help them, not shame them. So I tell her, "Let's wait. Right now, the board of trustees can claim ignorance. Let's give them a chance to act as true fiduciaries. Hell, let's appeal to their egos. Let them look like heroes, swooping in to save the day."

Lexi snickers, "Let them save us from the disaster they helped create?"

"I hear you. I just think an attack could sink the whole school and all the kids in it."

She acquiesces, reluctantly.

■　■　■　■

As word about our decision to withdraw from GCA leaks out, it becomes hard to ignore the variety of reactions: certain friends stand by me while others disappear or position themselves for neutrality. I recognize now that I miscalculated who would do what in some cases—maybe most cases. Either I'm a terrible judge of character, or it's impossible to know somebody until the shit hits the fan and people reveal their intentions.

The most confusing response to me is the neutral one. I realize most onlookers don't want to lose friendships or social standing over one girl's unfortunate situation. Part of me understands that. But the other part feels betrayed. People might think they're being impartial, but it sure doesn't feel that way to us. A reluctance to engage allows the abuse to continue. It condones and enables. So, neutrality, in all practicality, isn't neutral. There's no middle lane, and Hannah and I don't feel safe around people who try to drive down the center divide.

The more I encounter people who look away from our pain, the more I grasp a new truth: some of the people I thought I knew might never have existed in the first place. They were mirages I created by projecting traits onto individuals that I wanted to believe were there. I remember giving a toast at a friend's birthday party, appreciating how "solid" and "reliable" she was. Most others spoke of the trendy setting or an amusing memory, but I applauded her character. Now that I look around, this friend is nowhere to be found.

I guess I'm not only mourning the loss of a happy childhood for my daughter; I'm also struggling to process the loss of these people I thought I knew, these friends I thought I had.

The fallout continues.

Golden Nuggets

L exi hugs me as I step into her home. She's hosting a dinner for several women, a few of whom I recognize from my kids' schools and many more I do not. One familiar face belongs to Melanie, whose family left GCA last year, not long after she suggested I was being gaslit by Richard. I make a beeline for her.

When I ask about her son Luke, she lights up. "He's great. A whole new kid." And then she uses the word "thriving."

I'm thrilled to hear this. I want to believe in second chances— that Hannah can get a new start too. "It must make you feel good to know you made the right decision."

"Well, yes and no."

This isn't the answer I wanted.

She explains, "I mean, yes, because he's doing so well. He's starting to feel safe again, and he actually wants to go to school. But it also makes me so *angry*." She says this last word with gritty emphasis. "When I see how different it can be, I'm furious about the way they allowed him to be treated there. And I'm upset at myself for letting him stay so long."

She looks exasperated just remembering everything that transpired, but she lights up when she says, "Our new school doesn't assume he's the problem. They help him with his weaknesses, of course, but the approach is totally different. We're now leaning in *hard* to his interests and strengths. It's made *all* the difference. In his confidence *and* in his performance. In everything!"

This sounds like a golden nugget of wisdom to me.

Over the course of the evening, and a glass or two of wine, I learn the issues among us are varied, yet the authenticity remains consistent. And refreshing. Nobody presents a shiny veneer. This kind of honesty is both shocking and disarming. I can let my guard down here!

I'm also impressed by how reasoned and thoughtful the women are. Maybe their understanding of how it feels to be cast out for having a unique child—to be scrutinized and assessed constantly—prevents them from doling out judgments haphazardly. And maybe their familiarity with quick dismissals has taught them to express their cases judiciously. They know they need to be more measured and articulate than others if they're going to be taken seriously.

I'm also thrown by the way the women respond to one another. I'm used to apathy, judgment, and dismissal when I try to share my concerns. Yet when one of these women speaks, nobody says simply, "Huh." Or "Oh, it'll be fine!" Or, "That hasn't been my experience." There are no devil's advocates, taking the opposing position just for the sport of it.

Instead, I witness compassion. Whoever is speaking is validated with phrases like, "That's brutal." Or, "Oh, what horse shit." Or, "Trust yourself. You know what you saw." As far as I know, none of these women took counseling training, but they might as well have. Maybe they learned the importance of empathy "on the job" while parenting unique kids?

A mother soon discusses her daughter's speech impediment, a source of relentless mockery. The girl resists meeting new people because she's embarrassed to say her own name. Given that "th" and "r" are some of the last sounds to develop, her daughter Catherine calls herself "Caffeine." It doesn't help that she's hyperactive and acts like she drank a bottle of Red Bull each morning. The mom is half-crying and half-laughing when she explains, "I was so careful about choosing her name. I made sure her initials didn't stand for or rhyme with anything negative. I considered all possible nicknames. I thought I was set!"

A woman with warm eyes asks, "Does she like the name Cate?"

"That's her cousin's name, and my sister-in-law is pretty proprietary about it, so it's not an option for us, sadly."

Another mom talks about her daughter's epilepsy, which isn't noticeable to most people on most days. But she's in high school now, and her doctors advise against things like swimming unattended or drinking alcohol. All the women in the room who know her agree she's a very cool girl, but her mother insists her daughter's differences cause her teenage peers to exclude her. And they ensure she's aware of what she's missing by posting pictures of themselves partying together across social media.

We're all nodding our heads. Each of us is undoubtedly considering how our own children's differences make them vulnerable to mistreatment and exclusion.

A mom sighs, "I wish I could tell you mean girls outgrow this bullshit. But it's often a learned behavior, reinforced at home."

I choose to believe girls can evolve, but I admit it's probably harder without constructive guidance, and especially when parents normalize snarky or judgmental comments.

Another woman interjects, "It's not just the girls. Boys can be awful too. Some of you probably remember in grade school my son flapped his arms when he got excited. But he's a junior now and rarely flaps. But it doesn't matter. Some kids still call him Bird Boy. Moms too, to your point." She looks at the woman who lamented poor parental role-modeling and adds, "I should have given Michael the opportunity to reinvent himself by transferring him out after middle school to a different place for high school."

A mom confirms, "It's just so hard for kids to get out from under a perception once it's been set."

"Especially if the culture supports the behavior. I mean, if the adults aren't addressing the bullying in lower school, they're definitely not going to address it in the upper school."

I'm disappointed to realize how pervasive and enduring the cruelty can be.

Melanie, the ex-GCA mom says, "And since they don't deal with the child who's being intentionally hurtful, except maybe with a wrist slap, it's the gentle ones who are forced out."

I nod. Hannah will slip away while her aggressors remain.

Another mom laments, "It's heartless. They actually blame the *bullied* child, even on the way out. The message is: It's *you. You* are the problem. *We* don't need to change. *You* do. And to the kid's parents, they imply: Your child is unique, so he just needs to learn to deal if he wants to succeed in the real world."

I finally venture into the fray and ask, "Have you guys noticed how often people suggest our kids need to conform to 'the real world'? And the irony of that?" Everyone's looking at me, a few with unsure eyes, so I clarify, "I mean, in the *real* 'real world,' everyone is different. But people use the concept of the 'real world' to justify *denying* people's differences. And even ridiculing them. But expecting kids to be the same—to fit in cramped boxes—is actually what denies reality. And ends up being just plain cruel."

I'm grateful to receive an "Amen" and a "Seriously" and at least one "Exactly." The affirmations feel both foreign and liberating.

Another mom pipes in, "What are we supposed to do? Just give these children back when we find out they weren't built the way others expect? I mean, *honestly*, what options do we have? Besides hiding from all the judgment."

"Oh, you don't have to hide. They isolate you before you get the chance."

The room fills with another chorus of "exactlies" and soulful nods.

The situation is especially confusing when parents see their kids' idiosyncrasies aren't necessarily problems in and of themselves. Too often, differences become problems when the world is unwilling to support unique ways of being. Case in point: Hannah isn't dysfunctional in her own right. She's actually quite capable in many ways. But she has become dysfunctional in a school that doesn't allow for her distinct beauty, that actually mocks and taunts her for it. I wonder for the umpteenth time, *Are the kids disabled, disordered, and dysfunctional? Or are our attitudes?*

One woman dives into the deep end by confessing, "I'm scared to die, not for myself, but for my child. I buffer him from a difficult, judgmental world. Who will keep him safe when I'm gone?"

How many of us haven't wondered the same thing?

Lexi notes a need and offers, "More wine?" Several women hold out their glasses.

With more wine comes more truth. A mom talks about being among peers who offer little empathy or support. I relate when she admits, "It's hurtful when my own friends ignore what I'm trying to tell them. I mean, if *they* can't understand, who will?"

"That's why we have each other!" A woman holds up her glass to toast the room.

A conversation then ensues about how to talk to kids about their differences, and a mom admits it's hard, especially when even the experts can't agree on a diagnosis. She declares, "We finally realized there aren't enough classifications in the DSM to categorize Marcus."

I recall that even our neuropsychologist bemoaned the shortcomings of the *Diagnostic and Statistical Manual of Mental Disorders*, the tome used to diagnose learning differences (like dyslexia), attention challenges (like ADHD), and neurological variations (like autism) in addition to heartbreaking conditions like schizophrenia. And I collect yet another golden nugget of wisdom when she concludes, "We decided the process of figuring out how he learns is helpful. *Super* helpful. It pointed us in the right direction. But, ultimately, Marcus is Marcus. We need to focus on *him* as a whole person, not the limiting ways the DSM defines him."

Another woman agrees. "We decided to look to Liza's specific behaviors. The way she reacts in certain environments. Her own unique ways of being. Not some overarching label."

I deposit one more nugget in the bank.

As the women continue to share, I consider another irony. Schools stuff our kids into the "normal" box, but that doesn't work for some. So parents seek alternatives. And guess what happens next? The diagnostic system, and the DSM in particular, attempts to squash them into yet another set of boxes, many of which don't seem to fit so well either. I wish we could simply appreciate the rich, complex individuals kids were meant to be. If one is sick or in pain then, yes, let's treat them. But if someone is simply different, let's honor the individuality.

The woman next to me insists we need to start appreciating diversity early. She explains that she began teaching tolerance as soon as her kids could speak. "No, 'tolerance' isn't the word," she corrects herself. "Because we want to do more than tolerate one another, right? I actively *celebrated* differences. All types!" She says she was trying to help her boys see the value in others so they could be "good citizens," but then she unexpectedly found herself addressing their *own* unique ways of being after one child was diagnosed with dyslexia and the other with ADHD. She laughs as she explains how her boys were nonplussed when she tried to validate their individual learning styles. She guesses, "I'd probably normalized diversity so much, they didn't see their own issues as a big deal. In our house, differences are cool."

I smile as I realize her efforts to encourage her children to appreciate *others* ended up benefitting her own kids in multiple ways.

Melanie says, "I think a lot of us were taught that everyone is equal. So we should treat everyone *the same*. And be 'blind' to differences. But the effects have been so damaging. I'm now learning to treat everyone as equally *valuable*. But that doesn't mean they're the same. By appreciating the differences, we allow people to hold their fair space."

That just might be the biggest golden nugget of the night. A golden boulder, actually.

■ ▧ ■ ▧

On the way home, I feel energized. The evening was real. It was substantive. No one pretended everything's okay. But they also weren't dour. They were candid yet still had gratitude for the blessings in their lives. Lexi's friends were so much more interesting than the people I know who project a curated image and conceal the gritty parts that give depth and definition.

I was especially moved to see women caring for one another *and* for each others' children. I wonder, *Does it take having a quirky kid to appreciate other quirky kids? Is experience a prerequisite to empathy?*

I consider the many people who've shown up for me over the past few months. I admit, not all of them have kids with learning differences or anxiety. But as I tally, I note almost all have experienced a trauma or serious difficulty in their lives: sexual assault, death of a loved one, debilitating disease, discrimination. They have survived pains and abuses I wouldn't wish upon anybody. But as a result, they're now more understanding and compassionate. They are stronger and fuller and kinder.

I recall a friend once noting, "People who've suffered often have bigger empathy muscles." I'd stored this image because I appreciated the association with strength. Empathy is a muscle we can flex. It represents power.

Then I consider my friends who've endured pain but, for whatever reason, didn't show up for Hannah. Maybe empathy is not a foregone conclusion. Maybe personal hardships cause some people to shut down toward others. I think I remember reading as much in the research.

This understanding makes me appreciate all the more the people who actively care for others. And for the first time in months, I arrive home feeling less alone. Maybe I've finally found my people.

Throwing Down

I'm feeling high. After dropping the kids at school, I spend the morning basking in my alliance with my new friends. I now not only have my truth-seeking wine club comrades, I have the support of an additional group of women, all of whom are in the child-rearing trenches with me.

I move through the day not only content, but maybe even with a little kick in my step. But thirty minutes before pickup time, I receive an email from school. Megan is succinct:

Hannah was teased about ticks again. We are handling it with Lauren's parents.

I'm ready to jump out of my skin. *Handling it? The same way you handled the previous dozen tick incidents? And all the other bullying?*

There is no more trust. All goodwill has been squandered. Suffocated. Obliterated. I will no longer believe words that don't coincide with meaningful actions. My anger swells, almost beyond my control.

I am ready to THROW. FUCKING. DOWN. Those bastards.

I know my anger is ugly. I know I risk legitimacy if I let others witness it. But I no longer care. They disgust me. I've tried to play nicely in their sandbox, and my diplomacy only enabled my daughter's victimization. I'm no longer playing by their rules.

GAME.

ON.

After putting my kids to bed, I print off fifty pages of emails and letters documenting Hannah's bullying over the previous two years. Despite my rage, I find the restraint to redact the names of all children (even Hannah's tormenters) to emphasize the fact that I don't intend to blame the kids. I'm focused on the system. I even strike a Sharpie through the parents' names. I stay focused on my original objective: to find a better way. I believe we've all been let down by an administration that enables abuse—a culture that abandons kids, parents, and teachers too.

There's no way our letter is going to sit on my desk any longer. I make no further edits but attach the printouts as an Appendix—proof that bullying exists so they can no longer look the other way.

The next day, I head out in the muddy, mucky sludge left over from last week's snowstorm to hand deliver a copy of the letter to every single trustee, including Lauren's father. I do not discriminate. Besides, his name is redacted so he can feign ignorance if he chooses.

I have had it.

I then ask myself, *Why now? What made this the final straw? Was it this one last tick incident?* But there have been so many before. *What put me over the edge?*

It's almost impossible to ignore the juxtaposition of this new round of bullying against the afterglow of the previous evening. Before, I was alone and isolated. But last night, I was welcomed into a community, a group of interesting, thoughtful women. And throughout the evening, it became overwhelmingly clear that our experiences with bullying are not isolated. At least two former GCA mothers referenced the systemic bullying at the school. And I recall conversations from weeks ago, when even Hannah's doctors acknowledged GCA's longstanding problems.

It was easy to gaslight and silence me when I was siloed. But I'm not alone now.

I email my therapist to tell her I delivered the letter. I ask:

How do you think they'll respond?

Gail replies with therapy speak, telling me she expects "they will have cognitive dissonance." I recall from my empathy research that this is the discomfort people feel when confronted with the possibility that their actions might not match their self-image. She explains the trustees most likely consider themselves to be good people, so "they will have trouble wrestling with the fact that kids were allowed to be bullied under their purview." She says the board members can resolve their dissonance in one of two ways: either *authentically* (by contemplating how they might have missed the mark and endeavoring to behave differently in the future) or *inauthentically* (by justifying, and even doubling down on, their past actions).

Then, perhaps preparing me for the fact that I might not get the result I want, she concludes:

Sometimes our role is to till the soil, sometimes to plant the seed, sometimes to nurture the sprig, and, in a few circumstances, to witness a harvest. I hope you honor the role you have played in any case.

Well, I have definitely tilled the soil. I am fucking caked in dirt, burned from the glare of the sun, and bruised by the abrasive clods that haphazardly churned upward from the plow.

I am a wreck.

I am depleted.

But, I realize something else: I have done my part.

Still, lurking in the back of my mind, no matter what I do or where I go, the same question circulates in my mind: *How will they respond?*

Heard

Megan calls to report Lauren received a one-day suspension. This "solution" doesn't begin to repair the damage or comfort me about sending Hannah to school next week. Yet, finally, there is something.

I wonder why, after two years of egregious behavior, the school finally decided to take action now. Did they hear about my letter to the board?

I soon learn that Richard is traveling with his wife out of state so he had nothing to do with the suspension. Maybe, without his formidable presence, the staff finally felt able to enforce a consequence for these relentless, hateful acts. Maybe the teachers are at their wit's end too.

When I finally reunite with Hannah at pickup, she's distraught. I tell her that Lauren was suspended, and she responds, "Lauren will probably like that. She doesn't like school. She'll probably just get to play all day."

I think, *She's so frickin' smart. It wasn't enough for me either.*

I recall when my cousin was suspended for three days many decades ago. His father, my uncle, instructed, "You have wasted your tuition and devalued your education, young man. Over the next three days, you will work to earn back the money to compensate for the loss, and you'll have to double down when you return to school to catch up on the learning you missed." My uncle reinforced the school's punishment, and my cousin never got suspended again. What are the chances Lauren's parents will react similarly? It seems Hannah might already know.

We drive home, which must feel like a safe haven to Hannah. I hate that she's learning to distrust the outside world, but I'm grateful she has at least one refuge.

When we arrive, Jake seems to pick up on the tension and becomes increasingly focused on a Lego set. I try to settle his nerves and remark, "It looks like you're working hard!"

He responds, "I'm rebuilding my fortress." I appreciate his constructive effort, especially since yesterday he was all about blame, insisting someone keeps destroying his castle. Given how sprawling his creations can become, I advised that it was most likely knocked over by the vacuum cleaner or an accidental passerby.

A few hours later, I call the family to the table for dinner, but Hannah lags. I head to her bedroom, but on my way I'm distracted by movement in the family room. When I peek in, I spy Hannah's hand hovering over Jake's Lego structure.

"Hannah! What are you doing?"

"Nothing!" She jolts upright.

"Hannah, that's not nothing. You're ruining Jake's castle. He's been working hard on that! What on earth are you thinking?"

"I don't know. He just thinks he's so great."

"So you've been destroying this on purpose?"

Hannah is normally a rule-follower who cherishes order. And she loves her brothers. But she's become a human wrecking ball!

My anger rises in Jake's defense. "Hannah! This is just mean! And you've been doing this for weeks, haven't you? On purpose." And then I'm forced to realize that my own daughter is exhibiting bullying behavior. After years of being a victim herself, she's now striking out at her brother to manage her own insecurities. Will the repercussions never end? I stop yelling and sit down to help my daughter understand the drivers and consequences of her actions.

Before I finish, Hannah interrupts to ask, "Mom, does this mean I'm a bad person?" She looks frightened when she adds, "I don't understand why I'm acting this way. I don't feel like *me* anymore. Why? Why am I doing this? What's happening to me?" She looks absolutely terrified.

I offer, "You know, sometimes, when people do mean things, it's because they're not feeling very good about themselves inside. Do you think that's what's happening here?"

She nods and then lets her fear and sadness escape with deep, heart-driven sobs. This child doesn't recognize herself. She asks again, "Am I a bad person?"

I answer her the same way I would respond to the girls who terrorize her at school, "No, Honey. You are not a bad person. You are a child. And you have a good soul. We're all working to become our best selves, and you are on that path. There's a big difference between being a bad person and demonstrating bad behavior. What you did was wrong, but when you make an effort to correct your mistakes, you show you are a good person, the same kind, loving person you know yourself to be. That *I* know you to be. So let's show Jake how much you care. Okay?" We then make a plan for her to apologize to her brother and ask how she can attempt to repair the damage.

Jake, however, is not easily consoled, nor does he want to give her an easy out. He refuses to forgive Hannah.

I explain to Hannah that Jake's anger is reasonable, and she'll have to work hard to regain his trust. It will need to be earned.

I also later help Jake understand what drove Hannah's actions so he knows her behavior was more about her than him. He insists, "It's still not okay!"

I agree.

■　■　■　■

The next morning, I hear from the board chair, Priscilla. Finally, a recognition that our experience might be worthy of discussion! After years of nonresponse, things are happening quickly now. I delivered our letter two days ago, and the executive committee wants to speak with us next week. Priscilla proposes we meet in the school office, but I suggest a neutral location. We agree to book a conference room usually available in the local community center.

I also receive an email from Hannah's art teacher, who monitored the playground this morning in someone else's absence. She tells me she told Daniella and Lauren that they are "not allowed to approach Hannah without her permission," that Hannah is "in charge" of deciding when they can interact. She tells me Daniella and Lauren said they wanted to apologize for the tick incident, but the teacher told them they could only approach Hannah "when she's ready."

Wow. This is amazing—and consistent with my reading on bullying prevention and restorative justice. She's helping Hannah reclaim her power and her rightful place in her community. She's not letting things advance on the aggressors' terms, not even apologies. *Fucking brilliant.* I wonder if personal experience motivates her. *She really gets this!* And I wonder if anyone will give her the opportunity to share her wisdom with other educators. The whole school could benefit.

■　▪　■　▪

The morning of our meeting, I'm nervous. I pull boots over my sweatpants to take the kids to school, but then I return home to change. I don't need to wear a suit, but I want to be taken seriously. On my way out the door, I grab a pair of sunglasses. The risk of glare is low, given the muted light in the February skies, but I want the shades to shield my eyes, just in the case things don't go well.

When Jim and I enter the conference room, it's fuller than I expected. Half the board can't be on the executive committee, can it? I soon realize the chair invited a few additional trustees, those who have day jobs as lawyers. I pause but then feel bolstered by the fact that we have good intentions and truth on our side.

Jim takes the lead. Even though I've driven our effort to this point, I know they're less likely to dismiss a male when discussing such emotional issues. It's annoying that I need to take this tack, but I'm used to it. And I need to be practical if I want to make any progress.

We take about fifteen minutes to describe the culture that allows bullying to thrive and how much pain it inflicts on our family and others. We reiterate that we aim to be constructive, and we believe in the school's mission.

Jim notes that while Richard was thoroughly unresponsive to our situation, we're not vilifying the school as a whole. We believe the institution can deliver on its promise of graduating young global citizens *if* it addresses the problems thoughtfully and transparently.

We also recognize that not all children have the same experience at GCA. It's somewhat of *A Tale of Two Cities*. Those who are different, who enjoy less power, are cast aside, while the rest live a completely different experience, often ignorant of the pain endured by the degraded families. And these "second class citizens" know that if they speak up, they will be marginalized even more. We explain how parents feel there are no reasonable means to solve serious issues.

One of the board members, Emily, whose son once had regular playdates with Jake, says, "We were just so sad to get your letter. I'm so, so sorry." Her words knock me over. Her validation and empathy are the first we've received from someone in leadership. Ever. Yes, two teachers over two years, Sonia and Leslie, showed they cared. But they had no power, so they couldn't reinforce their words with actions that might actually help.

212

Priscilla augments Emily's words with a real action plan. She explains, "We're in the process of hiring an independent investigator to learn more about your concerns. GCA doesn't want to be seen as a school that tolerates bullying." I'm relieved, but I also recognize she's talking about appearances rather than underlying issues. I also take note when she fails to look me in the eye as we leave.

When Jim and I exit the community center, I throw my sunglasses in my bag. I don't need them. Yes, I'm nervous, but I also feel released from a colossal burden. For months, we've drowned in confusion and sorrow. I was bewildered when people heard about or saw a child in pain and did nothing. Their silence caused me to question my sanity. *Am I irrational and off base? Meanness is bad, right? Why is my family standing all alone here? Why won't anyone help?* The apathy also caused me to doubt humanity itself. *Are people really this uncaring?*

But now we've taken action, and those around us responded.

I do taunt myself with questions like, *How did we come across?* And, *Were we credible?* And the always present, *What will happen?*

But I can't help but notice a little spark of joy. My insides are giddy, bouncing to exclaim, *I'm no longer complicit!*

I didn't turn my back on kids in pain. No matter what happens, when I look back years from now, I'll be able to tell myself and my children that I tried.

And if they ever want proof, I'll show them my manifesto.

The Inquisition

The next day, I receive a text from Heather to me and Ellen that reads: *As you know, the board is running an investigation. We can't talk til it's done, but we're thinking of you!*♥♥

The emoji is probably inspired by Valentine's Day tomorrow. Ellen adds: *Yes, thinking of you!* ♥

I want to feel good about this, but their texts seem a bit trite in light of the letter I delivered to each of their homes last week. Is this really all they have to say? They're both now privy to extensive documentation of Hannah's years of bullying, and I get heart emojis in return? I can't help but think how emojis help people avoid emotion as much as express it.

Still, I hope for the best. We've been friends since our children were born. Heather and I used to stroll our babies together. That must count for something. Right?

A few minutes before pickup, Paula calls to see if I'm available right after school. *Finally!* I think. She's acknowledging our reality.

I collect Hannah and Jake and lead them to the playground. When I don't see Hannah's tormenters, I ask a friend to watch my kids while I head to the office. Paula smiles when I peek through the door marked VICE HEAD OF SCHOOL. "Hey there, Kayla! Thanks so much for meeting me!" After more pleasantries, she continues, "Lauren's parents came in this morning. They're upset

214

because they think their daughter's being misunderstood. They say Lauren's very sensitive and feel she's being mischaracterized. They requested that Hannah be separated from Lauren at all times."

I question slowly, "And . . . what did you say?"

"We agree Hannah needs to stay away from Lauren. The teachers have been instructed to ensure this."

"So Hannah's the problem here? She's the one who needs to be contained?"

"No, that's not what I'm saying."

"Really? Because that's how it sounds." My emotions are rising. After all the requests I've made to have Hannah separated from Lauren, and after all the promises broken in that regard, now Lauren's parents are being heard—and Hannah has been deemed the problem. I'm incredulous. "Is this because Greg's on the board and we aren't? This seems like a bit of favoritism toward trustees, don't you think?"

She's immediately defensive. "We just think a separation is a good idea for all involved."

How easily the tables are turned. How swiftly the school moved to protect the aggressor and characterize the bullied child as the problem. Just last week, Lauren was suspended for bullying Hannah, and now Lauren needs to be protected? The administration appears to be doubling down on its stance that Hannah wasn't bullied. I can't wait for the investigation to expose the truth. And, in the interim, at least Hannah will finally be separated from both girls. Still, I'm furious.

I march out recalling I once trusted Paula. I believed she was concerned for the students who were struggling. But now it's clear I gave her too much credit. I projected goodwill and caring traits onto her, just as I did onto some friends. I see now that Paula is one of the enablers. She, too, is an active participant in Hannah's pain.

■　■　■　■

We soon learn the name of the board's investigator: Arnold J. Howard. I pull up his website and see he's a lawyer, and his homepage quotes Voltaire: *Judge a man by his questions rather than by his answers*. Does this mean he believes his interrogation process delivers truth? Or does he manipulate people by posing specific questions to get a desired result? I reach out to Priscilla, noting my concern, and she assures me the board is committed to a truthful inquiry. She insists Howard is the best.

Howard can't meet us immediately because he needs to complete his current case. Apparently, the board had difficulty hiring an investigator with expertise in the education field because all qualified professionals are engaged in a nationwide scandal involving several prestigious universities. Just before our meeting with the executive committee, news of "Varsity Blues" broke, and the public is outraged by the extent to which a large number of wealthy parents committed fraud to get their children into college. While none of the named universities are in the tri-state area, it seems experts from New York are parachuting in to manage the crisis, so we'll have to wait our turn.

And while we do, I can't help but wonder if Howard is helping the universities pursue the truth the American public is demanding or if he was hired to protect their esteemed images and limit their liability.

Again, Pricilla confirms Arnold J. Howard is "one of the good guys."

■　▩　■　▨

Almost a month after learning about Howard, he finally reaches out to explain his process. He's all business as he requests copies of the documentation we supplied in the appendix of our letter "without names redacted."

I tell Howard I feel uncomfortable disclosing the names of the students—and I'm somewhat surprised he doesn't already know them, especially since a good portion of the documents were sent to GCA email addresses—but he insists there can be no investigation without my transparency. When he promises to respect children's privacy, I forward the unmarked papers.

Before we hang up, Howard tells me he needs only Jim or me to participate in an interview, and I know I'm the one for the job. After all, I've been leading this process the whole way, and I'm more intimate with the sordid details.

When I finally sit down with Howard, I'm surprised by his youthful appearance. I guess I'd expected someone more experienced looking.

Howard invites me to sit across from him at the long table. His appearance is stern, with his gray suit and crisp tie, but his voice is less imposing, and he beckons me to share my story.

Recalling events that my mind had sealed away in a tight little box is arduous. This compartmentalization helped me manage painful memories, but now I'm being asked to relive them. I'm a bit annoyed, wondering why he needs me to repeat things I already documented in the appendix of my letter. Is he looking for more detail? Or trying to poke holes in my account?

Howard must sense my insecurity and apologizes for pursuing his line of questioning. He says he regrets it's "just part of the process" and almost seems like a regular guy. Then he asks, "Can your daughter be available for a meeting?" and my protective instinct ignites.

I wonder if he would allow a parent to be present, but then I decide it doesn't matter. "You have over fifty pages of documentation, and I can point you toward several adult witnesses. Why do you need to interrogate a child? Don't you think she's been through enough?"

His tone is no longer amiable as he repeats that it's all "a standard part of the process." He adds, "But the choice is yours."

I wonder if this is true and if he intimating that the investigation will fall apart if I don't follow his demands. I decide right then and there I don't like him. Until this point, his questions were asked in a warm, unthreatening voice. But his tone is now mono-tone, maybe even challenging. It's the opposite of the one I used last night when I was crisis counseling. If he had suggested that a child psychologist or a behaviorist meet with Hannah, I might feel assured. But this lawyer appears more interested in procedures than children, so I decide, *There's no way in hell he's getting near my daughter.* I feel depleted going through this line of questioning. I'm not going to make Hannah suffer through this too. So, what? They can decide if they believe a nine-year-old child?

Concern flares again when we discuss the others affected by the school's culture. He asks, "Can you give me the names of the other students you claim were bullied? The ones in the other grades."

I shift uncomfortably in my seat as I'm asked to involve others. I don't have a right to out them, and, besides, shouldn't my story be sufficient? Apparently, it's not, so I insist, "They require anonymity first," I explain. "They're worried about ret-ribution, especially since the school is responsible for their kids' recommendations to high school. Can you create a venue where they'll be protected? Maybe an anonymous survey or a hotline? I know several other schools have done so."

He persists, "Our process requires full disclosure. We need to interview them and compare what they tell us to what Richard and other administrators say."

I'm confused. This statement is contrary to what I've read— that institutions benefit from providing confidential means for people to share their experiences without fear of reprisal.

I almost ask, "So you're going to take my statement directly to the very people who are at the heart of the problem?" But I bite my tongue and resolve to maintain the other families' pri-vacy. It looks like I'm in this on my own.

As the meeting wraps up, Howard has one last question for me. "What do you want? What do you think would be a reasonable outcome?"

I respond, "What do you mean? I think we've made it clear that we're hoping the school will make changes to prevent bullying."

"What do you want to happen to the girls you say bullied your daughter?"

"Honestly, I don't know." I shrug. "It's so late. If someone had intervened two years ago, their behavior could have been managed. But now bullying is so normalized. The culture of the school needs to change."

"So you don't want them expelled?"

"No, I don't think we should throw kids under the bus. We need to fix the system."

"Are you sure there's nothing *specific* you're asking for? What do you want *personally*?"

Is he alluding to financial compensation? I won't even dignify that with a response. I've made it clear all along that I'm not looking for a payout. If I wanted that, I would have sued months ago.

But I concede. "Actually, there is one thing I would like. I would like for an adult in a position of power to apologize to my daughter. To tell her that she shouldn't have had to endure years of bullying. I would like for somebody to recognize her pain and her right to dignity."

Howard nods his head and closes his laptop. The inquisition is complete.

Breaking the Seal

I must have rehashed my interview with Howard in my dreams, particularly his request for me to name the other families at school contending with bullying, because as I awake, an idea strikes me. I won't name the people *currently* suffering at the school. I will guard their identities, at least until Howard can offer them some sort of protection. But maybe there's another way. Maybe I can provide a list of people who *already left* the school. They might be willing to speak more freely given that they, like I, don't depend on the administration anymore. I call a few friends to confirm the names of at least eight families who are believed to have withdrawn their children over the past eighteen months in response to bullying. That's over one student per grade, probably the one with the least social power. (I worry that, now, the students on the next lowest rungs are in precarious positions.) I could probably uncover more names if I kept investigating, but I feel this number should be sufficient to confirm the systemic nature of the problem.

Over the following days, I reach out to the mothers of the departed children. Each one is surprised to hear from me. From the outset, I recognize the disillusionment in their voices. I hear their fear and humbled resignation. I'm saddened when they express guilt over how their own child was bullied. At times, I hear myself in their shaky voices.

When I tell them about the school's investigation and ask if they would consider participating, most are tentative at first. "Is it safe?" they ask, hesitant to relive their traumas. Their kids are now doing well in new schools, and they want to stay positive.

As we talk, they re-experience their anger over the humiliating ways in which their families were treated. Each mother I speak to explains how her child was regarded as the problem. Each one hints at how alone she felt. Each one tells me she was somehow made to feel in the wrong for speaking up. Many describe the condescending ways in which Richard addressed them. "And he has no training in education, child psychology, or human behavior!" seethes one of the moms. "What is he doing looking down at me! I'm a trained psychologist!"

I don't push. I've just experienced the effects of recounting painful experiences, and I don't want to slice open their jagged wounds. Most have retreated into smaller, softer environments, and they remain distrusting.

Still, in the end, eight moms agree to speak on the record. They can't deny their yearning to be recognized. They want to feel legitimized and for their experiences and truths to matter. They particularly want to help prevent other children from experiencing the devastation their own children felt. And like my family, they need neither GCA's nor Richard's seal of approval anymore.

I email the parents' contact information to Howard, and he replies:

Thank you for the additional data.

I don't hear anything else for weeks.

■ ▦ ■ ▨

The lack of response is unsettling. This case shouldn't take long to investigate. I handed over reams of documentation. Howard's job was mostly done before he even started.

The covertness and the implication that I'm seeking a cash settlement also make me worry about Hannah's safety at school. Will the administration ally against her to protect themselves? I start talking openly to Hannah about not returning to school. There are only eight weeks left, after all, and next week is spring break. Maybe we should just keep her home after that.

So this is what it's come to? I muse. Truancy now seems favorable to life at the Global Citizens Academy.

As I rationalize the option of departing early, Hannah resists. "Mom, I want to finish what I started."

I find this admirable. I also find it consistent with the messages I received as I grew up. I was taught that "life isn't fair" and "one mustn't run from problems." But now I see a distinction: a shrewd decision to avoid toxicity and abuse is a far cry from shirking responsibility. I don't want my kids to take the easy path in life, but I *do* want them to have autonomy and believe in their right to protect and pursue their own well-being.

But Hannah won't budge. She says, "Mom, they'll make fun of me if I leave. They'll just tease me and say I couldn't take it."

"Honey, they won't tease you because you won't be there to tease. And anyway, we can't make decisions based on the mean things others might say. We need to make the choice that's right for *you*."

"But if I leave now, I'll miss all the fun activities coming up!"

She's not the decision-maker here, and I'm leaning toward pulling her from school despite her protests. Especially since I'm aware that her resistance is rooted in anxiety. Change is the enemy of anyone with an active amygdala. But then I speak with Hannah's pediatrician and therapist, who say we shouldn't strip her of agency, especially since Hannah was clear about wanting to finish up the year.

The eight weeks ahead feel like they might become the longest of my life.

■ ▨ ■ ▨

Spring vacation doesn't come soon enough. We escape south to the beach, where, every year, the kids love searching for shells, jumping over waves, and coloring in a cabana by the "quiet pool." (The designated family areas often feel too "chaotic" to Hannah.) This year, Hannah develops a new annoyance: the feeling of sand between her toes. Fortunately, her siblings are happy to hole up in their poolside "fort" together.

One evening, as I tuck Hannah into bed after a long day in the sun, she opens up. She's often more candid when the lights dim, so I settle myself on the bed as she says, "Mom, I don't want to go to GCA next year."

If I could do a flip, I would. I think, *Atta girl. You weren't going back anyway, but I'm glad you're now on board with the decision!* I let her believe it's her idea by saying, "Hannah, I think that makes sense. It seems to be a smart choice given the tough environment there."

But then she cuts me off, "Wait. But Mom . . . what about the other kids? Who's going to help them? Somebody should write a letter to the school!"

I have three nearly simultaneous thoughts. First, I'm amazed she's thinking of others while creating her own evacuation plan. I'm proud of her, and I start to take some credit—*My parenting has paid off!*—but then I stop. I don't deserve it. Not even close. She was born this way. She's a perceptive and empathic young girl, who has always been extremely in tune with her environment and the others in it. She's a gorgeous canary, and my job is simply to recognize her spirit and create space for her to fly.

The second is that she even considered the option of a letter. And then I recall that she saw her grandparents resolve a problem last year by writing a note to their cable company's customer service department.

The third realization is the most humbling. She has no understanding of the work Jim and I have been doing behind the scenes to support her. She doesn't know we already sent a letter to the board and so much more. Does she think we haven't done anything at all? That all adults—even her parents—think her experience is okay? I realize we've made a terrible mistake. In our effort to protect her, we kept her at arm's length from "adult communication." Yet, in so doing, we look no different from her teachers and school administrators.

So I decide to break the hermetic seal that separates children from adult issues. "Hannah," I tell her, "your daddy and I already wrote the board of the school."

"You did?"

"Yes. We are very angry about what's been happening. Bullying is unacceptable, and you never deserved that. Nobody deserves that."

"Really? I thought everyone was fine with it."

She crawls into my lap and starts to weep. I shut my eyes, envelope her in my arms, and resist crying myself. The guilt is staggering. *How could I have let her feel so alone for so long?* My intention was to fix her situation quietly so that she didn't think her parents were swooping in to rescue her, but instead, she felt abandoned.

For a long time, we sit nestled against one another. Eventually, sleep overtakes her, and I settle her under the covers. But before I head to our attached room, I promise to continue fighting for the other children being bullied at GCA, or anywhere else for that matter.

I won't give up.

Yearbooks

At the end of break, I count how many days of school we need to survive. The total seems doable after years of endurance. Yet, we recognize we might be succumbing to the classic pitfalls of an escalation of commitment. In my previous job, I saw countless clients continue to invest in doomed projects because they were hesitant to acknowledge their previous waste of money, time, and effort. At GCA, we feel so sunk that the risk of staying a few more weeks seems relatively manageable. So we tiptoe through each day, stay clear of unwanted attention, and remain hypervigilant. Some might consider us paranoid, but we feel it's the only way to survive.

Meanwhile, I'm still concerned the local public school might be too big for Hannah, so when a friend recommends an education consultant, I call immediately. After reviewing Hannah's neuropsych report, the consultant says she'd like to suggest an alternative.

I agree, "Yes, please!"

She delineates four criteria she believes are crucial for Hannah. First, she agrees Hannah would benefit from a smaller environment than our public school can provide.

She also notes Hannah needs a truly kind culture, "not just a place with inspiring posters on the wall," so she can "heal."

This word strikes me; it's both sad and surreal. A third party is confirming Hannah needs to *recover* from her school environment, a place that was supposed to help her thrive and grow. How did we get to this place? I recall a photo we took of Hannah on her very first day at GCA. The two dimensions somehow capture her exuberance; her beaming eyes and smile attest to her pride in being a "big girl," old enough to start elementary school. Hannah's enthusiasm reveals she trusts this place will be good for her. *To* her. The image now breaks my heart as I understand I failed her by allowing her to stay so long. She now needs to go to a place where she can "heal."

My mind is torn from the memory as the consultant lists her third criterion. She believes that, given Hannah's strong aptitudes and high intellectual curiosity, Hannah requires a school with solid academics or she'll be "bored out of her mind."

Finally, the consultant calls for a placement that allows accommodations. "If Hannah can have a calculator and a wiggly stool near the front of the room, she's off to the races." She then winds up her analysis by advising that the best fit for Hannah is a Jewish day school a few towns over.

"But we're not Jewish," I say.

"They don't care. Do you?"

"No."

I'm thrilled to learn a better fit for Hannah might exist, and I call that very day to schedule a tour.

While I'm grateful this door is opening for us, I also feel a nagging sense of guilt. Troubled children still remain at GCA. And elsewhere.

I've spent the better part of two years researching, advocating, agonizing, devising escape routes, background checking therapists, and driving kids to appointments (*way* beyond routine visits to the dentist and pediatrician). Caring for Hannah has been a full-time job. What are parents who work or who can't afford therapies and tuitions supposed to do?

■　▓　■　▓

A few days later, Hannah spends a "shadow day" visiting her prospective school, and I'm nervous to pick her up. *How did she do?* She's dealt with so much. *Can she trust others and let down her guard enough to let them see who she really is?*

My voice masks my concern as I ask, "Hey, Hannah! How was it?" We need a win so badly right now.

"Great, Mom. It's really official."

"Official" is one of Hannah's favorite words, sitting at the opposite end of the spectrum from "chaotic." She continues, "And Mom, they don't bully there." She sounds shocked, as if she didn't know this was possible.

Might we really be able to drop her at school one day without the fear of assault? Will she get to be a regular kid who can learn without the imminent threat of somebody demeaning her? And do I get to be a regular mom whose body doesn't clench from drop-off until pickup?

We cling to these hopes and enroll Hannah for the coming school year. We also start the paperwork to send Jake and Theo to our local public school.

So now we only need to endure the last few weeks of GCA. I'm pretty sure I could have persuaded Hannah to withdraw early if it hadn't been for the year-end events. She's most looking forward to the talent show. For weeks, she's discussed her desire to perform with a band. But she's still without a group, so I ask the music teacher to help her form one. When he doesn't follow through, I start crafting a speech to help Hannah face yet another rejection.

But soon enough, she walks into the kitchen and announces, "I'm going to do a magic trick!" Apparently, she's found her own solution.

Jake's disappointed his class is too young to be included in the exhibition, but he's pleased he'll at least know one of the stars on stage.

■ ▨ ■ ▨

The day of the showcase, Jim and I sit near the back of the auditorium. Hannah steps on the stage right after a sixth-grader plays a piano concerto as well as any adult I know might have. She then performs her twenty-second trick, bows, and descends swiftly.

I couldn't be prouder.

A few months ago, she couldn't take the stage to be President Taft. Soon after, she feared mercury was poisoning her water and food. She wouldn't leave the house as she was convinced ticks awaited her. She couldn't fall asleep because every creak signaled a tiger was stalking her. And she refused to shake people's hands to avoid catching communicable diseases. Yet, she just voluntarily stood in front of two hundred people and performed with grace. I'm overjoyed.

And then I overhear the piano player's mother say, "I guess they'll let anyone on stage. So much for a *talent* show!"

These are children, I'm tempted to seethe. But I stifle my disgust and turn away. No one can ruin this moment.

Hannah finds us, and I give her the hug of a lifetime. Her performance was nothing short of victory—a triumph over anxiety, fear, doubt, and yes, this whole damn place. The piano mom peeks at us over her shoulder; perhaps she thinks I'm overindulging my child with my huge display of affirmation.

I don't care.

■ ▨ ■ ▨

As our family continues to count down the days, I'm somewhat amazed we're coasting through. Nothing bad is happening. But I don't want to jinx us, so I don't verbalize my relief.

Over time, each of the parents who agreed to speak on the record with the investigator reaches out to me. They're curious to know when they'll be contacted. Puzzled myself—it's been weeks since I forwarded their names to Howard—I admit, "I don't know."

With only five days left of the term, our trusty teaching assistant, Sonia, informs me she met with Howard. This is the first sign I've received that he's working on the case. She tells me that during her interview, he asked leading questions like, "Can Hannah be overly sensitive?" and, "Isn't she a disabled learner?" and, "Does Hannah have difficulty working in groups?"

Sonia says she doesn't feel comfortable with these characterizations. She admits, "It felt like he's trying to build a case *against* Hannah." She tells me other teachers were interrogated as well, and they're nervous they'll be held responsible for the bullying. This is the last thing I need: teachers blamed for an environment they don't control, making them more likely to resent Hannah.

I'm incensed that the probe appears to focus on the nine-year-old target, as if Hannah somehow invited her own bullying. I email Howard, and I copy Priscilla, the board chair, to document my concerns. I begin:

> It has come to our attention that you are investigating our child.

I'm done being nice with my feelings, so I express my incredulity that they seem to be questioning the character and abilities of the bullying target, the person who was most injured. I go on to express my lingering disgust with his request to interview Hannah and my near disbelief that the eight families who agreed to speak on the record have not even been contacted.

Howard responds curtly:

> I disagree with your characterization of my interviews of witnesses. It is never my goal to cause discomfort. However, I appreciate that an investigation is inherently difficult for all involved. Further, I would like to clarify that I did not ask to schedule an interview with Hannah.

*Finally, I must remind you not to speak to those involved
in the investigation so as not to impede the process.*

I'm astounded. He's denying that he asked me about meeting
with Hannah? It feels like he, too, is gaslighting me. And who is
he to restrict who I can or cannot speak with? I respond, once
again copying Priscilla, expressing my frustration.

Priscilla finally emails:

*Thanks for copying me. I can't address any of the issues
while we wait for the investigator to complete his work.
All of us want what's best, and we believe this process will
help us move forward in a way that supports everyone.*

Something is very wrong. Priscilla is more wedded to her
process than a child's well-being. She's hiding behind Howard,
but her stance doesn't relieve her of accountability. Maybe she
hired him to build a case against us while she looks the other
way, but that would make him a mercenary or a hitman. And
her a . . . what? A mob boss? Employing somebody to do your
dirty work doesn't absolve you of responsibility. It just makes
you more duplicitous.

I recount. It's been over six weeks since I met with Howard.
We have just five school days left. The last few days of school
usually consist of cleaning out cubbies, honoring the graduating
class with timeworn traditions, and bringing teachers thank-you
gifts. I pray, *Please just let us get over the finish line.*

But my plea evaporates without a trace. At pickup on the
second-to-last day of school, I find Hannah with tears streaming down her face. She remains tight-lipped until she shuts
the car door, and then she sobs, "Mom! They left me out of
the yearbook!"

"What? Are you sure?" I take a moment to pull to the side of
the road. I now know that DWP (driving while parenting) is not

advisable when emotions are high in the back seat, and Hannah sounds like she's about to burst at her seams.

She yanks her yearbook from her backpack and yells, "Yes! They left me off of my class page and put me in the second grade!"

"With Jake?"

"Yes! So they think I'm a little kid!" She explains, "They saw I was mad, so they printed a new page. But it's flimsy. See? It's not thick like the others. And only *my* class got the new page. The rest of the school has the bad one with me missing in third grade. The whole school now knows that . . . I don't belong!" She is practically choking on her words.

"Hannah, I'm sure it was a mistake. I understand you're upset, but I really don't think anybody intended to hurt you."

"But *Mooooom!* You don't understand! *All year* they made me feel like I wasn't part of the class! And now here's proof! I wasn't included! Don't you understand?"

And then I realize, *damn it*. I've just committed a cardinal sin. In my effort to relieve her pain, I didn't acknowledge it. And now she's devastated *and* alone. *Again.*

Ugghh.

"I am *so sorry*. You're absolutely right. What they did was wrong. It's indefensible to be so careless with a book that means so much to people." She nods, and then I seize the opportunity to recognize a strength, and add, "You know, Honey, I'm impressed. What you just did was pretty amazing. You noticed the symbolism in the situation. The awful mistake is one thing. But it also represents how you've been feeling most of the year, and that makes it so much worse."

"Yes! Exactly!" And then she wails. Hard and looong. Her face squishes to create her dimples, and her mouth looks like a sad clown face with her plump, full lips curved upside down. I realize adults don't generally turn down the corners of our mouths when we're upset, and I wonder if the distress signal is meant to force us to take extra notice of children's pain.

After a few moments, Hannah whimpers, "Thanks, Mom, for saying that. I don't feel so alone." And then all sixty pounds of her crawls on top of me as she crams herself between my lap and the steering wheel. She's too big for this, but the point doesn't seem worth debating.

In time, she sniffles and takes a deep, unsteady breath. After releasing some anger, she's now stewing in her grief. She seems to understand precisely what's happened: for the rest of history, when people open this year's GCA yearbook, they will see that Hannah was not *there*, not really part of the class. We now have full-color proof that nobody cared enough to include her.

■　■　■　■

It doesn't take much to convince Hannah to stay home the last day of school. It's a half-day, most of which will be spent allowing classmates to sign one another's yearbooks. Hannah can't face this, and I don't make her. In fact, I don't send Jake either.

Instead, Hannah, Jake, Theo, and I sleep in and cuddle in my bed as Jim leaves for work. We watch cartoons, make pancakes, and slowly slide into the first day of summer. We are beginning the unwinding process, trying to distance ourselves from depths of pain. And we're praying for a new stage that might allow us to "heal."

I get indications the road will be long. As we settle into our new way of life, Hannah looks up from a book and declares, "Nobody likes me."

"Oh, Babe, *I* like you."

"You have to," she insists. And then she digs deeper, probably saying what she hadn't dared to say at first. "I don't like myself. I hate everything. Including me."

She peers at me through her rounded eyes until they dart down. Her bouncy curls frame her sweet face. For such a complicated child, she looks so innocent. And sad. So deeply and truly sad. It's heartbreaking to witness.

"Oh, Sweetie." I rush to envelop her in a hug. "You are *so* lovable. And so *lik*able." I wish I could transfer all her suffering to me. I would carry it gladly.

But my embrace is useless. She says, "I wish there was one person at school who cared about me. Who made me feel safe. Who liked me." She's asking for so little. And then she suggests, "Mom, you should become a teacher."

I consider the notion aloud, "Maybe I will."

"No. No." She backpedals. "No, don't. I need you to understand *me*. *I* need you."

"Always. I'm on your team, and I'm not going anywhere." I hold her tight, racking my brain for ways to counteract her feelings of inadequacy. But I know there's no easy solution. This will take time. Just as it took time to rob her of her dignity, it will take time to restore it. She needs new experiences to believe things can be different. That she is worthy.

And so, a new journey begins. And I try to make it as uncomplicated as possible. In fact, we have only one item on the agenda this summer. Months ago, I slated Jake for his own neuropsych testing during the first week of break. I feel conflicted about this. I don't want to define my kids solely by any diagnoses, but I also want to understand their specific needs. I believe there's power in knowledge. Yet, I realize this knowledge is tenuous. As a dear wine club friend noted, "These aren't blood tests. There's a lot of subjectivity involved." And I recall how one of Lexi's friends lamented how sometimes "even the experts can't agree on a diagnosis." What does this say about the evaluations' reliability? Especially for particularly unique children who can't begin to be defined within the limited number of official classifications?

Still, I decide I'd like to be engaged in a flawed process that at least endeavors to uncover my child's particular nuances than acquiesce to a system that has grossly neglected kids' individuality. I'm a little frustrated because I believe that if schools acknowledged and appreciated differences in the first place, far fewer kids would need to get tested to have those differences accommodated. But because the system isn't equipped, philosophically or practically, I need to take extra measures to help people "see" my children.

I haven't told Jim about my plans. I can hear him asking, *"What's the point of testing a kid who's doing just fine?"* Maybe he's right.

But, ultimately, I'm swayed by my newfound understanding that *no* child is "average" or "normal," not even kids like Jake who can contort themselves to fit expectations. I'm actually curious to learn what might make Jake different—what sets him apart as uniquely interesting. I want to nurture *that*.

Obscure Apologies

I breathe in summer vacation like a free diver breaking the water's surface after an interminable period submerged below. But I know I'm not entirely in the clear. I need to be careful about where I take my kids. A surprise encounter with Hannah's tormentors or any of the adult conspirators will only set us back.

In some sense, I don't have to work too hard to avoid certain people. Even good friends, especially Ellen and Heather, have vanished. Apparently, the direction from the executive committee to ignore me matters more than our friendship. The realization is crushing.

While they avoid me, a few other trustees do not.

The second week of summer break, I spy one across the yard at a local park as my children explore the play structure. I sense the trustee is aching to talk, and sure enough, he makes his way toward me. "I'm so sorry this is happening, Kayla. I don't think the board is handling this well," he admits.

I ask, "Did you tell them that?"

He responds, "No, I'm not in a position. This is being handled by the executive committee. We were just told not to associate with you until this is done. So please don't tell anybody I spoke to you. I just want you to know I'm sorry about all this."

There it is again: the opacity. And the priority of process over humanity. And the fear of disobeying authority or veering from a group stance, even as his gut pushes him toward an alternative.

Not long after, I bump into another board member, and she asks, "How are you?"

"Fine, thank you. And you?"

Without answering my question, she probes again, "How's Hannah doing?"

"Well. Thanks for asking." I won't give her more than that. There's no way she's getting access to my daughter. It's been months since we delivered our letter with the thick appendix detailing Hannah's mistreatment. She should have an idea of how Hannah's doing. But I've seen no sign of concern or compassion until this point. If she really cared, she would have reached out earlier. The duplicity makes me stiffen.

"Kayla, I just want you to know how fine I think your family is. You've been such great supporters of the school. I can't believe it's come to this. I'm so sorry that you're leaving."

"Well, we don't feel like we have a choice."

"I know. It's not right."

I give her a chance to explain. "Then why didn't you do anything? Why didn't you say anything?"

She responds, "I will if I get a chance."

I'm annoyed. Do these people really think their sympathy is meaningful? I sense they're apologizing to relieve their guilt more than to support my family. If they truly cared, they would have done something to help. Instead, we're left hanging. They're blurting confidential admissions with no corroborating action. The effort feels empty and self-serving.

I wonder, *If an apology is offered in obscurity and no one's around to hear it, does it make a sound? Did the apology even happen?*

Denial

When I meet with our neuropsychologist to review Jake's evaluation results before the fourth of July break, Michelle begins, "Usually, I have a good idea of what I'm getting into with each child. I mean, before I've even seen a kid, I've reviewed surveys from teachers and caregivers that give me pretty good insights into each little guy. But once in a while, I'm surprised." Her eyes penetrate mine as she raises an eyebrow. "This is one of those times."

Michelle continues, "Jake's teachers describe how well-adjusted he is. How capable he is in class and how kind he is on the playground. I saw the same thing here. He's super sweet."

I nod and smile. "There were no red flags. Maybe it was silly for me to test him. I just didn't want to neglect him after spending so much time focusing on Hannah last year."

"It's a good thing you brought him in. Jake is dyslexic."

I can't contain my surprise. "What? The teachers say he reads above grade level. How's that possible?"

She explains that at young ages, some children slip under the radar by using clever "compensatory strategies," like memorizing stories and interpreting illustrations. "They're smart," she says. But in third grade, kids "go from learning-to-read to reading-to-learn." When schools up the ante, it becomes much harder for students with dyslexia to fake it. But then she suggests, "Actually, Jake's dyslexia might have gone undetected for a while. Mostly because he's what some people call 'stealth dyslexic.'" I have no idea what she means, so she explains, "Jake scored extremely high in some areas that help him excel in the classroom. Like this. See his verbal reasoning score? It's quite significantly above average. Multiple standard deviations."

Hmmm, I think. *Hannah has high verbal reasoning too. I guess my kids aren't all that different from each other after all.* And then I laugh, "Looks like my family knows how to rock the ends of the bell-shaped curves!"

She smiles. "Jake and Hannah have both significant strengths and growth opportunities."

"That's a kind way of putting it," I recognize gratefully.

She continues, "While Jake has some impressive strengths, we still need to be careful because he also has some areas that will slow him down and frustrate him. Like decoding. See?" While I know these evaluations aren't blood tests, the score that sits significantly below the others is hard to ignore. Michelle prods me. "If we don't give children like Jake tools to address their weaknesses and leverage their other capabilities, they'll get anxious. And we know where that can go."

I sigh, "Yeah. I'm all too aware."

Michelle then hints it's good we left GCA, and then she advises against our public school too.

I'm confused. "You just told me he has dyslexia. The public school won't support his learning difference? I thought they had to by law."

Michelle concedes the situation is complex. Schools aren't necessarily required to provide their students with fitting resources. Instead, they need to provide a "free and appropriate public education," the meaning of which can be quite arbitrary. Basically, schools are obligated to help students perform near "average," even if that's nowhere near their potential.

I imagine scholar Todd Rose shaking his head in disgust. The whole focus on averages ultimately dumbs down our expectations and inhibits kids' evolution into their best selves.

I counter, "But you said that kids like Jake often end up suffering from anxiety when their learning difference isn't addressed properly. We both know the implications of that!"

She agrees and explains that very capable kids, even those who score significantly above average in some areas, start believing they're "stupid." Michelle laments, "And then all the wheels fall off the cart." She tells me that, unfortunately, in some districts, a child needs to fail for two full years—that this is the only way to "demonstrate a need"—before the school will make appropriate resources available, even ones with minimal cost. She explains learning advocates call this a "wait to fail" policy. And of course, by the time students are failing, the stakes are higher. Not only are they struggling in school, they're likely coping with anxiety and depression too. Truancy and delinquency are also common. So intervention becomes much more complex. And costly.

I sigh in disbelief. "This is ridiculous."

She doesn't disagree. I feel yet another pang of guilt when Michelle says, "So let's look at Jake's options." He's lucky to have them, and more kids should. I want to brainstorm how, but Michelle steams ahead, noting, "There's a specialized school about twenty miles away that focuses on dyslexia." I promise myself to find ways to consider the larger problem, but for now I allow Michelle to focus on my son. She says, "The school could be a great option for a year or two, just to give Jake the tools he'll need to set him up for the rest of his educational career."

I'm not excited about a thirty-five-minute commute, and I'm worried about focusing solely on a weakness. I recall my friend Melanie talking about how much her child benefited from "leaning in hard" to strengths.

So I'm relieved when Michelle adds, "There's also a parochial school that recently hired a reading expert trained in dyslexia."

She then laments that there are few other options. Apparently, most schools don't really understand how to identify or support dyslexic learners, so Jake would need to get a reading tutor a few days each week after school.

Jake is an agreeable child, but he's mentally exhausted after a full day of school. That doesn't seem like the best time to grow his brain. And he would kick and scream if I told him he had to go to reading practice rather than play sports or see his friends. I'd force him if necessary, but it sounds like an unhappy, draining process for the both of us.

As we wrap things up, Michelle asks, "How's Hannah doing?"

I explain my intention to have a low-key summer—to avoid scheduled activities and kids who might feel threatening.

I assume Michelle will like this plan, but she frowns. "Are you sure you want to isolate her?" She tells me about a summer program that helps kids build confidence and social skills. And then she encourages, "It could be a great way to give Hannah a boost before she enters her new school in the fall." So I add one more thing to my to-do list. But first I need to finish packing for our trip to the beach for the Fourth of July holiday.

■　▧　■　▧

When we finally arrive, the kids dash to the shore, where they shriek and play for hours. They crash swiftly that evening, giving me the perfect opportunity to pour two glasses of wine and share Jake's evaluation results with Jim.

He's incredulous. "But the teachers say he's doing just fine! He's reading above average!" He falters when he looks at my face. By now he knows I hate comparing children to contrived, arbitrary standards, so he slows down and admits. "I don't get it."

I explain, "Apparently, Jake's been able to compensate. Or a fake it."

Jim's not easily swayed. "But he doesn't spell backward! I don't believe it."

I get the instinct to dismiss what I'm saying. Why believe what we can't see? Why fix what isn't broken? Why subject Jake to labels if he can pass as "neurotypical"? But I'm not as enamored with "average" or "normalcy" as the world seems to be, and I feel this new data could help us ward off some pretty serious misunderstanding and pain in the future.

I sigh. "Babe, not all kids with dyslexia present the same." Jim has a male friend who was recently diagnosed with breast cancer, so I remind him, "Just like all cancer patients aren't the same. There's huge variability in each condition. There's huge variability in any human characteristic, really. Right? Isn't this why healthcare is evolving toward 'personalized medicine'?" I quip, "Now if only we could get the education system to consider 'personalized learning.'"

Jim smiles and nods. And then we sit down to go through the evaluation notes together. While he was initially unwilling to accept this new information, he adores his children and will do anything to support them. Even if it means adjusting the way he sees the world.

Thank goodness. Love will lead the way.

Hierarchies and Needs

I like the idea of sending Jake to a well-rounded school that understands dyslexia rather than one that's dyslexia-specific. Yes, he's dyslexic, but he's also so much more. If reading were the only concern, that would be one thing. But my son loves science and the arts and math, and the dyslexia school doesn't have strong programs in those areas. I think Jake is more likely to thrive in a place that can see *all* of him, that can "lean into" his strengths. So, when we return from the beach, I pull up the website of the parochial school Michelle recommended. I'm thrilled to see it refers to learning "differences" rather than learning "disabilities." I consider this language choice a telling indicator, maybe even an important bellwether. To confirm as much, I call an old friend whose kids attend the school.

"It's fabulous," she insists. "Great values. And as they age up, they remain good kids. No drinking. No drugs. I highly recommend it."

So I start completing the online application. At the end, up pops a contract that looks like it might take five sheets to print. I see all the standard stuff about deposit payments and privacy protocols. But I'm set back when I'm directed to initial phrases like, *We believe boys and girls should dress according to their birth gender.* And *We believe a marriage is defined as . . .* And at least ten other declarations regarding gender and sexual identity.

I've never seen anything like this in a school contract. I feel tense and disoriented, especially since I've seen many churches of this school's denomination waving rainbow flags out front. *What is going on?*

I've come to this school because my child is unable to access an education that suits him elsewhere. Even though his learning difference is common, we've received both implicit and explicit messages that it won't be accommodated most places.

And I'm weary from my prolonged campaign to ensure Hannah is treated with respect. People acted as though she didn't deserve basic civility or compassion because she's unique. And now I'm supposed to sign a document that insists another population of children doesn't deserve dignity either? Yes, the issues are distinct, but I'm viscerally offended, as if this hits me personally, even though my family happens to fit the "norm" the school desires in this case.

I don't feel comfortable signing the contract as written, so I insert into the "Additional Information" section: *We believe in supporting the rights of all children and their families, no matter their gender identity, sexual orientation, or other difference.*

I realize I'm likely sabotaging our odds of admittance, but I just don't see how I can endorse the contract without a significant amendment. Can I really say it's okay to diminish and exclude certain students after all we've been through? I'd like to believe I wouldn't have signed the contract even before our demeaning experiences at GCA, but I've learned that personal exposure can strengthen understanding. *And* the empathy muscle.

So here I am, flexed and flummoxed. And a bit angry too.

I hold off on submitting the application and text a photo of my addendum to my friend whose children attend the school.

She calls a few hours later and doesn't hesitate to jump into the matter. Her urgency suggests she's trying to save me from myself. "So, Kayla, about your application . . . I just wouldn't include a note. It might ruin your chances. I think you should keep it clean."

"Clean?"

"Yeah, you know. I mean, it's such a great school. This isn't the time to ruffle any feathers."

I consider her analogy. Don't birds purposefully "ruffle feathers" to get rid of harmful debris? Wouldn't that be a good thing to do right now? I've known her a long time, so I'm not shy when I say, "But the contract is discriminatory."

"Really? I don't think they mean anything by it. They just want to be clear about expectations. And they don't want to get into a political mess."

Mess? I wonder, *How is discrimination "clean" and supporting people's individuality a "mess"?* But I say instead, "The contract has all these clauses, starting with not allowing girls to dress in boys' clothes and vice-versa. I would have been screwed if I'd gone there when I was little! And it goes on to discuss who can marry whom and a lot of other stuff."

"Don't be ridiculous. They let girls wear pants. But they're probably worried about getting into awkward situations. You know, with locker rooms and bathrooms and stuff."

"But it's discriminatory," I repeat. "And prejudiced."

She's quick to her defense. "I don't think most people there discriminate. They're good people. And most are fine with gay rights. But a few have strong opinions, and they have influence. So people just stay in their lane and let it go."

I now know how possible it is for a small minority to wield so much power, enough to make a majority stand down from their own beliefs. The books called this "pluralistic ignorance," and here it is playing out in real life. The school's minority is so vocal that people assume its opinions are widely held, even if they aren't. And so the majority remains silent, and the cycle continues.

Or perhaps it's worse. Maybe most people at the school *do* support discrimination, but they choose to let the few vocal people lead the effort and cower behind them.

My friend circles back to the purpose of her call. "I really think you should delete your note. You just don't want to rock the boat."

There it is again: the phrase "rock the boat." She's full of analogies today, and this one I've heard a lot lately. It was used not long ago to try to convince me to remain quiet while my daughter was being bullied. And now it's being employed to encourage me to hold still—to be complicit with discrimination against other children. *Children!*

My friend gushes, "It's a really great school. The best. You'll totally love it. And the new learning specialist is phenomenal."

I see what she's doing. She's reminding me that I benefit personally by staying quiet because the organization has resources my child needs. After all, I don't have many options for Jake. Most schools don't have experts in dyslexia. It's a terrible choice I'm being forced to make: Do I send Jake to a school where he can learn? Or do I stand up for our values of inclusion and compassion?

I consider a framework I've employed since it was taught to me in college. Maslow's hierarchy holds that some needs are more fundamental than others and must be addressed first. The concept usually helps me prioritize my efforts and make decisions. But both my child's education and other children's well-being are important to me. It doesn't seem right that I'm being forced to choose between them.

As I weigh our options, my irritation rises. I was initially upset about the contract itself, but now I'm offended by an even more insidious challenge: a system designed to appeal to a privileged group, one that fits a mold. Constituents can access valuable resources and benefits, as long as they remain complicit with the exclusion of others.

I ask my friend, "Did you sign this contract?"

"I don't think they had it when we applied. I don't know. I'm sure we signed paperwork, but I don't really read those things." So by not being diligent—by not endeavoring to understand the system—she remains at peace. Her kids get an education because she doesn't ruffle feathers or rock the boat. And even with my prodding, she remains serenely ignorant.

Although, maybe I *did* hit a nerve because she's now justifying the school's position by repeating, "I think they're mostly just worried about restrooms. They'd have to build separate facilities for what, just a few transgender kids, at best? They can't afford that. It's just too hard."

I realize the bathroom issue is multi-layered, and solutions do cost money. So I acknowledge, "It's complicated, but wasn't that same logic people used to avoid creating bathrooms for people in wheelchairs?"

She insists, "This is totally different."

Is it? It doesn't feel so to me. I have no intention of implying that the struggles our society imposes on transgender kids are identical to the ones forced on children with physical impairments. But some of the tactics used to deny both populations feel eerily similar.

My friend just suggested we don't need to support civil rights because it's "hard." Her rationale holds that if a situation gets complicated or forces us to reconsider our historical practices or affects our pocketbooks too much, we can move on to other concerns.

But I'm not willing to move on.

I tell her, "I just don't think I can sign it." I would be a hypocrite if I joined an institution that devalues individuals after spending months trying to advocate for the just treatment of my own. I try to explain, "How can I send my kid, in good conscience, to a school that permits discrimination and intolerance?" As the words escape my mouth, I realize she probably thinks I'm judging her for sending her own children to the school.

She counters, "You're wrong. The school is very welcoming of differences. They have Black people. We're not talking about real discrimination. This is different."

I'm pretty sure that an acceptance of a few people doesn't get you off the hook for excluding others. And given what I've seen so far, I wonder just how genuinely the school supports the unique needs, cultures, and backgrounds of the individual children, including those of different races. It seems more likely that people are welcomed as long as they assimilate to the expected norm. After all, wouldn't each family have had to sign the same contract I'm being asked to sign now?

I consider how I might convey all this to her, but then I realize it's unlikely anything I say will matter. I pointed out the discrimination, but she remained steadfast. She's taken her stand. She doesn't believe inclusion includes *everyone*. For her, exceptions can be made. But this doesn't seem kind *or* intellectually honest to me. I just don't see how it's possible, in a civil world, to justify dismissing some people while simultaneously embracing others. A lot of mental gymnastics and inconsistent logic would need to take place in order to reconcile the disparate treatment of who's in and who's out.

I decide immediately: there can be no carve-outs to decency or social justice. We either accept one another's unique identities, or we don't.

I also decide Jake is going to the dyslexia school. I'll figure out some way to enrich his exposure to science, math, and the arts. But I can't assume he'll just *figure out* compassion, especially if the adults near him role model bigotry. After all, I don't want him just to tolerate others. I want him to celebrate others. I'm prioritizing *humanity* in our hierarchy of needs.

I sigh as I realize the practical implications. With Hannah at the Jewish school, Jake at the dyslexia school, and Theo at the public school, we're going to have a hectic driving schedule. I'm tired just thinking about it, so I head upstairs to find Jim.

I need his buy-in, especially since he'll need to help shuttling the kids across town.

I unfold my line of reasoning, but he cuts me off. Jim doesn't need the entire evolution of my thinking in order to confirm we don't want discrimination demonstrated overtly for our kids.

So I pull up the application for the dyslexia school. It's not the perfect solution, but at least it will allow me to look at myself in the mirror tomorrow morning.

And who knows? I might even like the look of my ruffled feathers.

A Wider View

With decisions made about the upcoming school year, I assume I can relax, but a window on the world was just opened and I can't close it again. The view widens when Jim and I watch the nightly news together, and the images become even more vivid when I read articles exploring the complexities of the previous night's reports.

One evening, a news anchor reminds me of a deadly school shooting that occurred a few months ago. And he reveals some newly uncovered information: five months before that fateful day, a parent wrote a letter to the school voicing concern over a culture of drugs, violence, and bullying. The parent noted similarities to the environment at Columbine leading up to the massacre there. The reporter explains that school officials responded to this clairvoyant letter by filing a lawsuit, citing "defamatory statements."

My heart almost stops. I was hoping I was paranoid when I consulted a lawyer before sending my letter to the board. I didn't want to believe schools actually sued concerned parents. But apparently, they do.

Holy shit.

Over the course of several weeks, I'm disturbed by the frequency of news reports related to bullying. Were they always here? Or am I just noticing them more?

I learn about a girl who took her own life after being taunted and forced to perform sexual acts. School employees evidently knew she was threatened almost daily but didn't intervene or even notify the girl's parents.

I hear about a boy who was ridiculed by students over the course of five years. They called him cruel names, made fun of his speech impediment, and urinated on his clothing. The boy eventually stood up for himself and fought one of his bullies, whereupon the school, finally, did take action. Yet in an astonishing twist, administrators suspended the targeted child rather than the kids who abused him for years. A court is now awarding the family millions of dollars, pointing to the school's negligence, which left the student little choice but to defend himself.

More stories come from across the country, but the congruencies among them are clear. Most often, the bullied children are deemed "different," a classification that somehow justifies their mistreatment, even to adults. Many of the schools or districts had policies against bullying but simply failed to enforce them, often because they refused to acknowledge the behavior in the first place or take meaningful action once it was identified. Administrators also neglected to create safe, anonymous mechanisms for reporting abuses. And when people came forward anyway, officials demonized them and demonstrated more concern for public image than for the harmed children. At times, formal, explicit policies actually prioritized the protection of the school and the perpetrator over the victim.

As I follow the news, my ears perk, and I stop breathing momentarily, sometimes even when the word "bullying" isn't mentioned. The cases are distinct from mine, but I continue to sense something familiar. I'm not exactly sure what I'm identifying, so I listen more carefully.

Many reports feel surreal, like a horrible kind of déjà-vu. I can't keep track of the incessant accounts of the *hundreds* of young gymnasts molested by their team doctor, or the *thousands* of Boy Scouts abused by their leaders, or the *thousands more* children assaulted by priests. And there seems to be a never-ending string of stories about exploitation at boarding schools. Each report makes me feel nearly apoplectic. The stories have recycled for years. Why can't they stop?

After a while, I point to the screen and tell Jim, "See? There it is. Again! It's different. But it's the same!" He looks confused, so I direct, "Look how people *responded*!"

I recognize that our own experience with bullying on one small campus in Northeast America hardly matches those of families contending with powerful national organizations that normalize and systematize molestation. But it's getting harder to ignore several disturbing consistencies, each of which enables the scourges to continue, often for *decades*.

As with the reports on bullying, in almost all of these other instances, the governing bodies prioritized their own reputations over the well-being of the minors in their care. Authority figures seemed more concerned with what the perpetrators could lose (jobs and esteem) if they were ousted rather than what their targets have already lost (safety, dignity, trust in their communities, their very childhoods, and so much more). Many institutions even created formal, albeit covert, systems to conceal abuses and to inhibit the reporting of wrongdoing. These cover-ups enabled the accused to maintain their positions or simply move to new locations, where they could assault a new round of unsuspecting children. Meanwhile, their victims forever grappled with the consequences. They were often even expected to continue operating in the very same environments as their abusers. No matter the context, the apathy exhibited toward the children and their families is revolting. They are ignored, silenced, and shamed routinely.

It all feels too much to bear. And as Jim and I keep watching the nightly news, I'm unable to ignore the fact that children aren't the only ones affected.

I hear about low wage-earning women harassed at work and people raped on university campuses and athletes victimized by coaches and soldiers sexually assaulted while serving our country and minorities across the board attacked with countless forms of discrimination and cruelty. All too often, the individuals who speak up are discredited while people in a position to help remain passive. The wronged individuals are often cast as pathetic, untrustworthy, irrational, or wanting of the assault. Their reputations are shot, while their abusers move on. In the workforce, the abusers might even be promoted.

And I witness *repeatedly* how the broader public fails to recognize, believe, or support people who've been assaulted. I wonder how this happens so easily, so I start mining the incidents for insights. Of course, each atrocity is unique, and each mistreated individual and community is deserving of its own platform. But it's hard to ignore that many of the *tools* used to silence those seeking help are often eerily similar.

When people first report wrongdoing, they are regularly *ignored* and *doubted* and *denied,* even when evidence or proof exists. I saw this at GCA, and now I'm seeing it across the news. Typical responses include trivializing and gaslighting. People are told they are "too sensitive" and advised to "just get over it" or, my favorite, "don't rock the boat."

When injured parties (or whistleblowers) don't stand down, they're often then *demeaned* and *ostracized.* They're even dehumanized, and their unique traits are used as justifications for their mistreatment. Another crafty technique involves *flipping roles*, whereby victims and survivors of abuse are put on the defense. Unrelated past events are considered somehow relevant and are used to divert attention from the case at hand. All the while, the aggressors are characterized as the victims who are being wronged or unjustly threatened.

If the injured parties don't give up and plead for recognition, even after being degraded in these ways, the tactics used against them escalate. Threats and legal vehicles like non-disclosure agreements are employed to *silence* and *conceal the truth*, giving those in charge the opportunity to *rewrite history* and create entirely new (albeit false) narratives. For those who can afford them, there's always an attorney or public relations firm willing to take a fee to help orchestrate a smokescreen, no matter how duplicitous and unethical. And the cases are often difficult to investigate because the organizations' senior management and boards are regularly active participants in the cover-ups.

I've been dismayed to see reports suggesting that some of the initial in-house reviews of sexual assault allegations at national broadcasting agencies were, in fact, shams, making a mockery of their own mission: to be trustworthy investigative news sources.

I hope the GCA trustees are watching the television at night, just as we are, and that they aim to hold themselves to a higher standard. After all, we aren't cogs in a big corporate wheel. And we aren't strangers. It's easy to demean people when there's no personal relationship. But they *know* us. And the letter I delivered to the GCA board contained fifty pages documenting Hannah's mistreatment. Will this evidence suffice? Shouldn't it? Or will I be summarily dismissed and ignored *again*, like these others I'm witnessing?

I try to take comfort in the fact that we shared nothing but the truth with the trustees, and they expressed concern. They even hired a consultant, and that consultant engaged enough to ask what our family needs. I was clear that the only personal restitution we want is for an adult to acknowledge Hannah's very real experience—to tell her she didn't deserve her years of bullying.

As I continue to listen and read, I get confirmation that others have similar hopes. No matter the abuse, survivors voice a consistent, disabling need to be heard and acknowledged. They are not asking us to suspend reason. They are asking us simply to consider their stories in earnest and, ideally, to recognize what happened is wrong.

I recall my first night of crisis counseling and the girl who was being molested by her father. At the time, I guessed she was going to live with me for a long while, and here she is in my thoughts again. She was suffering not just from physical assaults but from emotional ones too. That evening, her greatest need was to be believed. Yet, even her own mother—the woman who probably loves her most—denied her.

The news demonstrates how regularly people are deprived of validation or an honest reckoning with their very real truths. The dismissiveness is knee-jerk. Few bystanders even *try to consider* what survivors tell us, and few policies or norms veer us back on track. I recall my research into empathy and remember that our brains, driven by our rash, impetuous amygdalae, protect us from others' pain, even if it means ignoring it and betraying our kinder selves—our own values and ethics.

I consider what a different path would look like, one in which we acknowledged people's experiences from the outset. Now, institutions often respond only after media attention builds or hordes of people band together to demand justice. Maybe this is why the GCA investigator has refused so far to contact the parents willing to corroborate my story with their own? He knows it takes masses of people to force institutions to take responsibility, which perhaps he has been hired to help GCA avoid.

But shouldn't even one person's report of abuse be worthy of attention?

Unfortunately, the news keeps telling me no. It took over *sixty* courageous accusers to speak up over the course of *thirteen* years to finally win at least one case to convict Bill Cosby. (Even this ends up being overturned.) And *eighty* brave women and *several* daring investigative journalists were needed to bring down Harvey Weinstein. And how about the *countless* young athletes, scouts, and parishioners who have yet to see justice? And the *endless* reports of racial discrimination and aggression that have been—continue to be—dismissed until, or even when, cell phones document the gross violations of justice. Again and again, people in need are disbelieved. They remain unseen.

What does this mean for us?

In coffee bars and across social media, my peers express disgust at people and institutions enabling abuse, either directly or through their complicity. We are quick to judge people and situations "over there." And yet, when a mother reports bullying right here at their very own school, what will happen? Will they believe her? Or will GCA follow the national model?

It seems like we might have a small but potentially powerful case study.

Camp

"But why do I have to go? I thought I was gonna get to relax this summer! I only have a few weeks left of break!"

"Sweetie, I've heard great things about this camp. Michelle says they're really kind, and the whole goal is to help you have fun with friends. You deserve to feel safe with your peers."

She resists, but I send her anyway.

Just before 8:00 a.m., I roll my car into the parking lot and see the camp director, Marie, whom I met earlier in the summer at a meeting she requested to verify that Hannah is a good fit for the program. Marie opens the door to let Hannah outside and greets me, "Hello again!" She then turns to Hannah and says, "You can call me Ms. Henderson!"

Several employees flutter about getting campers acclimated, and I take comfort in the fact that they're all trained in psychology. Hopefully, over the course of the week, Hannah will gather strategies and insights to help her acclimate to her new school . . . or participate in any group setting, for that matter.

Later in the day, when Hannah climbs in the car, I ask, "How'd it go?"

"Terrible!" she proclaims.

I suppress my exasperation. Must she resist all efforts to help her? "Can you give it a chance, Honey?"

"Those kids are weird! Mom, they're seriously strange. I think they might be crazy."

I'm not okay with these characterizations. I've spent the better part of two years promoting the worth of all children, and now my own daughter is violating one of my core tenets: All kids deserve dignity. So I say, "Honey, that's not okay. Each one has something valuable to offer the world."

But she insists, "Mom, I think they're deranged."

Where on earth is she getting this language?

Before I can lay into her, she asks, "Mom? Is *my* brain okay? Am *I* deranged?"

This pivot leaves me flabbergasted. "Honey, no! What do you mean?"

She explains, "We had a whole-camp assembly today. And Ms. Henderson made each kid stand up and talk about themselves."

Really? Many of these kids have social anxiety. And they were asked to speak publicly? On day one? I verify, "By themselves? In front of the entire camp?"

"Yes, alone." Before I can ask more questions, Hannah elaborates, "We had to say our name, where we go to school, what our diagnoses are, and what we need to work on."

Wait, what? Their diagnoses? Even this word sounds too mature coming out of my child's mouth. Some kids aren't yet experienced enough to understand the weighty concepts and the stigma behind words like "disorder." Even I, who have spent years researching the issues, am still trying to figure it all out.

Nothing of this sort was discussed when I met Marie earlier in the summer. So to take it upon herself to instruct the children to speak about their diagnoses in front of strangers? Isn't that a violation of HIPPA law? And just plain decency? Not even twelve-step programs force participants to speak on the first day!

I tell Hannah, "I don't think all kids there have official diagnoses." I want her to know that this wasn't meant to be a camp for the "deranged." And I wonder aloud, "What happened if a kid didn't list a diagnosis?"

She explains, "Ms. Henderson said it for them, and she also listed problems the kids need to work on if the kids didn't say it themselves."

WAIT. WHAT THE HELL IS HAPPENING HERE? I thought this was a camp for children who've been mistreated and bullied and demeaned elsewhere. Some have social anxiety; some are on the autism spectrum; some have other challenges. And this was supposed to be a compassionate place where kids could feel safe and learn helpful strategies for surviving social settings. How is this helping? It sounds more like public shaming!

"Hannah, did Ms. Henderson ask you to share your interests or strengths?"

"No, she just told us to say our problems." She then clarifies, "Well, actually, when she left, another counselor asked us about things we like. But I didn't want to talk then."

Of course not. The director of the entire camp had already signaled what was important. She didn't even stick around to hear the positive things kids might say about themselves. To her, the campers were nothing more than "diagnoses" and "problems."

I try to process all Hannah is telling me, but she isn't done. She directs, "Mom, I think you need to call a surgeon. Something's wrong with me. I think I need a brain transplant." With this revelation, her bottom lip quivers and she bursts into tears.

Holy shit.

When we get home, I shoot an email to the neuropsychologist who recommended the camp. I'm livid but hopeful she had no idea something like this might happen. I also want her to know the effect on Hannah so she doesn't give similar advice to other families.

An hour later, Michelle calls. She sounds mortified as she says, "Oh my God. I'm so sorry. I feel awful. Since I recommended the camp to you at the beginning of the summer, I've heard some other complaints." She explains she just learned the founder retired last year, and in her absence, the culture of the camp has changed drastically. She apologizes again and again, and her concern feels palpable. She's struggling right alongside us.

Later that night, I consider how embarrassed I was when Hannah degraded her peers. She called them "weird" and "strange" and "deranged." I realize, *How could she think otherwise?* First impressions matter, and the campers were being taught to present themselves to the world by their weaknesses. Each child was reduced to a diagnosis, spurring my own child's disgust—not just toward others but toward herself as well.

As I tuck her into bed, Hannah begs, "Mom, please don't send me back."

It's an easy request to honor, but I become even more concerned when she says, "It was scary there. Some of the kids were really mean. There was a nice kid on crutches. I think he has something called CP? But those mean guys tried to knock him down and take his crutches."

"Oh, that's awful! What did the counselors do?"

She reports what I should have known: "They didn't see. The kids did it sneakily."

After shutting Hannah's door, I call a friend who told me she almost sent her child to the camp a few years ago. She admits, "Well, we tried to send him because Leo's school said he had ODD. But Leo refused to go." I'm tempted to laugh at the consistency of a kid with oppositional defiance disorder refusing to comply with orders, but I'm too annoyed to be entertained—especially since I've learned that kids are often mislabeled with ODD way too quickly. If adults fail to understand how a child is feeling—what he struggles with—why wouldn't he act out? I recall Sweet Sonia, the fabulous teaching assistant, who regaled the importance of the ABCs, or rather, understanding the *antecedent* of a *behavior* before dolling out judgments and punitive *consequences.*

I can't stop thinking about this child who was physically assaulted at camp. I decide his mother should know, and if the camp isn't aware of what's happening, who can tell her but me? I text my kids' favorite sitter and resolve to find the boy's mom the next morning.

When our sitter arrives, I head toward the garage, and Hannah protests, "Mom, you said I don't need to go!"

I respond, "You don't have to. But I do." She looks nervous, so I say, "I'll be back in a bit. Maybe an hour." And I speed off to camp, where I spy a woman in the parking lot pulling crutches out of her trunk. With no other crutches in sight, I make my move. The mom closes her trunk and heads toward a passenger door, but I intercept her before she can pull the handle.

"Hi. Umm, I know this is awkward, but I wanted to introduce myself. My daughter is Hannah. I think she was in your child's group?"

"Oh, hi! I'm Amber!"

I tell her my name and admit I'm embarrassed I don't know her child's.

"Spencer!" she says in a way that conveys deep pride and love.

I explain that I'm worried about being intrusive, but my daughter shared some information I thought she should know. "That I'd want to know," I say. And then I convey all I heard.

Amber looks dejected as she shakes her head. "I just don't know what to do." She admits, "Something like this happened last session too."

"Why did you send him back then?" and I immediately wish I could rescind my question. It sounded accusatory and judgmental, even to me. My crisis counseling taught me to avoid the word *why*, but now it lingers between us, unbottled and difficult to recapture.

Amber doesn't miss a beat as she explains she's "at a loss." She needs to work, and her son needs a place to go. She looks thoroughly defeated when she says, "There just aren't any other options."

I strongly believe our schools and systems should not segregate people based on differences. We all benefit from diversity. But I wonder if I've come across an exception. If kids have been so mistreated that they require treatment, maybe it makes sense to ensure the program is, first, built around compassion and dignity, and, second, designed to support kids' very specific needs. Should we send children struggling with impulse control and anger management to the same program as children recovering from emotional and verbal abuse, as this camp seems to do? Each child deserves support, but clearly, different kids have different needs. Even children with the same diagnosis are often quite unique. I recall reading a neurologist from UCSF explain that initial evidence suggests there are multiple phenotypes of dyslexia, for example, and each one should be addressed differently.

I feel a pit in my stomach as I watch Amber escort Spencer to the camp entrance. It must kill this loving mother to leave her child in this place. It hurts just to watch. In fact, I'm so upset that I don't notice the camp director approaching me until she says, "Hello there! Ready for another day?"

I try to contain my anger as I turn to address her. "I'm glad we ran into each other. I was hoping you could help me understand the philosophy behind forcing kids to stand up one-by-one and introduce themselves with their diagnoses and problems."

She looks taken aback, but just for a moment, then quips, "It's important to normalize their diagnoses. They all have them, so we discuss them in public from day one so the kids know they're in like company. It helps them face their reality and is comforting to them."

Comfort was the last thing I saw last night. My kid literally wanted a brain transplant!

She continues, "Kids are usually relieved to be given diagnoses. The world suddenly makes sense to them."

I've heard this trope several times by now. The idea of the happy diagnosee seems to please officials, but it dismisses the complex rush of emotions people actually feel. Yes, children can be relieved to learn they are not "crazy" or "lazy" or "stupid," as people often imply. It can feel vindicating to know there is an actual name for one's struggles and perhaps even an understanding of the physiological differences that cause them. And caregivers can finally access an argument to counter the assumption that their child's behavior is a result of bad parenting. But diagnoses induce other feelings too, like confusion, embarrassment, fear, anger, hopelessness, and shame. And each person experiences these emotions differently.

I attempt to convey all of this to Marie, as well as the impact her exercise had on my child, but she only gets more defensive. And then she goes on the offensive asserting, "Parents who resist diagnoses just don't want to see their kids' issues."

Oh, wow. She's actually proclaiming that the people who deal with their children's idiosyncrasies day in and day out don't regularly get frustrated, annoyed, and overwhelmed by the challenges? That they don't even "see" them?

I then feel assaulted by subterfuge when she starts to deny Hannah's reports and insist that she gave the kids the opportunity to talk about their strengths. But I've already seen and heard enough to know something very troubling occurred. And I believe my daughter more than I believe this person. My skin is crawling, the same way it did when I sensed Richard slithering around the truth.

So, I turn my back and promise myself never to deliver my child into misguided hands like these again.

Never.

Ever.

The Final Blow

Almost twenty-one weeks after I sat for six hours with Howard, Jim walks in the room with a certified letter in the mail. No phone call. No personal words. And apparently, no humanity.

Jim fumes, "This is bullshit! Don't read it. It'll just piss you off. They're assholes."

So I leave the envelope sitting on his desk, where it stays a few days as I try to give myself space and focus on my family. I still need to recover from the camp experience, and I'm not sure I have the fortitude to reconnect with the pain of the previous few years as well.

But over the next few days, the envelope taunts me. In a moment of weakness, or maybe a spurt of strength, I pick up the letter and read.

Dear Jim and Kayla:

We are writing to inform you of the results of the investigation into your claims of bullying at the Global Citizens Academy. We realize the process was long, but it was also thorough, a sign that we are deeply committed to our school's mission and the well-being of all students.

As you are aware, we engaged Arnold J. Howard of Howard Consulting LLP to perform this investigation. We are pleased to report that his thorough and independent process found no incidents of bullying at the Global Citizens Academy.

This outcome is consistent with our deep understanding of elementary school pedagogy, which holds that bullying is highly uncommon at this age. Mr. Howard confirmed that while some disruptive classroom behavior occurred, nothing was atypical for a cohort of the age in question. Mr. Howard also determined that GCA staff responded swiftly and appropriately each time you reported a concern. If anything, the investigator found that Hannah's high degree of sensitivity and complex learning profile, as documented by her neuropsychologist, cause Hannah's perceptions to be skewed. We believe Hannah's unique challenges underlie her difficulties with peers. We wish her luck in her new school.

Please note that nothing about this document constitutes a waiver of privacy rights or attorney-client privilege. We appreciate your effort in supporting this independent investigation.

Sincerely,

Priscilla Williams

I sit in shock. Their lies are blatant. I think about the large appendix I forwarded to Howard. It included multiple emails in which teachers themselves used words like "target" and "bullying behavior." It also included the letter from the school-recommended developmental specialist who advised administrators to implement a bullying prevention program after his visit. Any investigation would have found that there was no response to his letter, and that, to this day, there is no official bulling policy. And school files, if they are kept, would have documented Lauren's suspension and the reasons behind it.

I peruse Mr. Howard's "findings" on the following page. Inexplicably, his notes make no mention of meetings with the faculty who observed the attacks on Hannah nor with families who were willing to speak on the record about their own children's experiences.

I also notice the line asserting "attorney-client privilege" placed hypocritically before the phrase "independent investigation." And I'm confused by the language claiming "nothing about this matter constitutes any waiver of privacy rights." Are they referring to the school's rights? Or the child's? I signed no non-disclosure agreements. What privacy do they need ensured?

I am galled by the infringement of *Hannah's* privacy. I shared her neuropsych report with teachers in good faith with the expectation they would use the information to help Hannah learn. Instead, they breached confidentiality and used the material to hold her responsible for her own bullying. The betrayal is unconscionable. They are blaming—and shaming!—the victim.

My worst fears are confirmed. They never had any intention of getting to the truth. I hoped the board was distinct from the administration—that they had children's best interests at heart—but now I see they are all in bed together. And they followed the same playbook used by so many people and organizations before them. It didn't matter that they knew me or that we belong to the same small community. The board hired a lawyer to ask me the "right questions" and execute a cover-up.

I should have seen straight through their intentions when I learned the investigator was a lawyer, not a child psychologist, nor an expert on bullying, nor a behaviorist, nor someone with a civil rights background. They engaged a lawyer, so we got a legal response. Of course.

Howard was a mercenary employed to construct a new narrative. Truth was not the goal. Obfuscation, attacking the whistleblowers, and soiling our family's reputation was. I'd recently read a rape survivor's lament that "it takes a certain kind of person" to be willing to accept payment to lead a process that *revictimizes* an injured party. I guess I shouldn't be surprised that somebody like Howard exists, but I'm still stunned that GCA would hire him. Trustees probably hoped that by engaging someone else to do the dirty work, they wouldn't be responsible. I know better. They *designed* this sham.

I'm embarrassed that I was so easily duped. I can imagine the board's smug satisfaction over their success, tricking me into trusting them. But for what purpose? We stated several times that we wanted "to support the school" and to "help it prosper long into the future." If we intended to sue, why would we even bother writing a letter? Wouldn't we just head straight to the courthouse? Even now, their letter still doesn't prevent us from suing. So why did they spend so much time and money creating a dishonest account? It serves no purpose but to humiliate us.

I'm so angry, I contemplate changing course and calling the attorney who was gunning to take our case. How ironic! The trustees pursued this path to avoid a lawsuit, yet their behavior makes me want revenge in a way I never contemplated before!

I take a deep breath to contain myself. I want to stay true to myself and my original intention: to help children and families who are mistreated. I realize if I take legal action, I'll feed their storyline that I'm a risk, not a person who cares.

So I brace myself, will myself, to stay calm.

I consider the history of our experience with bullying at GCA and the many rounds of defeat. The first transgressions were the incessant jabs at Hannah's right to belong. The hits were cruel, but not unique. Bullying happens everywhere. The perpetrators simply needed guidance and structure to learn how to behave appropriately.

The second blow came when the adults—Richard, Paula, Megan, Priscilla, and even close friends—rejected Hannah's reality. It was an uppercut to our dignity, and it hurled us to the mat. I was unprepared to see the very people empowered to help young children turn their backs on the most vulnerable.

But I surprised them all when I pulled myself up. (How dare I?) So the board itself orchestrated the final body blow, sending us flying out of the ring for the final count. I can see Priscilla flexing her muscles, gloating, "Down goes Kayla!"

This last round debilitates me, particularly because so many people were engaged. The entire institution attacked us, all because we asked leaders to be accountable for what was happening on their watch. Challenging the powers-that-be to take responsibility, it turns out, is a brutal and devastating contact sport.

I stuff the letter back in its envelope, and I seal it away. At the same time, I smother an ache that's been tugging at me—pulling me under—for months. I've resisted it as I've clung to hope and the belief that, in the end, people will care for one another. People are good. People will help those in need, especially children.

But now I have incontrovertible proof: Nobody did.

I step into the kitchen and ask Jim to take the kids away for the day. "Somewhere. Anywhere." I need to be alone.

Once they're all out of the house, I head outside and lie face-down on an unpadded metal lounge chair. It should feel uncomfortable, but I don't sense any pain. I can't breathe well, but it doesn't seem to matter. I don't adjust my head.

And then, a groundswell overtakes me resonating with loud, strange noises. I momentarily consider gagging them to regain control, to "soldier on." But I'm awed by the primal depth of the sound, and I don't want to fight anymore. So I succumb.

After a while, I turn my head slightly and note the sun blazing above me. I realize this kind of intense heat and light should assault my senses, making my glazed eyes sting and my confused head ache. But I feel nothing.

I have no idea how long I spend in this void, wailing but numb to my surroundings, somehow disassociated from the intense physical outpouring of grief, mourning a world I thought I knew—that I'd come to trust—but apparently doesn't exist. At least not for my child.

In time, I remember my family will be returning, so I wipe my face with the bottom of my shirt and pull myself up. I don't have the luxury of wallowing. I have kids.

So I carry myself into the house, dazed. Somehow naturally anesthetized.

When my family arrives, I go through the motions, but Jim sees something is wrong. He tells me to lie down while he fixes dinner.

He never fixes dinner.

Hours later, after putting the kids to bed, he joins me.

I concede, "I think I need medication."

He nods.

No Words

I was so distracted by the board's letter yesterday that I forgot to check in with my newish friend, Beth, who reached out to me last spring when she heard I was concerned about bullying. Her son has been bullied over the years—first because of his brown skin tone and then for just about everything else—and as the school year wrapped up, he was battling depression. Beth was nervous about sending him to camp, and she's been a wreck in anticipation of his return.

I text:

How'd it go?

She's quick to respond:

Amazing. He said it was the best experience of his life!

When she explains it was the first time in years that he felt seen and heard by the adults around him, I can't help but note the contrast between our two camp experiences. I ask how her son's camp made the kids feel so comfortable.

Very simply, she writes. *But it was also very intentional. They just let him do him and encouraged other kids to do the same.*

I jot this nugget in my journal and make a mental note to take some time later to consider how we can design environments that allow kids to be true to themselves. Beth knows I've been journaling, so she brainstorms with me for a bit, and then she asks how my writing's been going. *Has it been cathartic?*

I'm not sure what to say because the truth is I've been struggling. Journaling was supposed to help me release stress, but instead, my mind feels distended by a tangle of thoughts and feelings that intertwine and conflate, to the point that it's hard to know where one begins and another ends. How am I supposed to separate the effects of bullying, learning differences, anxiety, isolation, betrayal, anger, guilt, and shame? I'd hoped to find clarity, but I confess:

My writing sucks. It's too jumbled. I'm just too tired to think straight.

Evidently, this deserves a direct conversation. My phone rings, and my friend says, "Kayla, take it easy on yourself. Look, you've been through a lot. That letter from the school was enough to knock anyone down. And fatigue is a classic symptom of depression. It's probably just one of your body's ways of coping."

She hit a nerve, so I reveal more. "I can't drive by the school anymore. When I'm running errands, I take the long way just to avoid it. And I find myself dodging situations where I think certain people might be. I even resigned from community boards I *love* so I don't have to sit in a room with the people who hurt us." If these individuals didn't care to support me before the board sent its letter, they're definitely not going to now. I find this especially troubling because, after reading the science behind cognitive dissonance and normative social influence, I understand that most of the people involved have likely constructed a line of reasoning that enables them to even justify their callousness toward my family.

But I don't want to belabor her with research. So instead, I divulge, "I see Hannah struggling too. She mentions GCA constantly. She asks to meet with the administration to present her own ideas about how to run things differently so other kids aren't hurt. It's so very Hannah, but I know it will just drive the nail deeper into the coffin."

"She's a good kid," Beth says.

"I'd hoped the school would at least honor my single ask of Howard—to offer an apology. She wants one so badly, but *that's* clearly not gonna happen." I stare out the window as I relay these thoughts. Summer is tipping toward fall, and soon the new school year will be here. I admit, "Hannah's confidence is shot. She doesn't even want playdates anymore, especially if I'm not around. How am I supposed to get her ready to start a new school?"

"Sounds like PTSD. For *both* of you."

The assertion sounds dramatic. Post-traumatic stress disorder is big stuff, something rape survivors and soldiers who've witnessed unfathomable violence suffer. How can we possibly be in the same category? We're struggling with something; I just don't have the language to explain what.

I've read that the Sami people in northern Scandinavia and Russia have at least 180 words for "snow" and "ice." They are also believed to employ about one thousand terms for "reindeer." In the Arctic, there's a need to understand the variety of weather, terrain, and fauna because of their impacts on people's lives. If a vocabulary reflects the priorities and values of a community, then our lack of language to describe our very own experience seems pretty telling. What happened just doesn't matter to most.

■　▧　■　▧

That evening, I get a call from one of the ex-GCA mothers who was willing to speak on the record. She tells me Priscilla called her to follow up on reports that she was "upset" with her daughter's experience at the school.

I confirm, "Priscilla? Howard, the investigator, didn't reach out directly?" I think I know the answer. But I want confirmation.

"No, just Priscilla. I thought it was odd and wasn't sure about her motive. Can I trust her?"

I sum up the situation quite easily. "No."

Let Go of the Outcome

My wine club is scheduled to meet tonight, but I'm not sure I'm up for it. I've had a few days to digest the letter, but I'm still a shell of myself. I don't think I can fake it and abide by the Code. And then I realize, I probably don't need to. This group has always been a safe haven where we keep it real. So, I force myself to go.

It takes little time for the ladies to see straight through me. "Kayla, what's up?" they ask. I see the alarm on their faces, and I don't mask my defeat. In a monotone voice, I share the board's findings.

Amy is the first to react, "You're kidding. So they're saying the culture *they* created isn't the problem? Hannah is? That's outrageous!"

"I know. There's tons of documentation. But the school ignored all of it and instead just blamed Hannah."

Susan says, "It's so upsetting. They're blaming a nine-year-old child? Because she's different? Do they realize they're implying that only some children are worthy of decency, and the school gets to decide which ones?"

Monica's shocked. "I don't know what to say. I am so, so sorry. We're here for you—"

Maria interjects, "Thank God you've left. Let's celebrate

273

your kids and all the good that's ahead of them. Onward and upward!" I'm not ready for this kind of positivity, but I realize she's trying to help. Or, maybe it's too hard for her to sit with my pain.

Kara, ever the bulldog, barks, "You should depose them, just to fuck with their asses."

Robin agrees, "Yeah, sue them. It would be fun to watch them perjure themselves. Or maybe an oath in a court of law is what they need to finally start telling the truth."

Susan adds, "They gave you a gift. Do they even realize what they did? Their letter documents *in writing* their pattern of lying and avoiding responsibility. And they made a case for their own ignorance. Bullying doesn't happen in elementary school? Pleeease!"

I respond, "I don't want to sue. I'm just so tired." A round of conversation ensues about the upsides of litigation, but I cut my friends off, "I don't want to spend any more time on this, especially not in a courthouse. I just want to have a normal life with my family." I feel robbed of such a basic thing.

When Robin asks how I plan to reply to the letter, Maria advises, "Don't dignify them with a response."

I slump as I consider her directive. "So I'm supposed to just roll over and let them treat Hannah this way? It's not okay." She deserves to be defended.

Amy asks, "What do you hope to accomplish by responding? They made it clear they're fine making an enemy. Now it's between them and their god—if they have one."

But I'm not sure I can just let it go. I explain to my friends, "I want to say, 'In treating this like a litigation process, you have missed the *entire* point. We thought we were pretty clear about our intentions with you. We were trying to help the school and the children who are hurting. And then, ironically, you responded by demeaning and shaming *a child*!'"

Amy wonders, "Would you consider leaving this to the

universe to play out? It has brought you so much pain. Let some higher force handle it."

I'd like to believe that could happen, but I've lost faith in karma.

And when Monica asks, "Isn't Priscilla's daughter dyslexic?" I lose more faith in compassion. A fellow parent, one who should understand and support learning differences, is the one who led this charge on my daughter?

I'm incredulous. "Are you kidding me?" But then I realize she probably designed some sort of convoluted hierarchy in her mind that allows her to believe her child is deserving of respect while mine is not.

The ladies go on to berate those women who don't support other women in life, and I don't disagree, but I stay quiet. I know it wasn't just the board chair who behaved so egregiously. The entire group was complicit.

I guess I shouldn't be surprised. I recall my empathy studies, which revealed how people tend to turn their backs on uncomfortable situations in order to diminish their own distress. And I remember how social scientists like Solomon Asch demonstrated that people purposely override their better judgment to conform with group opinion. And I recall how researchers like Stanley Milgram demonstrated how average people will do terrible things to one another when directed to do so. In our case, every single board member signed on to the process that demeaned Hannah and shamed my family. Even friends.

I feel torn among betrayal, resignation, and anger. I realize I can't change people, but my soul wants them to care. And I want my own caring to matter. I wanted to make a difference for those kids who are aching. But they're still there, unprotected.

■ ▩ ■ ▩

The last week of summer break, I have the good fortune to be invited to a clinic taught by tennis Hall of Famer Gigi Fernandez, and she gives me some perspective I need to move forward. After spending the morning teaching strategy on the court, she talks us through "the mind game" at lunch. To impart her wisdom, she takes us back almost two decades, describing how she and her partner entered Wimbledon seeded in the top spot but blew their opportunity to take home the trophy when Gigi's partner double-faulted in the finals at match point.

Gigi still looks incensed as she says, "Recreational players might miss both serves, but at the Grand Slam level, especially at match point, pros don't. We let them win that day without even forcing them to hit the ball!" Gigi then reveals the devastation wasn't complete. When she returned to the locker room, her partner informed her that she was teaming up with another athlete to finish the season—one of the very women who just defeated them. Apparently, the two players had forged the new alliance before the day's competition even started.

Gigi admits she felt both betrayed and frantic, and then she recounts her thoughts at the time: "My partner, who failed at the most crucial moment, is dumping *me*? What am I supposed to do?" Gigi had little choice but to join forces with one of the only players available: the other athlete among the foursome who was dumped that day as well.

Gigi explains how the two scorned-but-now-united women reached Wimbledon's Championship match the following year. Staged for poetic justice, they were up against the very partners who jilted them the year before. But vengeance was elusive; they found themselves down 1-4 when play was halted by rain. Gigi left the court fuming, aching to win so badly that she called her sports psychologist, who directed her, "Detach from the outcome."

She fumed, "I can't *detach* from the outcome! The outcome is what matters! We need to show them who they messed with!"

But he remained firm. "Gigi, just play each point as it comes. One at a time."

When the rain stopped, the four athletes returned to Center Court, and Gigi complied. She didn't focus on the endgame or consider how much the match meant to her. She didn't envision her vindication or her former partner's comeuppance. Instead, she played each point one-by-one.

Gigi has the audience on our seat edges by the time she reveals that, in a dramatic turnaround, she and her partner took ten of the next eleven games to win the championship. She smiles as she explains how this one-point-at-a-time strategy ultimately enabled them to conquer three of the four Grand Slams that year. And over the following seasons, Gigi and her partner never again lost to their former partners in a Grand Slam. Not once.

I think, *Okay, Gigi, I hear you. Let go of the outcome. I can't ensure global justice or even the emotional safety of children at one school. I don't have power over that. But I can play one point at a time in a way that acknowledges my hope for a kinder world.*

Shalom

On a still evening just after Labor Day, Jim, Hannah, and I file into an assembly room for a family orientation at her new school. After a few minutes, the women running the reception table allow Hannah to join their efforts. Nine-year-old, anxiety-prone Hannah, the new kid, is now checking in other families, welcoming *them*.

The head of school greets us and announces their theme this year: "Everyone Counts." It's a double entendre, based on the fact that a federal census will launch after the winter break. But for us, the phrase symbolizes so much more. Maybe Hannah can be a worthy member of society here. Maybe her differences won't preclude her from belonging.

As if reading my mind, the head of school confirms, "We aim to honor the sacred nature of the community and the sacred nature of the individual. Here, everyone has something to contribute. Our goal is to bring out the unique light in each child. We celebrate each one because every single one *counts*. And together, our society shines brighter."

I'm deeply grateful to be joining this community, especially since it has no obligation to open its doors to us. As far as I can tell, we're the only non-Jewish family in the room. We could easily be "other," but they spread their arms open. In the presence of such generosity of spirit, we are humbled.

I think back to how lonely and humiliating it felt to be effectively excommunicated from the school we once considered home. Our dismissal was not only embarrassing but ungrounding. I still feel afloat and wonder if this new place will ever provide an anchor.

As teachers take turns presenting, I steal glances at my daughter, still standing by the reception table assisting latecomers. She adjusts the pencils, ensuring their straight alignment, and I worry people will notice her peculiar tendency. Will we be outed before the first day of school even starts? I surveil the room and spy the head of school observing her. He watches intently. Then he smiles. He actually looks amused. He sees my child's idiosyncrasies, maybe even her diagnoses, yet he doesn't judge them. Instead, he accepts her as she is. Without even saying a word, he demonstrates his authenticity. "Everyone counts" here.

So, in this unfamiliar gathering hall full of mostly strangers, I start to let down my guard. I don't know these people, and we don't practice the same religion. But they are showing me that their principles aren't just platitudes scrawled across posters pinned to walls. I allow myself to wonder, *Are we finally safe?*

The head of school wraps up his remarks with his final blessing for everyone in the room: "Shalom."

Shalom, I agree. *Peace. And thank you for giving us hope.*

■　▨　■　▨

On the drive home, Hannah raves, "I really like that school. Isn't it great?"

Jim concurs, "I spoke with some of the teachers. They're really impressive. So experienced!"

"And there are no bullies!" Hannah rejoices.

I want her to be prepared and forewarned, so I'm tempted to explain that no school is immune from bullying. But while some schools tolerate bad behavior, others don't. And some schools have cultures conducive to cruelty while others create environments that make it less likely.

I stop myself. Don't we all deserve a break? Especially Hannah? Maybe I can just let her rejoice in the notion that she might not be targeted this year. Hope has to be one of the most restorative forces on Earth, and I won't deny anybody, especially my children. After all, they are my own hope.

The next day, Jim and I enter Hannah's classroom for our "Entry Parent Conference." The teachers tell us they like to meet new parents to understand each child's needs. They want to "start building the relationship between home and school so we can coordinate and help each child thrive."

I'm not used to being treated like part of a team. I try to relax, but as we talk, the teachers must sense my guardedness, my hesitancy to believe things can be different here.

The lead teacher says, "I understand you're nervous. You both are likely facing some PTSD after your previous experience."

Wow. The acknowledgment of what we've gone through, and actually calling it PTSD, grabs my attention—in a good way. This kind of validation is an unexpected gift, deserving of a beautiful poufy bow. I almost can't believe it's for me.

She continues, "Please just know it's my goal to demonstrate to you that we care about your child. And I'm committed to creating a safe place for her to learn. Not just with my words but with my actions. I realize it will take time to earn your trust, but I'm committed to it."

My spine begins to uncoil as my daughter's new teacher states, "No child should have to go through what Hannah experienced. It's the opposite of what schooling should be. And the impacts can be indelible. Last year, I had a new student in a similar situation. I mean, of course, he had his own unique learning profile, but he had also been bullied at his previous school. He spent the first month in my class with his hands clasped to his head. He wouldn't look up from his desk. He just braced himself." My core tightens again while my stomach sinks. She continues, "At our year-end conference, his mother was astonished. She said her child was a completely different person. Confident. Risk-taking. Laughing."

"Not bracing his head?" I ask.

"Not even close. In fact, he ended up taking the lead in one of the school's spring performances. We just need to show these kids that people care, and then they can blossom."

My hope soars. And the walls enveloping my trust begin to erode.

■ ▓ ▓ ▓

On the first day of school, Hannah asks me to walk her to her classroom. We arrive a few minutes early and see we aren't the only ones. About seven children are gathered outside waiting for their new teacher to unlock the door. I can tell Hannah is nervous, but she's also willing herself to be strong. To see so much fortitude in one small being is striking. Her earnestness. Her willingness to try to integrate into a new community. It's so much to ask of a little girl after all she's been through.

But I suppress all emotion. I will be her rock today.

Hannah stands at my side but doesn't hold my hand. She's doing this on her own today.

Then one girl lifts her head and greets, "Hi, Hannah." Her peers join her gaze.

"How do you know my name?"

She explains, "We met at your shadow day last year. Remember?"

"Oh, yeah." Hannah smiles. And she moves toward the group of girls. They show her a page in a book they hold among them, and then they giggle together. I pull out my phone and snap a picture. I'm not trying to capture a significant event. In fact, quite the opposite. I'm trying to document the simplicity, the ease. Last year, no children greeted Hannah when she walked into her classroom. On some days, she was met instead by fake bugs in her cubby. Or berries from the schoolyard smashed inside. But today, she's met with kindness and several smiles.

I text the picture to Jim and receive his quick reply: *I'm crying.* He gets it. Today, Hannah gets to belong.

Healing

While school is going better than I dared to imagine, I find it's not a panacea. We still need to venture into our surrounding neighborhoods on evenings and weekends. Landmines exist there, but we have no idea where. Even simple reminders—like running into former classmates at the ice cream store—upset Hannah. What used to be a fun place for my family is now anything but.

I learned about neuroplasticity over the last few months but hadn't fully appreciated the practical implications for our family. Now I understand that each time Hannah was exposed to bullying behavior, her anxious response became more engrained. So not only did the bullying impact her well-being at the time, it affected her future. She now doesn't trust the world to be safe. She has morphed from a curious, joyful participant in life to a wary little commando, bracing herself against future assault. I can almost envision Hannah donning camouflage as we leave the house, preparing to surveil her surroundings. It feels like Hannah's very childhood ceased when she was targeted and adults showed so little concern.

And the effects don't end there. One of the most confusing aspects of this whole ordeal is the sense that Hannah and I are stuck in a continuous loop, even though we left GCA three months ago. We're trapped in a time warp dealing with the repercussions of her experience and the board's "investigation" while those around us move through their lives with ease. Our world stands still while others march on. I'm told this is a classic element of PTSD.

Fortunately, we have a few close friends who rally around us, but most don't. When we run into old GCA acquaintances, many act occupied and divert their gazes. It's surreal to realize we're expected to shrug our shoulders, accept the shame, and head to a new school to start over while few others reach out to see how we're doing. This has an upside: I don't have to waste time on fake relationships. I can focus on my kids and help them get to a better place. But even this isn't clear-cut.

We don't want to teach our children to run from problems, as moving to a new school might appear. And we don't want to commit what Alcoholics Anonymous refers to as a "geographical"— taking the same struggles to a new location without addressing the underlying causes. So, I try to be introspective and own our part—but only our part. I decided last year that we shouldn't force Hannah to endure avoidable cruelty. We all have a right to opt out of unhealthy situations. Claiming your agency isn't failing or giving up. It's being smart and brave.

Since I'm not sure how to balance all of these concerns, I call on my therapist, Gail. I give her an update on the last few months, conveying the rollercoaster of emotions—from a deep, dark hole to some semblance of hope—and I admit to feeling debilitated at times. I ask her opinion on meds. I realize I probably should have asked earlier, soon after my soul seemed to leave my body as I broke down on that hard chair. But I've been focusing my limited energy on helping Hannah.

Gail shakes her head. She says that anyone would have been upset by the school's letter—that my response was not abnormal or dysfunctional. She acknowledges how devastating things have been, but she also points to all of the constructive efforts I've been able to make in the past few weeks. So, we agree to hold off on meds for now.

I then ask, "But how do I help Hannah heal when I'm still reeling myself?"

She directs, "Let's put your oxygen mask on first."

This is a gift since I've spent months prioritizing my family. But with her encouragement, I indulge and confess, "I'm so angry this situation robbed us of such special years. The kids are finally out of diapers and not yet teenagers. I realize raising kids is never easy, but this could have been a really special time, and it's been anything but. If only the school did what it said it would do."

"It's shameful," she acknowledges. And she asks how I've been processing my anger.

I fess up. "I guess I haven't really. I try to stay calm for Hannah's sake, but I feel rage—and so much more—just below the surface." I tell her I have horrible nightmares about losing my daughter in markets or of her getting kidnapped. And I have dreams where I'm completely alone and everyone is against me, no matter what I do or how hard I try. I wake up with my jaw clenched, and my body remains stiff all day.

My therapist explains that dreams are important tools for processing our lives because they help us turn current events into past memories. She says many people suffering from PTSD have trouble doing this.

This is now the third person who has used the term PTSD in reference to me. First, it was my friend Beth, then Hannah's new teacher, and now this expert. I assumed the first two were using the term colloquially, casually. But it feels different coming from my therapist's mouth.

Gail goes on to explain that people suffering from PTSD often live as though what happened a long time ago is likely to occur again today. "This is why retired soldiers might hear a loud noise—say a book slamming on the ground—and react as if a bomb went off." She says if my dreams don't help me process my family's "trauma," something called eye movement desensitization and reprocessing might help both me and Hannah.

She then describes the EMDR process, in which a therapist instructs patients to watch a light moving side-to-side, causing the patient's eyes to simulate REM sleep. Meanwhile, the therapist helps the patient talk through painful experiences, allowing them to become stored in memory banks, away from current realities.

The whole thing sounds a bit hocus-pocus-y to me, but at this point, I'm willing to try just about anything. So far, Hannah and I have employed tactics like meditation, mindfulness, and deep breathing. We've even worked to instill gratitude into each day by listing ten things we appreciate before going to bed. These strategies help a bit, but not enough.

Gail then validates that my anger is normal and understandable. She says, "It's healthy to feel anger when you've been wronged. I'd worry if you *weren't* angry." But she warns, "People who've been through betrayals like yours also often deal with shame. And people who were bullied or victimized, like Hannah, have an especially hard time coping with that shame. Shame is debilitating."

I remember renowned researcher Brené Brown saying as much.

My therapist continues, "It's important to help Hannah understand that what happened is *not her fault*. Her mistreatment reflects on the people who allowed it to happen. Not her."

We then brainstorm ways to help Hannah work through her emotions. I say, "I've been journaling, but what can she do?"

Gail notes that many people benefit from writing letters to their accosters even if they never intend to send them. She shares that one client drafted a letter to her dead dad, putting in print how damaging his actions were and all the things she wished she had had the opportunity to say before he died. The letter even included how she wished her father could have responded—what actions he could have taken and the very specific things he could have said to acknowledge and help relieve her pain.

I say, "Hannah keeps telling me she wants to speak with Richard to tell him how to run his school better . . . and with the board to help them understand the effects of bullying on kids. She doesn't love writing the way I do, so I don't know if a letter will appeal to her. But she's still so desperate for validation, for an apology. Unfortunately, I'm pretty sure the school won't meet with her like she wants. Jim and I already tried, and we got nowhere. Everyone was just so *awful*."

My therapist makes me reconsider when she asks, "Were they all? Is there *one person* who might meet with Hannah and give her the chance to share her feelings?"

I recall the one trustee who expressed empathy at our meeting last spring. Emily said, "We were just so sad to get your letter. I am so, so sorry."

I tell Gail, and she proclaims, "Wonderful!"

So, later that night, I reach out to Emily and ask her "mom-to-mom" if she could do this favor for us, for Hannah.

She agrees right away. There's genuine warmth in her voice as she promises to email me dates when she can meet with Hannah. That night after climbing into bed, I list ten things I'm grateful for. Emily is at the very top of the list.

■ ▩ ■ ▩

A week passes, and I don't hear from Emily. I assume she's been busy settling into the new school year, and I don't want to pester her. So I wait a few more days before I shoot a quick text.

Later that night, Emily calls. She's profusive. "I'm sorry it took me so long to get back to you! It's been hectic around here!"

I empathize with how busy the transition from summer to school is. And then I tread lightly as I ask, "I hate to impose, but is there a time that would be convenient for you to meet with Hannah? I doubt it would take more than fifteen minutes."

She stammers, "Well . . . about that . . . I've been thinking since we last spoke. You *know* I want to help Hannah, but I just have this weird feeling about it. I'm probably not the right person."

It takes a moment to absorb this blow. "Can you tell me what worries you?" I wonder if she, too, thinks I want to sue, even though I've been clear about my intentions. All I want is for someone to validate my child.

She explains, "At the end of the day, because I'm on the board, I don't feel I can speak to Hannah in the capacity of a mom."

"Okay, then would you be willing to speak to her as a trustee?"

Emily hesitates, "I do want to help. But it's just a crazy risk for me. I can't ethically meet with Hannah. I'd have to tell the board. It's awkward. It breaks my heart, Kayla. I just don't know what to do. My heart's pounding. I'm so sorry. I don't think I can do it."

This was supposed to be our saving grace. The chance to have at least one person, besides her parents, tell Hannah that she's not to blame for her mistreatment.

I've never been one to beg, but I need this. My family needs this. "Feel free to tell the board. We're not hiding anything. We're just hoping for some compassion for our nine-year-old." I wonder if she'll change her mind if she understands where I'm coming from. "A psychologist suggested we need to help Hannah get some sort of closure by having somebody speak to her to confirm that bullying isn't okay, that she shouldn't have to endure that."

Emily repeats, "I just can't meet with Hannah. I'm so sorry. This whole thing is gut-wrenching."

I'm ready to explode as I scream in my head, *Gut-wrenching? For you? You have absolutely no idea how gut-wrenching this has been.* Emily has not been the one trying to convince her child she is worthy of common decency. She hasn't spent three hours some nights trying to help her daughter fall asleep. She hasn't had to medicate her child just to reduce her anxiety so she can do everyday things other people take for granted, like eat, sleep, and step outside.

I'm so angry, I can barely contain myself. I will myself to speak rather than yell the words I wish I could say to the whole board. "We poured our hearts out to you, and all we got in return was a certified letter. Nobody even bothered to talk to us. The irony is the letter we sent wasn't to protect our own child. It was to advocate for *others*. But you guys responded by demeaning us and denying *any kind* of bullying. At all! Even though there's *reams* of evidence. A child was *suspended* for bullying Hannah. Multiple families are begging to share their experiences. Yet instead of listening to them, you deny all of us and shame the victim. In our case, you shamed A NINE-YEAR-OLD CHILD!"

My anger can no longer be tamed, so I hang up the phone without giving her a chance to respond. I don't think I've hung up the phone on anyone in my entire adult life.

I plow from my kitchen to my bedroom and back again feeling like I just might jump out of my own skin. I'm so upset that I can't be still. I break open the pantry door and scan the shelves. Isn't food supposed to be a source of comfort? But everything on the shelves looks disgusting. I can't do anything. I can't even eat.

I'm not just angry. I'm humiliated. And I'm incapacitated. I can't help my daughter. And now my body can't help me. My very nerves are fighting to jump off my bones. I don't blame them. I don't want to be me either.

As I pace, I resent that the school still affects me this much. *I want to be calm, damn it! How can these people still have this much power over me?* I realize it's because I wanted to believe that even though the school betrayed us, a single person (the one I had identified to be the kindest) would be compassionate. But even she cared more about defending the institution than the well-being of children.

That night, I lie in bed. I don't list any sources of gratitude. Emily definitely wouldn't make that list anymore if I did. Instead, I hear her say over and over:

"... *a crazy risk* ..."
"... *it's awkward* ..."
"... *my heart's pounding* ..."
"... *gut-wrenching* ..."

And then I realize, *Oh my God. I was talking to her amygdala.* Her fear overrode her entire sense of humanity.

It's little solace, but at least I understand.

Betrayal to Courage

I need a break from this town, so the next evening, I take the train to meet Jim for dinner at a chic little bistro in SoHo. I'm in search of a distraction, and the vitality of the city is the lure I crave. We order a drink while we wait for our table, and I spy an acquaintance nearby.

After we chat with her for a bit, I recall that she advocated for survivors of sexual assault in a previous job. So I cut from the small talk and tell her I've been thinking a lot about the ways our society regards people who've been abused. I say, "I just can't believe there isn't a more universal understanding of how to support people who've been mistreated."

She reminds me, "That's exactly what I've spent my whole career trying to do."

I know I'm preaching to the choir when I say, "You get it, but shouldn't people more broadly understand how to respond to those who've been victimized? Shouldn't people know not to ask rape survivors what they were wearing on the night of the rape, as if any answer could justify sexual assault? I mean, I don't care if she's lying naked in the middle of the street! You don't get to rape her!" Jim slips away to check on our table, probably relieved to escape, but the woman across from me is nodding, so I continue. "And what about the way the system treats parents whose unarmed kids were just shot in the back? I read yesterday about a child who was murdered and then his body was taken for drug testing while the shooter walked free with no testing. I can't imagine how that felt to the parents." I know this is enough to convey my point, but I'm upset and on a roll. "And what about court systems that allow lawyers to interrogate assault survivors and smear their reputations as if *they* are the culprits? I mean, it should be against to law to revictimize people that way!"

"It's criminal," she agrees.

I then acknowledge that I'm particularly sensitive to the issue because we've been going through some difficult stuff with Hannah, and I've spent months trying to understand how and why we treat people the way we do. I tell her, "I've been looking for some sort of guidelines for responding humanely to people who've just had their worlds blown apart. I would have thought that the police, the military, the education system, or *someone* would have some basic protocols that the rest of us can learn from, but I can't find anything at all."

She suggests, "Look up Jennifer Freyd and her research on institutional betrayal. Maybe it'll help?"

I thank her just as Jim returns to let me know our table is ready.

He raises one eyebrow and offers a goofy grin, as if to ask, "Are you ready to have fun?" I nod, crack a smile, and grab his hand feeling a little guilty that I allowed my ongoing exasperation to creep into our date night.

Apparently, not even the energy of the city can distract me from our family's saga—or my newfound mission. Or, maybe, its vibrancy is what inspires me.

■ ▧ ■ ▨

Upon my next reunion with my computer, I type "institutional betrayal Freid" into the search engine. Fortunately, my spelling error doesn't prevent Jennifer J. *Freyd*'s impressive body of work from appearing. I soon learn she and her team coined the term "institutional betrayal" in an effort to enhance the limited vocabulary available to address victimization and trauma.

I'm beyond grateful. And intrigued. So I keep reading . . .

The literature explains that institutional betrayal occurs when organizations fail to support those individuals who are dependent upon it. The concept applies to both actions, such as explicit policies and overt behaviors that unjustly harm people, and inactions, like failing to prevent or react reasonably to offenses. Researchers have shown that the institutional response is critical because it can exacerbate trauma—often severely.

While Freyd's work initially focused on sexual assault, several researchers have since demonstrated that institutional betrayal is relevant to a wide variety of abuses that occur across schools, businesses, healthcare systems, religious organizations, the military, prisons, and more. In fact, several experts, like renowned brain development scientist Bruce D. Perry, are acknowledging that "trauma can arise from quieter, less obvious experiences" like humiliation, shaming, and marginalization. Freyd notes that evolutions in understanding required daring and outspoken individuals to force the psychology field to look anew at dated stances.

I realize, *Maybe I need to do the same.* To this point, I've been hesitant to use terms like "trauma" and "PTSD" to describe my family's experiences. These words feel melodramatic and even ridiculous, especially when I consider extreme contexts like war or rape.

But today, my psychologist's advice reverberates in my head: "There is no Olympics of pain; nobody wins for hurting the most. There will always be somebody suffering more and somebody suffering less. Honor your own experience. Don't smother it under the traumas of others."

So I admit that, while my family is not at war, both Hannah and I are exhibiting signs that are commonly associated with PTSD. We avoid certain people and places, have upsetting dreams about the bullying and the school's response, feel detached from our community, are hypervigilant about potential threats, and are uninterested in activities we used to love.

I'm not surprised when I read studies that show betrayals perpetrated within relationships can be more harmful than abuses committed by strangers. Of course it hurts more to be wounded by a friend than a stranger. But institutional betrayal takes this concept a step further by revealing how institutions can aggravate an individual's trauma, often significantly, when they fail to respond appropriately. For example, research documents that targets of sexual assault in the military have worse health outcomes than those who suffer from sexual assault in the civilian environment.

When a person is violated by an individual, either known or unknown to the assaulted party, the effect can be traumatic, but when an *entire* institution is complicit with the abuse, the devastation can rise to a whole new level. The survivor is initially overwhelmed by one person's wrongdoing, but then the anguish is compounded by the realization the entire community effectively condones it. This understanding can trigger feelings of isolation and despair. It can also cause people to doubt basic goodness and humanity itself. Because of this, institutional betrayal is extremely toxic, leading to higher rates of dissociation, anxiety, depression, sexual dysfunction, PTSD, and suicide.

I'm once again reminded of my research on neuroplasticity when I read analogies between institutional betrayal and secondary concussions. Neurologists have shown that athletes who experience brain trauma can be more susceptible to future concussions. Effectively, a lower threshold can be set, aggravating the potential for consecutive injuries. Similarly, an assault to one's psyche can cause a person to be more sensitive to and impacted by successive betrayals. As a result, effective, compassionate responses by institutions from the outset are crucial.

Throughout her writing, Freyd documents a common coping

mechanism in traumatic situations called "betrayal blindness," defined as "the unawareness, not-knowing, and forgetting exhibited by people towards betrayal." In a previous life, I might have doubted that a victim of a serious offense could actually forget or reconstruct traumatic events to appear more benign, but now I understand how individuals might have trouble recollecting details after an attack, especially if authority figures or people they trust are doubting them or are developing alternate storylines. (And even more so if aggressors spend time grooming their targets into trusting them.) Understandably, the phenomenon of "betrayal blindness" is most common when survivors' well-being depends on preserving certain relationships or social systems. If admitting to an assault threatens their own safety or standing in a community, individuals can be more inclined to deny their understanding and toe the party line.

The research lists several factors that perpetuate institutional betrayal in an organization, like tolerance for abusive behavior, dismissal of reports, retaliation against those who speak up, refusal to implement protocols and meaningful consequences, and the prioritization of reputation over member well-being.

I realize, *Damn it. We experienced every single one.*

It looks like I finally have some language to wrap around what my family is experiencing and to explain why GCA's reaction feels strangely similar to the disturbing responses to trauma I've witnessed across the national news.

I'm especially bowled over when I learn that Freyd created an acronym that quite succinctly describes the common ways people treat victimized individuals: DARVO—*deny* the aggrieved party's experience; *attack* the words and character of the person claiming injury; *reverse victim and offender* so the perpetrator is cast as the aggrieved party and the target as the aggressor who's unfairly taking down the offender.

I sigh. *Check. Check. Check.* We experienced each one. Our efforts to advocate for Hannah were *denied* at every turn. And the school administration *attacked* us passively by casting us as not credible, while the board attacked us directly by victim-shaming Hannah. In suggesting Hannah was the problem, the board wasn't alone. The vice head, after all, called me to her office to explain the *roles* had been *reversed*. Hannah was deemed the tormentor who had to stay away from the children who bullied her for years. These DARVO tactics, and the fact that so many people were engaged in them, feel far more treacherous than Hannah's initial playground assaults. The latter were instigated by two children—the former by an entire community.

I take a seven-question survey Freyd and her colleagues designed to help institutions uncover, or identify a propensity toward, institutional betrayal. I then look down to see that I checked every single box. *We were betrayed at every turn.* I sting from this realization but also feel energized to have the language—*finally!*—to describe our difficult reality, so much so that I email Dr. Freyd to thank her.

I doubt she has time to respond to a stranger, so I'm surprised to find her name in my inbox a few days later. We end up talking on the phone, and she shares updates on her research. She also expresses empathy for Hannah's experience. But I don't want to stay stuck in this world of betrayal, so I ask, "What can we do? Where do we, as a society, go from here?"

She tells me about Institutional Courage, a program she created to help organizations "become sources of justice, support, and recovery—rather than betrayal—through accountability and transparency." She lists the fundamental principles and several supporting strategies, and I soon realize Dr. Freyd is providing the guidance I've spent weeks trying to find.

At the outset, she recommends engaging experts to educate community members on both the causes and effects of victimization. (After all, how can we prevent what we don't understand?) She also endorses explicit, consistent policies to both prevent and respond "sensitively and humanely" to each and every report of abuse. (No DARVO-ing allowed.) Her guidance reminds me of my counseling training, where I learned to use empathic listening skills, bear witness, and validate. When Freyd endorses tools like anonymous surveys, I recall the many times I begged the school to provide safe venues to report offenses. Freyd also notes the importance of not only being accountable but apologizing for all wrongdoing. This part burns because I know Hannah will never get an apology from GCA. As she summarizes, Freyd cautions that the work is never done. Policies must be monitored for effectiveness on an ongoing basis. And leaders must dedicate resources, "not just good intentions," to their efforts.

I thank Freyd for finally providing the guidance I've been seeking. And I admit that the aspect that's been disturbing me most is people's instinctual reluctance to believe survivors. I'm troubled by the ways we even demonize those who've been injured, enabling perpetrators to absolve themselves from all responsibility. I recall how dear friends reported victimization (like sexual assault or flagrant discrimination) and were subsequently cast as attention-seekers, troublemakers, or overly sensitive wimps. I tell Freyd I consider this unfair because, in fact, each one of my friends was motivated by a desire—a nagging awareness of a moral obligation—to protect others from similar offenses. I believe their efforts were brave and heroic, yet they were treated like treasonous villains.

Freyd agrees. "Those who do speak up demonstrate fidelity to, not a defection from, an organization's ideals and durability. We should be celebrating whistleblowers, not condemning them."

I thank her profusely for taking the time to talk with me, and after we hang up, I open my notebook to jot down several thoughts that have percolated for me over the past few weeks. Freyd has many powerful guidelines for responding to people who've been injured, and I now have a few ideas of my own. I expound:

- Managing abuse is a delicate process requiring compassion. Too often, the instinct is to defend the transgressor and the institution and DARVO the victim. We must counteract these trends, but we should not swing to the opposite extreme. The community deserves non-delayed due process, not an instant condemnation of the accused.
- To maintain integrity, organizations should appoint an unbiased, qualified, legitimate response team designed to pursue truth, not simply a lawyer or public relations strategist to protect one side or defend the status quo.
- In egregious cases and with the survivor's input, institutions should hire an advocate with the expertise to counteract "betrayal blindness" and DARVO.
- If misconduct is reasonably confirmed, transgressors should be encouraged to right their wrongs. All individuals, but children and young adults, in particular, might need guidance and support doing this.
- Since victimization often entails a power differential, policies and practices must rebalance control and re-empower those who've been traumatized.
- Action plans and leaders must respect survivors' autonomy and avoid the arrogant assumption that others know what victims need better than the victims do themselves. Survivors' needs should weigh heavily in determining the appropriate response.
- Survivors should be given time and flexibility to recover without loss of privilege, position, or rights.
- Survivors' future safety must be assured; too often, they are left with no option but to withdraw from their communities while their aggressors remain.
- Without exception, organizations should get survivors' permission before releasing information to the public that could reintroduce shame or trauma.

- When a community member victimizes another, the institution should reaffirm *publicly* its values and policies, leaving no doubt about its commitment to humane conduct.
- Organizations should instill checks and balances to avoid abuses of power, limit conflicts of interest, and protect the institution's mission. Trustees should be more than patsies.

I feel good about finally having some tenets for responding to people in crisis, which include both Freyd's published guidelines and a few of my own ideas, but my head hurts when I think about what it would take for GCA to implement any of them. From the outset, the school's response seemed to be the antithesis of what I spent the last hour discussing with Freyd.

When I told her how GCA brought in a lawyer to investigate our case, she exhaled deeply. She acknowledged that lawyers bring great strengths, but when they overshadow other professionals, an institution's goals and even its legitimacy "can be compromised quite easily." She observed that lawyers are generally risk-averse and hired to protect against the downside. But institutions with socially minded missions are hopefully the opposite. She noted, "Ideally, they are forward-thinking, audacious in action, and committed to the greater good. As a result, they benefit from engaging experts who can promote these higher values." She concluded, "When you operate out of a place of fear, you miss the opportunity to be courageous and compassionate."

I agree. And it seems to me that you also lose your soul.

What Did You Say?

As I continue to look for new ways to help Hannah recover, I read memoirs, like Chanel Miller's *Know My Name* and Bryan Stevenson's *Just Mercy*, which detail terrible ordeals, most far worse than our own. Yet their brave accounts help me process the nuances and complexities of my family's experience. I also read exposés like Ronan Farrow's *Catch and Kill* and John Carreyrou's *Bad Blood*, which detail how systematically leaders can discredit whistleblowers and cover up truth, all while associates remain passive and complicit. These judicious narratives help me parse through our own gaslighting and give me the confidence to affirm my family's truths.

The egregious affronts to decency throughout these books are shocking, but so too are simple, routine practices. For example, in *Know My Name*, Miller's lawyer says they will avoid choosing female jurists for her rape trial. The attorney explains that women tend not to empathize with sexual assault survivors and instead look for faults in the victims. Apparently, they hope to distinguish themselves so they can believe the same thing could never happen to them.

I share what I read with Jim and ask him, "Do you think this is why my friends on the board isolated me? And didn't stand up for Hannah? Do they need to paint her as different or strange or undeserving and me as crazy, coddling, and over-reactive so they can believe this won't happen to their own families?"

"Hmm. Maybe." Jim ponders more and nods. "That actually makes a lot of sense." He then asks, "Haven't Ellen or Heather reached out to you? I mean, since we sent the letter?"

He doesn't usually inquire about my female relationships. As a result, his question feels like a validation that I'm not ridiculous to expect something more from friends.

"I haven't heard a peep in five months," I admit. I trusted they would be our allies. Instead, they appear to have behaved more like the female jurists.

Jim wonders, "Do you think they want *you* to approach *them*? Now that their process is done?"

I'm confused. "That's a little strange, don't you think? The injured party needs to be the one to reach out?" I reconsider. "I guess I could." But that doesn't feel safe, so I say, "I think I just need to accept the fact that they didn't value our friendship in the way I hoped. And they didn't care about Hannah." It seems my daughter is not the only one who needs to rethink and reestablish her relationships.

■　▧　■　▨

As I continue reading *Know My Name*, I'm amazed that somehow, even at her lowest points, Miller appreciates any evidence of humanity. For example, when she reviews the police report of her rape, she doesn't focus solely on the assailant; she stops to consider the two Swedish men who intervened. Miller reminds herself that she was not alone by the end of her assault. Two good men acted to protect her. One of the Swedes rushed to check on her while the other tackled and yelled at the assailant, demanding, "Say sorry to her." Even in the heat of the moment, he understood the primal need for an apology.

I'm relieved to know people like this exist in the world. But I feel something else too.

Could it be?

I'm jealous.

How is that possible? My child wasn't the victim of rape, a trauma far greater than Hannah's. But it seems I want something this survivor has. I want some Swedes.

Or Norwegians. Or Fins. Or Danes.

Or Indians. Or Nigerians. Or Malaysians. Or Belizeans.

Or even Americans.

Really, anyone willing to take a stand to help others will do.

■　■　■　■

Before bed that night, Hannah asks when we can see her friend Ava. "I love Ava," she says.

"I know you do, Honey. I'll ask her mom when we can get together again."

But Hannah has a thought she hasn't completed. She asserts, "If anybody *ever* tried to bully Ava, I'd say, 'WHAT DID YOU SAY?'" Her voice is accusatory and unyielding. One hand is on her hip and the other is pointing firmly at the imagined antagonist. Her brows are furled, and her aura is undeniably intimidating, even to me. Hannah continues, "There is NO WAY I would let anybody say anything mean about Ava. NO WAY!" Then she lowers her voice to ask timidly, "Mom, what did you say to the kids who were mean to me?"

Oh, God. My heart sinks to the floor. She's not trying to hurt me, but I'm skewered. Mostly because, down to my depths, I know she's right. I did not do enough.

Hannah continues, "Did you yell at them?"

"Your dad and I had very strong words for people at school and on the board. We had many meetings to try to make them understand. We told them very firmly that what was happening was wrong, that things needed to change. Immediately." Even to my own ears, these words sound insufficient.

And, apparently, they're also not what Hannah was looking

for. She redirects me, "No, Mom. Did you yell at the *kids*? At Daniella and Lauren."

I flash to a conversation I had with another mother a year ago. She told me that when her son was bullied and the parents of the aggressor did nothing, she found the kid on the playground and threatened, "If you mess with Will again, I will rip your arm from your socket and stand here and watch you eat it. Do you understand me? You will EAT it. Got it? NEVER bully my child again."

I remember considering this alternative but only for a moment. I knew Daniella and Lauren could call my bluff, and I couldn't imagine threatening a child like that, even though I admired this other parent for having the guts to do so. I also still wanted to believe there were constructive methods adults could employ to resolve the situation. But now I know it's impossible to work with a system that refuses to acknowledge a problem in the first place. And by trying to collaborate, I fed my daughter to the wolves.

Hannah pulls me from my thoughts, questioning me again, "Mom? What did you say?"

I try to explain. "I can't yell at children, Honey. My job as an adult is to behave maturely. I would have loved to impose consequences on Daniella and Lauren, and I tried to work with the adults to make that happen. I know it wasn't enough, though. *I am so sorry*, Hannah. You did *not* deserve what happened. I tried my hardest to stop it, but it kept happening. I'm *so, so sorry*. Dad and I enrolled you at a new school because we don't want this ever to happen again."

"Why didn't you send me some place else earlier?"

"I tried. Remember? You were sure you wanted to finish the year." But then I slow down. I don't want her to feel responsible for her own mistreatment. "I think we were all hopeful that the school would do the right thing. They promised they were going to make things better. But now we know they lied. I'm just so glad you're out now. And I'm *so sorry* that your daddy and I trusted the school and didn't take you out earlier."

I look in her eyes and see something I'm unprepared for: resigned disappointment. She knows her parents failed.

My whole life, I wanted to be a good mother. And now I have unequivocal proof that I failed my child. This recognition is crushing to me. It must be for her too. I wonder, *Is this one of those coming-of-age stories, when a young girl learns she can't count on her parents or anyone else around her, for that matter? So she resolves to take care of herself from this point forward?* I suppose this kind of self-sufficiency is good, but it's not how I expected her to earn it.

I want to tell her again and again how much I tried, but it doesn't matter. I allowed the system to manipulate us all, and Hannah's not going to get the outcome she needs.

I want to rewind time. If I could start over, I would yell at every single person who allowed my daughter to be mistreated, *"WHAT DID YOU SAY? How DARE you hurt my daughter this way! How DARE you ignore the other children!"* I want to steal my daughter's voice and yell from the mountain tops, *"There is NO WAY you can do this to kids. NO WAY! SAY SORRY TO THEM!"*

And then I realize something else.

Apparently, I have raised a Swede.

Okay. Maybe she raised herself. I haven't earned the right to take credit. But there she is. Our very own Swede.

Apologies

After Hannah's rant, I can't deny she still craves an apology. Yet, even though experts like Freyd keep extolling the virtues of atonement, they remain elusive to us.

Truthfully, I wish Hannah wasn't so laser-focused on an apology. Her desire makes us pitifully dependent upon others. I'm tempted to tell her to "just get over it," but I've learned by now—through counseling training, research on compassion, and even personal experience—just how demeaning and counter-productive that phrase is.

I decide that rather than push Hannah to "get over it," I should help her "move through it," so she can escape our time warp and advance forward.

But how? I know we can't force others to care or be contrite or listen to their conscience. So what *can* we do? Why does this need for an apology have such a stranglehold on us?

I decide to submit to my modus operandi. *Why stop now?*

I find reams of research that endorse apologies as important tools for maintaining constructive relationships and promoting civilized societies. And while many institutions resist them for fear of increasing liability, studies show that apologies can actually decrease the risk of lawsuits. People feel less aggressive and retaliatory when they are heard and cared for.

This logic rings true to me. I never felt more like suing than when the school's board refused to acknowledge Hannah's experience and instead blamed her for her own abuse.

As I read further, it's clear that, at best, Hannah's peers delivered hollow, insincere "I'm sorrys." But forced contrition is meaningless. As Molly Howe states in *A Good Apology*, "When we teach [children] that saying the words 'I'm sorry' is all an apology takes, we miss an opportunity for them to learn about repair. We could instead raise the question[s:] . . . How can we fix what got broken? How can you make up for what you did?"

This sounds more constructive to me.

Unfortunately, kids weren't the only ones who missed the opportunity to repair damage. Most adults around us did nothing. And the few that approached me offered words that felt empty and self-serving. The research helps me understand that they were more akin to "fauxpologies," expressions that avoid accountability and any sincere demonstration of remorse. I learn fauxpologies are concocted quite easily by adding words like "that," "if," "you," or "but" on the tail of an "I'm sorry."

*"I'm sorry **that** it ended up this way."*

*"I'm sorry **if** I did something wrong."*

*"I'm sorry **you** feel hurt."*

*"I'm sorry, **but** there was a lot going on."*

Rather than repair relationships, fauxpologies sow seeds of distrust. I can see now that the best word to put after "I'm sorry" is simply: "I." And that the next necessary step is to take meaningful, demonstrable action. As Harriet Lerner says in *Why Won't You Apologize?*, "The sincerity test of an apology is in the follow-up."

The more I read, the more I'm struck by how consistent the principles for apologies are with what I've learned about crisis support, bullying prevention, restorative justice, compassion, *and* institutional courage. Experts across the board talk about things like dismantling unjust power imbalances, validating the survivor's experience, reestablishing the injured party's sense of control and self-efficacy, and separating intention from outcome. After all, just because you didn't mean to hurt someone doesn't mean you didn't hurt them. The uniformity in findings from disparate fields confirms their relevance for me. I can almost feel the confused mass in my brain starting to unravel and align.

I stumble across the writings of Aaron Lazare and feel like he connects with something deep inside my soul when he writes about the specific psychological needs that underlie people's desires for apologies. This is exactly what I've been looking for! His work helps me identify and understand what Hannah is going through.

Throughout several articles and in his book, *On Apology*, Lazare notes that one of the most vital needs, especially for egregious offenses, is the restoration, affirmation, and protection of the injured party's dignity. I can't imagine how humiliating it was for Hannah to lose control of her own body that day on the playground when her worry meter registered "one hundred out of ten." Despite her pleas, classmates pricked and prodded her, convincing her that ticks were biting her. Her anxiety attack was a public spectacle. Although she might not have the words for it, I now have the framework to understand that she wants her dignity affirmed.

Lazare also writes about the need for a demonstration of a shared social code. Several experts agree that in order to feel safe, people must witness community members upholding and enforcing their common values. I sigh as I recall Hannah's experience. Rather than enforce social codes, the school denied Hannah's very reality. And when we called trustees to account, they compounded the injuries even further. Lazare helps me understand that in a functional community, the opposite happens: leaders and bystanders rally to ensure their standards are upheld, and they encourage, hopefully even mandate, wrongdoers to repair the damage responsibly. This doesn't just help the victim. The effort affirms the dignity of all constituents, perhaps especially the transgressor's. When we encourage people to right their wrongs, we demonstrate our belief in their ability to be part of a loving community.

Several psychologists agree with other needs injured parties crave, like an admission of the transgression and an acknowledgment that the victim was not responsible. These sound so basic, which is perhaps what makes this situation so mind-boggling and disconcerting. We feel assaulted all over again because no one will break ranks and assure us that what happened was wrong and that Hannah didn't deserve it—that she is not to blame for her own mistreatment.

I can admit that, in many cases, two parties each have a hand in a conflict, and they benefit from taking responsibility for their parts. But I've learned of a critical exception: in cases of victimization, targets are never at fault. Victimization is not mutual. In fact, victims often already harbor too much undue guilt. It's absolutely inhumane to suggest they should carry more.

Many of the scholars also note the importance of bearing witness. Over the last few months, Hannah pleaded for a chance to be heard, understood, and believed. She even begged to meet with the head of school and the board, such brave asks for a young grade-schooler. Unfortunately, even the "nicest" school representative refused to speak with Hannah. So she now feels untethered and insecure. With nobody acknowledging her realities, she doubts her own judgment and sanity.

I recall the judge who presided over the harrowing criminal trial of the gymnasts' predatory doctor, Larry Nassar. She took nine days to allow over 150 girls and young women to take the stand in the protection of her courtroom so their truths could be recognized. I now understand the importance of victims' impact statements and how creating a safe space for people to address their persecutors while others bear witness is a vital part of healing.

Jim and I were able to share our grievances, but the forum—that ridiculous meeting with the executive committee—was fraudulent. I now believe they asked us to speak, not because they wanted to help, but because they wanted to learn our account so they could annihilate it.

According to Lazare, another of Hannah's key emotional needs was never provided: a guarantee that her safety mattered and would be assured. Instead, she was targeted time and again. The school never attempted to institute protective measures or shift the power imbalance. Instead, they reinforced it. Hannah was told *she* was the one who needed to keep away from her aggressors, as if their well-being mattered more than hers. And I recall how stunned I was to learn that a bully's father was nominated to the board, bolstering her family's power over ours. The move signaled the school's true values and the fact that it had no intention of supporting kids like Hannah. No wonder Hannah is now hypervigilant, trusting almost nobody.

I'm blown away when I read *How Can I Forgive You?*, particularly when author Janis Abrahms Spring advocates for a "transfer of vigilance," which encourages offending parties to hold themselves responsible for ensuring a safe environment thereby enabling the injured parties to finally let down their guards. I sense the clouds parting and angels singing when I read: "Wouldn't it make sense for the offender to spend as much time earning our forgiveness as we spend struggling to grant it?" But of course, no such effort was made for Hannah. She still doesn't feel safe.

The more I read, the more I understand what happened. Instead of acknowledging Hannah's truth and right to dignity, they "othered" her. Even the adults judged her, so her peers felt justified in their mistreatment. After all, if the school psychologist can shame my daughter in front of her classmates by expressing disgust at her anxiety-coping mechanisms, why shouldn't her classmates follow suit? And if Hannah's lead teacher can withhold the tools she needs to function well in the classroom, why should the other students respect her differences?

I'm looking for solutions to help Hannah move on, but all I'm finding is evidence of how wronged she was. So what can we do? I feel good about leaving the school, but I sense much more needs to be done.

Over the years, I've heard people promote the power of forgiveness. It's suggested that offering it is the righteous, virtuous thing to do, even when the offending party is unremorseful. But this doesn't sit well with me. In fact, I find it curious that people often expend more effort encouraging injured parties to forgive than pressing aggressors to own up to their mistakes. I think this reveals a lot about the way we regard—or disregard—people who've been hurt and the ways we reinforce power imbalances.

So, I wonder, *If I encourage Hannah to forgive her unapologetic tormentors, will I really be helping her?* Or will I be implying, "It's just the way it is," suggesting she has no agency and that she can expect more of the same going forward? Will I essentially be directing her to be complicit with her own abuse?

Spring writes that forgiveness without a demonstration of remorse is "cheap" and inhibits personal growth, autonomy, and constructive relationships. And even though some people insist non-forgiveness is bad for one's physical health, Lerner clarifies that it's probably more accurate to say that "nonproductive anger and bitterness" are detrimental to well-being. But these harmful feelings can be addressed in many ways, not just through a one-sided absolution of wrongdoing.

I look to Merriam-Webster for clarification and am shocked to read its definition of forgiveness: *to stop feeling anger toward (someone who has done something wrong): to stop blaming (someone).*

Wow. That's not at all what I expected. And it feels so much easier said than done. There's no explanation of *how*, the hardest part. I reach out to a dozen friends to see if I'm the only one who doesn't relate to the definition. I text: *What does forgiveness mean to you?*

Within the hour, I receive a variety of responses that reveal just how diverse people's relationship to the concept is, and I sense culture and personal experience are highly influential. The most obvious discrepancies relate to the most crucial aspects: who's involved and what's the purpose of the apology?

Some friends agree with Merriam-Webster. For them, an apology is a process within the aggrieved person to release shame, anger, and bitterness. It really doesn't matter what the offending person thinks or does. Forgiveness is an internal, empowering means of self-healing.

Many others, however, have a different working definition. One friend even texts: *Webster is so flat it's inhuman.*

And another says: *I know a lot of people write about the importance of forgiveness in the absence of apologies, but from my perspective, that is something else entirely—not forgiveness!*

For these friends, apologies and forgiveness are part of a symbiotic process between two parties in the hopes of repairing, or at least moving forward in, a relationship. Forgiveness is a response to a sincere demonstration of regret and contrition.

As I read on, it's clear that forgiveness is a nuanced thing, affected by factors like the offender's age, whether the behavior is ongoing, the severity of the misdeed, and the level of remorse demonstrated. And I'm struck by just how passionately my friends feel about forgiveness. Several say things like: *I can't believe I haven't considered this more. It's so important!* And *I want to circle back after giving this more thought.* Several do. Their words make me think we, as a society, would benefit from deeper conversations on the topic as well.

In the end, based on my own experience and cultural influences, I decide I identify more with the working definition that says apologies and forgiveness are elements in a collaborative process of reconciliation. It's about maintaining a relationship, and I can't do that single-handedly. Trying to do so leaves me feeling vulnerable and positioned for future abuse. And it doesn't release the shame, anger, and bitterness I want to get rid of.

So how can we move forward when no apologies are offered?

A few scholars promote a path of "acceptance." In theory, I like this concept, but I agree when a friend says the word sounds too passive. She texts: *Are we really supposed to just* accept *what happened to us?*

I brainstorm for alternatives and home in on the word "release." This action sounds more proactive to me, like it might allow my family to move forward with a clear mind about what happened, let go of the idea that the past can be changed, and abandon any false hope that the people who hurt us will behave differently in the future. We also don't have to continue participating in the same dynamic going forward. We can have agency and mold our own paths. Releasing might also allow Hannah to transfer guilt and shame to the people who more appropriately deserve them: those who committed the offenses. And I hope releasing could enable her to disassociate from the label of "victim." Nobody should be defined by what others do to them. Instead, people should be defined by their own actions. In formulating her own identity, Hannah can be empowered to reclaim the dynamic, capable, worthy, and whole individual she is. Yes, she's more battle-worn, but she also might be stronger and more insightful. Her experience enables her to understand things other people don't.

While I sense my family will never forget or fully "get over" the awful things that happened, I hope we now have a framework for moving forward in a way that feels genuine and empowering. Each of my kids, all kids, deserve nothing less.

■　▧　■　▨

I ask Jim to watch the boys while I take Hannah to a nearby pond. Like usual, she's entertained by animals as they glide along the shore and asks, "Can we feed them, Mommy?"

She knows my answer: "We need to let them stay wild. Feeding them will hurt them. But, here, I have another idea. There's something else we can throw in the water."

"What?"

"I'm feeling a little weighed down. I sense you are too. I think we're a little too heavy." She looks confused, and I realize she might think I'm suggesting we weigh too much. I don't want to recall the days her classmates said she was "so fat" her arm was "going to fall off" and made her question her body shape, so I clarify, "We're carrying more than our share." I pick up a stone and say, "I'm holding this rock to transfer my pain and anger to it. I feel awful when people say mean things to me, and I'm tired of it. So I'm putting my sadness here." I clench the rock and continue, "The mean words came from other people . . . from their sad hearts. It's not mine. I'm not going to carry it anymore." I then sidearm the stone across the water. It skips a few times as if it's trying to stay afloat. But ultimately, the good earth's gravity sinks that nastiness right out of sight.

Hannah stands still, considering what I've done, but she doesn't respond. So I make another move. "And this one? It's not the meanness, but it's something that's strangely bothering me even more. It's the indifference. The apathy." Her eyebrows furl. I rarely adjust my diction for her, but once in a while, her precocious mind needs an assist, so I elaborate. "I feel hurt when people act like they don't care. Sometimes they stand there and watch while others are mean to me. I hate when that happens. It makes me feel so bad. But, you know what? The decision not to help comes from *them*. It's *theirs*. *I* want to care when other people are hurt. So this isn't mine." I take two skips sideways for momentum and hurl the rock as far as I can. Unfortunately, my arm isn't as lithe as I remember. My rotator cuff spasms as my arm extends, causing my throw to be far less glorious than I expected. The rock sails only about twenty yards and lands in a loud kerplunk. Still, I enjoy the satisfaction of the low, absurd noise, and I appreciate that the rock doesn't waste time gliding across the surface. This one sinks hard and fast.

Hannah smiles.

"You wanna try?"

She looks unsure as she picks up her own rock. I ask her what it represents, but she doesn't say a thing. Instead, she releases the stone across the air, and I pray it carries some of her pain with it. Again, the loud kerplunk reverberates, and Hannah's rock descends out of sight.

The stone pickings along the shore get sparse pretty quickly, so we take a few steps back to see what else we can find. And then I spy something unexpected. I lean over and direct, "Hannah, look!" My new stone is slightly pointed at the bottom and has two uneven lumps on top. I slip the heart into her pocket and declare, "This one we keep." She smiles.

We spend the next few minutes throwing rocks into the water. Sometimes Hannah looks unsure. Sometimes her face crumples with scorn. A few times, she looks satisfied. I imagine my own face displays a range of emotions as well.

When Hannah holds up a contorted rock with a crooked shape and a fissure down one side, I smile. "Oh, yeah. That's an ugly one. Let that one go. What does it represent?"

She retorts, "No, Mom. I'm keeping this one. It's different. And beautiful. I like it." She turns it over a few times, examining its complexities, and then she eventually slides the rock into her pocket, right next to the heart.

Yes, I think. *Keep that one. Absolutely keep that.*

Expert Opinion

G ood days with the kids bring me some semblance of peace. At times, I'm even able to suspend emotion and analyze the world with detached objectivity. When I do, I find human behavior fascinating. Yes, it can be devastating, but it can also be entirely, ridiculously astounding. People do some mind-bending things. And more remarkable: often, no one else blinks an eye.

I can't recall who wrote a study I read years ago, but I remember the central theme. The author analyzed market bubbles and crashes—everything from the tulipmania of the 1600s (which apparently wasn't as widely devastating as some have suggested) to the 2008 subprime mortgage crisis (which was). The researcher noted that in each case, people projected and warned others about the impending fall. (In *The Big Short*, Michael Lewis documented the ways some investors alerted authorities about the perilous conditions in the mortgage industry before profiting absurdly from the wreckage.) These heralds were often uniquely educated and distinctly positioned to see things laypeople couldn't. But when the harbingers sounded alarms, people laughed. The *masses* laughed. Skeptics even treated those who tried to caution others like eccentrics, or worse, like "lunatics." And then, well, we all know what happened.

I see the phenomenon playing out around me in everyday

life. People who know very little about an issue often feel completely justified dismissing others with more expertise.

I recall how both the head and the vice head of school—who, as far I can see, have no training in bullying prevention—summarily rejected my reports, even when I backed them up with research. They also refused to accept third-party expert training on the matter. The board, too, rebuffed legitimate accounts, all the while declaring bullying atypical in elementary school. Yes, the fear of lawsuits might have motivated their actions, but the instinct is common, even when no legal risks exist. For example, although Hannah's teacher had no training in neuropsychology, she snubbed a PhD's assessment that Hannah required certain accommodations to manage her sensory-processing issues and learn. Her doctor is highly regarded in her field, the best I could find, yet the inexperienced teacher negated her unequivocally. Smugly.

How is it that people feel so comfortable refusing the insights and understandings of those who are especially trained in the matters at hand? Wouldn't they like to gain relevant knowledge so they can be more effective themselves? It seems our amygdalae never go to sleep. People feel uncomfortable with what they don't know, so they instinctively dismiss the unfamiliar, especially if it's threatening.

Unfortunately, the tendency to negate experts isn't isolated to school. The news continues to document instances of people overriding authoritative scientific viewpoints and, apparently, feeling completely justified in doing so. And I see it around town as peers cast off even their own friends. Naturally, nobody knows more about one's life than the individual actually living it. Yet, all too often, when someone tries to discuss a personal experience, others with no involvement in the matter negate the person who just *lived through it*. When I alerted friends about our peers' troubles with racism, they asserted that the affected parents must have "misunderstood." My friends weren't present, but they assumed they knew better. The school's trustees did the same: when they buried my letter, they not only ignored reports of bullying, they rejected several references to racism. And in the process, their brains might have calmed down but a disturbing trend remained. The power imbalance endured.

After all my research, I understand why people feel comfortable dismissing others. But I still hope for something better.

I'm Sorry You

A few months into the new school year, I get a text. Out of nowhere. I'm only half realizing who it's from as I read:

Hey, been thinking about you. I hope all is well. Sending love.

After half a year of silence, Heather is reaching out.

What do I say? Why is she contacting me now? Is she finally checking in to see how my family is doing? My fingertips fly across my phone:

Wow. I'm surprised to hear from you after all that's happened.

Her reply is quick:

Just because we had different points of view doesn't mean I stopped caring. I assumed you wanted space, but I still consider you a friend. I drove by your house yesterday and naturally thought of you.

Hmm. She believes our separation was a favor to me? And after a little ride in her car, it's time to let bygones be bygones?

Well, I've got to give her credit. She was brave enough to reach out. Most others haven't been.

Or, maybe I'm not witnessing bravery. I reread her text and note her choice of words, which convey a profound lack of awareness for how I might receive her, especially after suffering through the consequences of her actions—and inactions.

Much of my generation was taught to raise our chins, to "suck it up" and walk back into the fray to resolve issues, even if it meant denying our own needs. We were trained to "be the bigger person," which implied taking whatever steps were necessary to repair a relationship, because relationships—and the maintenance of peace—mattered more than individual needs.

These philosophies were instilled in me directly and indirectly over almost four decades, but I sense my body resisting now. The last few years, some good therapy sessions, and a lot of research have made me question my programming.

And I see red flags. I see red flags all over the place. What's happening is not okay. I will not paint the red flags pink. I now know I can make a different choice. I don't have to repair a relationship with someone who demeaned me and my family. I don't need to be complicit with my daughter's betrayal. It won't make me a "bigger person."

I type:

Unfortunately, I don't think you realize how much pain you caused.

I don't expect to hear back. My words aren't exactly welcoming. But a few minutes later, I read:

I'm sorry you feel that way. I tried to be sensitive, but clearly I had a different point of view than you did. I'm sorry that it turned out this way.

Huh. The classically unremorseful, "I'm sorry *you*," cleverly diverting culpability my way. The phrase suggests *I* am to blame. If only my pesky feelings didn't get in the way, everything might be okay.

But that's not all. Unsatisfied with the "I'm sorry you," she tagged on the cleverly obfuscating "I'm sorry *that*," again denying any personal responsibility. It seems she believes we are all just victims of unfortunate circumstances beyond our control. *Oh well! We can wipe our hands of that unfortunate, little series of events now, can't we? Glass of rosé, anyone?*

How the hell do I respond?

I type:

You are referring to a "different point of view." I'm dealing with the consequences of the board's dismissal of our very painful reality. Not only did you conduct an incomplete, bogus investigation, but you actually victim-shamed our child!

I hover over the send button, but I know she won't be able to handle this. She's still saying "I'm sorry *you*." So I backtrack the cursor to start over.

I hinted at our painful reality, but she was unfazed. I wonder what would happen if I helped her *feel* what it's like to be on the receiving end of texts like hers. I could get her attention with something like:

I know your sister was raped by a boy she dated, and you feel guilty about not saving her. But I don't think you need to feel responsible. We all know how she flirts. And she dresses provocatively. They probably just had a few beers and got carried away, right? You know how it goes. I doubt it could really be called rape. It was a date, after all, right? Just my point of . . .

I start deleting before I finish. I don't want to prove my case by being as cruel as she's been. Besides, I don't think she'd allow herself to consider the analogy.

My frustration mounts as I reread her texts. Her commitment to her "point of view" is infuriating. She seems to think this is just a simple matter of differing opinions and the stakes weren't that high, so we should just agree to disagree. But the stakes were high, and her words now only continue the betrayal.

Damn it. I was having a great day until her text lit up my phone. I had moved *on*. I had released the pain. Or at least I thought I had.

I wince, embarrassed to admit how much I still want to be heard. To be believed. The realization that I remain exposed and vulnerable to others tears at a wound I thought was closing. This frustrates me. I sit up and reach for my phone. I guess I still have some fight in me. So I text:

I realize you have a point of view, but . . .

But what? It doesn't matter what I say. She has rationalized all her actions so far. Why would she stop now? She hasn't asked how I'm feeling. She hasn't tried to understand my experience. Instead, she remains high on her own logic. She seems quite proud of it, actually. She wasn't even present when Hannah was bullied. But she's still absolutely certain of her own "point of view."

And since there's no way for me to convince her otherwise, I need to find a way to "release" what happened . . . and what's happening now.

I type:

I have no words. You don't seem to understand, and I don't think I can be the one to explain it to you. Especially if you are going to chalk it up to a difference of opinion. Your words only continue to hurt.

This time, I hit the send button and turn off my phone.

I picture her reporting back to her friends that she *"tried"* to reconnect, but I was just *"too sensitive, too irrational."* I suppose I should care that they are likely to agree with her, but I don't have the energy, and I want to release them all.

This understanding bolsters me. I note that my body actually feels a bit more stable.

But then I'm betrayed by a single tear streaming down my face. It seems that while my mind knows that this friend, actually an entire group of friends, was lost to me months ago, I'm only processing the grief of it now. My path for reasoning and my path for feeling aren't in synch. What can I do but be patient while the laggard catches up?

I resign myself to this plan, but then I sense a new surge of strength and resolution. I'm even a little indignant as I ask myself, *Really? Will you really miss her? And the others?*

I feel a resounding, *No! You can't hurt my child and still be friends with me. No way in hell!* Conviction runs through my bones. This fidelity to my experience—to what I know to be true—is unfamiliar yet solidifying. I feel whole. Secure. I'm even a bit enchanted as I realize, I *like* this state of being. This sense of self.

I wonder if maybe the practice of releasing is not just about letting go but also about becoming more integrated within myself—allowing my feelings and my beliefs and my understandings to unite so that my foundation can stand firm. Yes, that sounds so much better and truer than anything else I heard today.

Mama Bear

Hannah is not the only one settling into a new way of life. Jake and Theo are relaxing into their new schools too. And Jake is loving his new co-ed flag football team, which I only agreed to when Jim promised there would be no tackling. After all I've learned about neurology, I want to safeguard his young brain.

My family stands on the sidelines while Jake scurries around the field. I lean down to show Hannah which little red jersey is his, but as I point, I watch her face go blank. She then perches both her feet on one of mine, clings to my torso, and burrows her head into my side.

"Mom! Lauren's sister is here!" It's a whisper that somehow screams in high alert.

I look up and, sure enough, spy Lauren's younger sibling on an adjacent field. She's probably six inches shorter than Hannah, but somehow the mere sight of this small child incites panic . . . and an instantaneous metamorphosis. A few moments ago, Hannah was confident and playful, showing little Theo how to use a camera to take pictures of Jake. But now, she's vying to climb inside me. If she could access my womb, I bet she would.

After situating Hannah at a new school, countless therapy sessions, and organizing activities like releasing rocks—and pain—into a pond, this sighting of a little girl, who's not even the actual perpetrator, has destroyed months of hard work in a matter of seconds. Hannah is now incapacitated.

"Mom, can we go? Please?!" She's trembling.

I know I shouldn't reinforce the notion that that this sibling is a genuine threat, but I suppose I, too, am overcome. I can't believe we're so easily undone, and I want to avoid more pain, so I turn to Jim and ask, "Sweetie, can you take Hannah home? I'll stay here with Theo."

He agrees, but we both shake our heads, depressed by how easily things fell apart. A beautiful afternoon just turned upside down.

■　■　■　■

The next weekend, I ask Jim to stay behind to meet the dishwasher repairman while I take Jake to his game. But Jim shows up with our two other kids in tow during the first quarter. He explains that the repair was cancelled at the last moment.

Hannah sidles up to me, tugs on my sleeve, and asks, "Mom, can we talk?" Her words sound urgent. I lean over, and she informs me, "Lauren's here. And I want to talk to her. She's on the playground. Will you come?"

My mind screams, *Oh, hell no. Can't we be done with this? Didn't we release all of this?* But I try to understand and ask, "What do you want to say?"

"I want to tell her that what she did was inappropriate."

Again, Hannah's using language beyond her years. And it seems she has more processing to do, more psychological needs to address in order to finally move forward. Maybe she feels that, with me nearby, she's in a safe space where she can speak her truth and lay claim to her dignity. Maybe she can finally deliver her own sort of victim impact statement. The experts say this is crucial. *How can I say no?*

"Okay. But what, specifically, are you going to say?"

"I want to tell her what she did was unacceptable."

"Hannah, that word is a bit mature. Can you say that what she did was mean?" I know her advanced vocabulary drives kids to tease her, and I want to limit the chance of more abuse.

She agrees, so I leave Theo with Jim, and she and I head toward the play structure.

But Lauren is nowhere to be seen. I assume her mom took her to another commitment, and I'm secretly relieved we might have averted disaster. But Hannah looks crestfallen.

After the game, Jim takes Theo, while I grab the hands of my other two, and we head toward opposing parking lots. The three of us only get about half way before Hannah stops in her tracks and squeaks, "Mom, look!"

I lift my head to see Lauren's father walking toward us. It seems he's the one in charge of taking Lauren's little sister home today.

Hannah's eyes plead as she begs, "Mom, can I talk to him?"

Oh, wow. I was not expecting this. She wants to approach a 200-pound adult? There's no longer any denying she needs to be heard. And maybe it's better to speak to a grownup. Who knows how Lauren might have responded, but an adult should at least be civil.

I direct, "Just say the one thing you wanted and then come back. Okay?"

"Will you come with me?" Hannah implores.

I worry my presence will overshadow her bravery, and I don't want to do anything to suggest I put Hannah up to this. So I respond, "Jake and I will be right behind you, but it seems this is what *you* need to do. Am I right?"

She nods, and I promise to stay nearby.

Hannah hurries toward what must feel like a giant, and Jake and I pick up our pace to remain about fifteen feet behind. As she reaches Lauren's dad, she taps his leg. "Excuse me?"

I almost laugh, thrown by her polite introduction.

Hannah continues, "What your daughter did was unacceptable."

So much for toning down the vocabulary! But she looks so polite and innocent . . . and still so strong. I can't help but be proud of her.

Lauren's dad looks down at her and then up at me.

I don't want Hannah to feel isolated, so I speak in a way I hope reassures her, "It was hard for *all* of us." I will not let her feel abandoned again.

Lauren's dad then shifts his gaze back down to Hannah and bellows, "You know, *Hannah!*" He's almost spitting her name. "It takes *two!*"

In an instant, Hannah deflates. Her shoulders heave forward, and she looks at me in shock. "Is he saying it's my fault?" Her upside-down clown face is in full effect. She sounds almost tortured as she begs me to help her understand, "Is he saying I deserved it?"

The vision of her looking so defeated, right after doing something so brave, wrecks me. I'm so enraged and desperate to put things back on track that I school him, "*Nobody* deserves to be bullied. Bullying is *not* a two-way street."

He then yells at *me*. "There WAS NO bullying!"

I, too, am now in disbelief. "You still don't take responsibility? Lauren was suspended for bullying. And you still can't own it?"

"No. I don't. *We* don't." He scoffs at Hannah, "You need to get your facts straight and leave my kid alone."

Holy shit. He's DARVO-ing her! Deny, Attack, Reverse Victim and Offender. Now that I've been taught, it's so much easier to identify. *A grown man is DARVO-ing a child.*

And now she's crumpled at my side. This was supposed to be her catharsis, the day others bore witness, but she's incapacitated. My eyes penetrate his, and with every fiber in my being I demand, "Look. What. You've. DONE! Look what you've DONE to this child!"

My anger swells, and I'm in full attack mode. I don't care who hears me, who sees me. I don't care that I'm dehumanizing myself. I have morphed into a full-blown mama bear. Not some cute little thing in a storybook. I feel the power of a full-grown, wild grizzly, ready to annihilate the human who just attacked my offspring. I have two years of anger pent up inside, and I let it escape. "YOU SAY SORRY TO HER!" I am more determined than I have ever been in my entire life, but he remains still. In the heat of the moment, I've forgotten that we can't hope for an apology, so I swell again, and with every particle of my being, I command, even more forcefully this time, "YOU. SAY. SORRY. TO HER!"

It's a risk, I know. Because if he doesn't comply, I have no recourse. What am I going to do? Beat him with my fists? But I go all in, stiffening every cell in my body, coordinating them to demand he take me seriously. I have nothing to lose. This is the only thing I want in the entire world right now. My eyes are surely hurling daggers.

He blinks. Do I sense confusion? Perhaps he's never seen a woman this mad.

He starts, "I'm sorry, b—"

And I cut him off before he can complete the offending "but." I will not give him the opportunity to demean her again, so I own every inch of the airwaves. He tries to talk over me, but I don't allow him even one syllable. He's blocking our exit, so I grab my children's hands and unleash a verbal tirade as we careen past him. "You are an a—" I hesitate to curse with my children at my feet, so I finish with, "awful, awful person!" I continue, my voice sharpening. "You stay away from us! From my entire family! If I see you within twenty yards of any of us, I'm getting a restraining order!" I know this probably doesn't make sense, but I passed reason long ago. I'm now just doing whatever I can to get my children to safe ground. I keep spewing words so he can't hurt Hannah again. He's already shown me what he's capable of, and I'm not sticking around to see how much worse he can possibly be.

We finally make it to my car, and I help my kids pile in, shutting the door to shield them from the treacherous world outside. Outside the car still, I finally allow myself a moment alone.

Damn it! Damn it! Damn it! Why did I let her approach him? I failed. Again!

Trying to control my trembling fingers, I grab the driver's door handle, drop into my seat, and seal the three of us inside. "Guys, are you okay?" I scan their faces, assessing the damage.

Jake nods with a blank expression.

And then Hannah proclaims, "Mom! I had no idea he was so *mean*."

"I'm so sorry. Are you okay?"

"Yes. But he was scary."

"What part scared you most?" I will go to the source of pain.

"He was yelling. Why was he yelling?"

"I yelled too. I didn't want to give him the chance to be mean again." But I'm curious. My mind is on such high alert that I can't think straight. "Who yelled first? I did, right?"

After the grizzly's escape, my ability to think clearly disintegrated. If an officer approached me at this very moment, I don't think I could recall the order of events. My mind is frantic. The nerves along my arms are electrified, and this loss of control unnerves me. If I can't remember the chronology of what transpired just a few minutes ago, how can rape survivors recount details to investigators hours later? Or in front of juries *months* later?

"No, Mom. He definitely yelled first. He's really scary." But Hannah is saying this with conviction rather than fear. She doesn't actually look scared.

I want to validate her assessment, but I also want to diminish his standing in her mind. I want her to "release" him. So I respond, "He's tall. And he yells loudly, but he's not strong. Strong people take responsibility for their actions and help children learn to as well. That would have been the strong thing to do."

She nods, and her apparent understanding makes me wonder if, perhaps, I've been protecting them too much. They're old enough to know the truth. So I concede, "Not everyone is kind out there. Some people act like real jerks."

They both laugh, surprised, and maybe a little thrilled, to hear me use this language.

And then we all fall silent as we process what just happened. I let the keys dangle from the ignition, aware I need to calm down before operating a two-ton vehicle.

From the backseat, Hannah finally breaks the silence. "Mom, thanks for what you said." I twist to look Hannah in the eye again while she continues, "Now I see what you were up against." She explains this with an assurance that makes me feel like she just aged thirty years in one fell swoop.

"Hannah, now that we know they'll never admit they behaved badly and truly apologize, can we just stay as far away from them as possible? They're not going to give us what we need."

"Yes, Mom. I want nothing to do with them."

"Me neither!"

Still shaken, I turn the key and begin our drive home.

■　■　■　■

Back at the house, the kids race upstairs, and I find Jim in the kitchen.

I report without preface, "I fucked up."

He's confused. "What do you mean?"

I repeat, "I fucked up." And then I explain, "I blew up at Lauren's dad. Right in front of the kids," and I recount the entire disastrous event.

When I'm done, I sink my head between my shoulders. *How could I have allowed our kids to face further abuse? How could I have let them see me lose control? It was a public spectacle.* I feel the failure throughout my entire being.

But my husband smiles when he says, "Honestly? I think that's the best thing that could have happened."

I must look perplexed, so he explains, "Hannah saw you defending her."

I consider the notion. *Was this meltdown between adults really something to be happy about?* It violated, on almost every level, the model of decorum I've been taught to pursue—the level of comportment that "good women" are expected to maintain. And yet, Hannah *did* thank me in the car.

Jim reasserts, "This is great!" And then he adds, "That asshole fucking deserved it. It's about time somebody called him out to his face."

I realize Jim is trying to give me all the credit, so I remind him, "Actually, it was Hannah who approached him first."

"Even better! A *child* finally told him what's right." Jim couldn't be more pleased. And then he notes, "Now we know where his kids learned how to behave."

"No kidding," I agree. But it's not a victory for me. My heart sinks for those children.

Jim notes, "I bet the school's refusal to acknowledge his daughter's behavior only emboldened him."

"You think so?"

"Definitely."

And I'm sad to realize he's probably right. Nobody's actions popped out of a vacuum. This was not just two adults yelling at one another. This was a whole system failure.

I take full responsibility for losing my cool. I'm not proud of it. But it might have been a long time coming.

■　▧　■　▧

Over the following weeks, Hannah recounts the confrontation multiple times, but I notice she hardly mentions GCA anymore. It no longer seems to have a hold on her. Perhaps she's starting to distinguish between the past and the present. The yelling at the park—people defending her—is her current reality. Not her years of abuse. Maybe she's releasing and moving forward.

She must be proud of her bravery. Not only was she willing to approach her tormentor but the imposing, booming overlord as well. After all the time I spent trying to help her, *she* showed *herself* that she is capable and worthy. She initiated her own catharsis.

I feel blessed to bear witness. The canary is taking flight.

Up and Out

I notice Hannah chewing on her hair less. She sleeps better. She laughs more. Life is not perfect, not even close, but she actually looks forward to school most days. Her doctor suggests we might want to consider tapering or perhaps even eliminating her meds. When Hannah asks for a playdate with a friend, I realize it's the first time in over a year that she wants to interact with a classmate after school. While she once held her head down—kept to herself to ward off blows—she now looks up and out.

I remind myself that we have embarked on a lifelong journey and, with unique children in particular, the path will continue to present twists and bumps. But our road is now traversable, and I'm grateful to be on it.

I consider that it wasn't just one thing that got us here. There are no quick fixes to the kind of mistreatment Hannah endured. A new school was necessary, but not sufficient. And maybe the concept of releasing played a part. Perhaps she has started to integrate what she feels into what she knows, to be more confident and grounded, the lesson I learned while texting with Heather. She also had a few emotional needs met that day at the park. Her journey has not been direct nor simple, but slowly, Hannah is moving forward.

I notice I might be moving forward too. I am still a bit untrusting, but I no longer feel like I'm in a deep, dark hole. I'm sleeping better, my neck aches less, and I can exercise more now that my back doesn't feel so misaligned. I, too, am looking up and out.

I do find myself close to crying sometimes, but the emotion is often a reaction to small acts of kindness. Things I used to think were merely "cute" now leave a lump in my throat. When I witness a young child caring for an injured animal or a stranger getting out of her car to help someone walk across the street or a teacher working extra hours to help his student feel more secure, I realize that feeling "choked up" is literal. I think some people use the word "verklempt" to describe the sensation, and I welcome the sweetness attached to it.

■ ▩ ■ ▩

The day before winter break, Hannah asks me to join a *shacharit* prayer service. She has attended this school for only four months and she does not know Hebrew, but today she will chant a section of the Torah in front of about seventy students and ten adults. She's no longer bracing her proverbial head.

Hannah practiced the prayer for weeks at home. She reviewed the English translation, but today she chants in Hebrew. Despite her limited familiarity with the language, she seems to appreciate the message.

I realize I'm witnessing the antithesis of Hannah's world last year when, despite being prepared and eager, she couldn't summon the confidence to present her president report in front of her class. I'm beyond grateful that she's finally found a real home where she can be supported, valued, heard, seen, and *known*— where she can be respected for who she is, all of her, including her differences.

When Hannah completes her reading, the rest of the children join her effort. As the swell of rhythm pervades the room, I'm reminded of cultural beliefs, as well as medical practices, that promote the healing powers of chanting. I see it in action in here.

The tempo literally shakes and releases joy from within the children. The vision of a room of students singing and clapping, sometimes in unison and sometimes completely—utterly, almost impossibly—off-beat, is fully and gorgeously life-affirming. My faith in our collective future intensifies as I smile at the girl, my beautiful, brave, singular canary, leading the effort. I appreciate that by allowing her to be here, this community proves the boundlessness of goodwill and humanity. Yes, around the world, and even very close to where I stand now, individuals have used religion—and many other belief systems—to justify judging and segregating people who are different. But here . . . today . . . this community accepts someone who doesn't fit their mold.

The experience is absolutely stunning. Here, "every single one counts." Hannah is not just tolerated. She is celebrated, as is every one of her peers. I can't imagine a God who would want anything different for the world's children.

I wonder, *What if we could all do this for one another throughout our lives?* This simple effort of valuing both our individuality and our shared humanity could have a tremendous outcome. More of us could experience something I was starting to think was unattainable, but I now know to be lifesaving:

Up and Out

שלום (Shalom)

Amani

शांति (Śānti)

和平 (Hoà Bình)

Maluhia

ᎣᏍᏓ (Dohiyi)

Paz

سلام (Salām)

Vakaçegu

Мир (Mir)

صلح (Solh)

Emem

和平 (Hépíng)

Pokój

Peace

Everywhere

With the first dusting of snowflakes, my kids beg for skating lessons. I wait in the stands catching up on texts and emails as I overhear two women. One is clearly distressed.

". . . crazy . . . frustrating . . . judgment . . . They say he'll *outgrow* it, but I'm not sure."

I've treaded these waters. With only a few words, I know there's a deeper story, an undercurrent. So, as unobtrusively as possible, I ask a simple question. And the dam breaches.

"How did you know?" Her eyes look both shocked and grateful.

"I've been there. I *am* there."

We talk for a while, and later that night, I email her some information—bits and pieces from my research notes and a quirky little story about a crate full of eggs—just to reassure her that she's not alone.

The following week, a woman who's been an acquaintance since childhood asks while our boys run around a play structure, "Do you know of a good neuropsychologist?"

I'm surprised she's so direct. Most people pose these questions in hushed tones, if at all. But I suppose our shared history makes me safe. And I've been open about my family's journey; I'm finding my transparency makes me a harmless place for inquiry.

I ask a question, and she's soon telling me about the isolation, the confusion, and "rocking the boat." I later email her a journal entry about a walk in the woods, and she texts: *You are my angel. Thank you for sharing. How did you know I was feeling all this? You mean I'm not alone?*

Not long after, I run into a friend in an occupational therapist's waiting room. She whispers, "I hear Daniella and Lauren were caught using school-owned iPads to cyberbully some classmates. And that Daniella was talking about suicide to her classmates. She actually asked their opinions about whether it would be better to drown or jump from a building."

Jesus. They're only in fourth grade. I take no pleasure in hearing this, especially since my crisis training tells me this nine-year-old has laddered halfway up the diagnostic tool used to determine if she's an imminent threat to herself. I wonder if anyone will hold themselves accountable if something awful happens to her. I hope the pit in my stomach isn't signaling the answer.

Before her son's session ends, my friend asks the receptionist for a pair of scissors and cuts the labels out of his jacket as she moans, "He's just so sensitive! Everything is difficult. Tags in clothes! Smells! He's driving me nuts!"

I ask a few questions to confirm my intuition. And then, later that night, I send the name of a book and a journal section I wrote long ago, near the beginning of our journey when I was just getting to know my daughter in a way I never expected. The experience taught me so much about myself as well. The entry is about a canary.

By now I'm so very familiar with the identifying marks that I sometimes detect the parents struggling to support unique children after they speak only a few syllables. I can't possibly know the details of their experiences, but I recognize their bewilderment. Their loneliness. Their exhaustion. Sometimes even their depression.

When I express understanding, parents seem to break at the seams. They need a release. To be heard. To be believed and seen. Most of the time, they work hard to abide by the Code and present a calm, competent image to the world. But when I offer them a space for private confession, they split open and liberate their truths, often in spite of themselves. One insists, "You should write a book."

I balk. *Hell, no,* I think. *My writing is for me. A private journal. It's not fit for public consumption.* But, if I dig deeper, I know my real excuse is different. I've seen what people do to those who reveal uncomfortable truths. I don't think I'm ready to set myself up for more judgment. Haven't we been through enough?

But as I move forward with my family, I keep spying canaries among us. They're everywhere! While many are vocal and glorious, not all are free. I'm sad to find some on ill-fitting perches and many forced into cages that weren't designed with their specific needs in mind. Some even have veils over them, often draped by loving, well-meaning family members in an effort to avoid the attention and ire of others. The children sometimes seem confused, angry, or anxious, and the parents often look lonely. So very lonely.

I see myself in these families.

And I wish I knew then what I know now: I was not alone. I was isolated right next to countless other parents experiencing similar challenges. We were all alone together. I can see it so clearly now.

I casually mention to a friend how many canaries I'm finding among us. And how I'm touched each time a parent lets down their guard to share their truths with me. I tell her I'm honored but surprised they trust me. I'm not any sort of expert.

She says, "I'm not surprised. Those who heal heal others."

Huh. I don't consider myself healed. A piece of me broke— maybe permanently—when I learned firsthand how apathetic people can be toward others.

But I realize this wound isn't incapacitating me anymore. I'm able to experience joy. And I appreciate kind acts more than I ever did before. And those quirky, fabulous children give me hope. I sense they're the ones who are going to force us to look at one another anew, in kinder, more compassionate ways. Not just with tolerance but with respect.

Again, a mother suggests I write a book, and I reconsider, *Could I? Should I?* I think back to my studies of apologies, and life in general for that matter, and I remind myself that it's not just about saying something in obscurity; it's about doing something meaningful. Unfortunately, speaking up also sets me on a silver platter for ridicule. And the truth is, I don't want to be exposed again.

But slowly, I evolve. I become less nervous about those who might demean me and my desire for a world that celebrates *all* differences. Instead, I start to welcome the notion of watching the critics *out* themselves. If people made an effort to trash me or my writing, then I would have a better idea of where the landmines lie. Part of me thinks, *Bring it.*

And I consider sharing all I've studied and all I've learned over the past few years so that other caretakers don't have to spend as much time behind their computers. Each round of parents shouldn't have to reinvent the wheel to honor their children's unique ways of being. They should be able to build off previous generations' learnings. I benefited from others' work. Maybe I, too, should pay it forward.

I lean closer still to telling my story.

But then I ask myself, *Do I have the right to expose* Hannah's *story?* She should be able to define herself, and I don't want to subject her to new and possibly more ruthless judgment.

Then I remember Hannah's first thought after we resolved to flee her toxic environment: "What about the other kids?" she asked.

She is my canary. She is my Swede. She has an intrinsic desire to make things right. To care for others. At each turn, she's wanted to help children feel safe, even if it required yelling at the top of her lungs. She knows who she is. And after a long road, she finally knows she's worthy.

When I ask her how she feels about me writing a book, she confirms she wants other kids to know their worth too. I ask the boys, and Theo shrugs while Jake asks, "Will it help people be nice to kids with dyslexia?"

I tell him, "I sure hope so," and then I tickle him. He has the most wonderful laugh I've ever known. Laughs like his change the world. It's certainly changed my world, and I would be devastated if anyone robbed him of it.

So, slowly, I start writing again, late into the night after my children fall asleep. Even after Jim has gone to bed, I find myself rehashing my journal, often seeing new ways to connect our experience to the research. Sometimes, I'm jolted from bed in the very early morning, and I rush to my computer to document the idea that startled me awake. The darkness beyond my windows is surprisingly comforting, even as my new task forces me to relive memories close enough to the surface to hurt, ones I tried to bury.

When I share chapters with other parents, they provide new insights I hadn't considered. And they encourage me to emphasize certain points that I was too shy or irresolute to make forcefully. This writing process continues to create meaning for me.

It's not easy, but I do it because I don't want other parents to know the deep, dark hole that once shrouded me.

I want to unlock the ill-fitting cages that house our canaries.

And I want *you* to know that you and your beautiful children aren't alone. Not even close.

As I said at the outset, we are in this together.

Postscript

This book was written in 2019 and later published in 2022. It reveals much of my thinking at that time as a white, heterosexual, cisgender woman without obvious physical impairments raising neurodiverse children in the United States. I have no idea how I will evolve going forward, but I hope that I do.

The other day, I found a childhood diary and was thoroughly embarrassed by a good portion of its contents. Maybe you've had a similar experience? The shame was enough to make me consider halting the presses on this book.

This is the risk of committing our thoughts and feelings to print. Our words reflect our understanding and interpretation of experiences at that time but not what we'll come to learn in the future. I pray you will have compassion for my mistakes and that we can use them to grow and reach for a brighter future together.

Recommendations
for Further Reading

ANXIETY
Freeing Your Child from Anxiety by Tamar E. Chansky
Anxiety Relief for Kids by Bridget Flynn Walker

APOLOGIES
How Can I Forgive You? By Janis Abrahms Spring and
    Michael Spring (focus: marriage)
A Good Apology by Molly Howes
On Apology by Aaron Lazare
Why Won't You Apologize? By Harriet Lerner

BULLYING PREVENTION
Bystander Revolution: bystanderrevolution.org
PACER National Bullying Prevention Center: pacer.org/bullying
Stomp Out Bullying: stompoutbullying.org
StopBullying: stopbullying.gov, especially "Misdirections in
    Bullying Prevention and Intervention"
Centers for Disease Control: cdc.gov/violenceprevention
    /youthviolence/bullyingresearch

COMPASSION
The Compassionate Instinct by Dacher Keltner et al.
The Empathy Effect by Helen Riess
The War for Kindness by Jamil Zaki

HIGH SENSITIVITY
The Highly Sensitive Child by Elaine Aron

INSTITUTIONAL BETRAYAL AND COURAGE
Center for Institutional Courage: institutionalcourage.org,
especially "Resources for Changemakers"

INTELLIGENCE
Ungifted by Scott Barry Kaufman

LEARNING DIFFERENCES AND ATTENTION ISSUES
Understood For All: Understood.org

For Children:
Fish in a Tree by Lynda Mullaly Hunt, a novel (focus: dyslexia)

For Adults:
*Forward Together: Helping Educators Unlock the Power of
Students Who Learn Differently* by National Center for
Learning Disabilities and Understood
The End of Average by Todd Rose
Parenting Bright Kids Who Struggle in School by Dewey Rosetti

NEUROPLASTICITY
For Children:
Your Fantastic Elastic Brain by JoAnn Deak

For Adults:
Limitless Mind by Jo Boaler

TRAUMA

What My Bones Know: A Memoir of Healing from Complex Trauma by Stephanie Foo

What Happened to You? by Bruce D. Perry and Oprah Winfrey

The Body Keeps the Score by Bessel van der Kolk

OTHER BOOKS THAT VALUE NEUROLIGICAL DIFFERENCES

Quiet by Susan Cain (focus: introversion)

Ten Steps to Nanette: A Memoir Situation by Hannah Gadsby (focus: autism intersected with other identities)

Raising a Rare Girl: A Memoir by Heather Lanier (focus: a rare genetic condition)

Uniquely Human by Barry M. Prizant (focus: autism)

Acknowledgments

Thanks to my family. I needed to write to make sense of this dynamic, messy, glorious world, and I appreciate the time you gave me to do so.

I'm grateful to each friend who read my unedited manuscript, offered advice, and related your own experiences. Your perspectives and insights highlight what fierce, brilliant, and caring individuals you are.

My life is forever changed by those of you who dare to seek justice, even as others try to tear you down. I will probably never meet the likes of Andrea Constand, Sybrina Fulton, and Tyler Shultz. Nor could I ever know the thousands of Scouts, parishioners, students, athletes, employees, soldiers, and citizens who demand their institutions be accountable for what occurs under their purview. You prove good people are willing to do hard things to make the world a better place. Thank you.

I am also grateful to those who supported an unknown debut author with a nontraditional story. While several people told me things like "You have no platform," and "You are trying to tackle too much," and "This doesn't fit a defined genre," others encouraged me. Brooke Warner is a courageous pioneer who built an entire business to create space for underserved voices, and I am honored to be on her team. Her colleagues Lauren Wise,

Cait Levin, and Laura Matthews worked wonders shepherding my manuscript through an exacting process.

Sages like Susan Leon, Caroline Heldman, and Jennifer Weis also helped me find my way.

Glennon Doyle, Eve Rodsky, Jennifer Rudolph Walsh, and Kim Scott might not even remember me, but their efforts to assist fellow writers, no matter how inexperienced, demonstrate their commitment to amplifying a variety of voices (rather than an echo chamber) and being true literary ambassadors. Thank you.

I was awestruck the moment I saw Luc Tuymans' canary, and I'm grateful he agreed to support this effort. Tabitha Lahr then translated his singular image to reflect central themes: unique individuals are gorgeous and they're everywhere. The world would be flat without creative geniuses like these.

Most important, I want to acknowledge each child who could never, should never, fit in a cage. Your undeniable beauty continues to force me to reconsider the tired, restrictive norms that, ultimately, limit all of us. May we break free from our confines and soar!

About the Author

Kayla Taylor graduated from a few respected schools and held some high-pressure jobs, but nothing has been more challenging and rewarding than raising her wonderfully inimitable children. She also supports organizations dedicated to improving pediatric health and education. In fact, she is donating her profits from the sale of this first edition book to organizations advocating for neurodiversity and mental health.

SELECTED TITLES FROM SHE WRITES PRESS

She Writes Press is an independent publishing
company founded to serve women writers everywhere.
Visit us at www.shewritespress.com.

Blinded by Hope: One Mother's Journey Through Her Son's Bipolar Illness and Addiction by Meg McGuire. $16.95, 978-1-63152-125-6. A fiercely candid memoir about one mother's roller coaster ride through doubt and denial as she attempts to save her son from substance abuse and bipolar illness.

Once a Girl, Always a Boy: A Family Memoir of a Transgender Journey by Jo Ivester. $16.95, 978-1-63152-886-6. Thirty years ago, Jeremy Ivester's parents welcomed him into the world as what they thought was their daughter. Here, his mother—with Jeremy's help—chronicles his journey from childhood through coming out as transgender and eventually emerging as an advocate for the transgender community.

Parent Deleted: A Mother's Fight for Her Right to Parent by Michelle Darné. $16.95, 978-1-63152-282-6. A gripping tale of one non-biological, lesbian mother's fight for shared custody of her children—an intimate, infuriating, and infectious story of perseverance, sacrifice, and hope in the face of debilitating adversity.

Stepmother: A Memoir by Marianne Lile. $16.95, 978-1-63152-089-1. Lile describes the complexities of the stepmom position, in a family and in the community, and shares her experience wearing a tag that is often misunderstood and weighed down by the numerous myths in society.

The ABCs of Being Mom: Advice and Support from the Mom Next Door, Birth through Kindergarten by Karen Bongiorno. $16.95, 978-1-64742-010-9. Written for loving but frazzled moms burdened by worry and confusion and in need of encouragement and direction, this handbook gives new mothers a bird's-eye view of the maze of parenting— providing the reassurance, practical advice, and guidance they need during their early years of motherhood.